An Introduction to People of Property

An Introduction to People of Property

R. D. Armitage

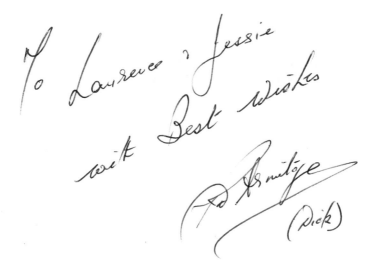

To Laurence & Jessie
with Best Wishes

R D Armitage
(Dick)

The Pentland Press
Edinburgh – Cambridge – Durham – USA

© R. D. Armitage, 1999

First published in 1999 by
The Pentland Press Ltd
1 Hutton Close
South Church
Bishop Auckland
Durham

ISBN 1–85821-718–0

Typeset in Bell 11/14
by Carnegie Publishing, Carnegie House, Chatsworth Rd, Lancaster
Printed and bound by Antony Rowe Ltd, Chippenham

Dedication of this book is to my wife for her encouragement, tireless patience giving advice and suggestions in so many ways, and for her acceptance of being a 'book-widow' for countless hours.
To Brenda

Contents

Contents

Acknowledgements

Without access to the works of previous writers this book could not have been written, and to those many authors grateful thanks is given. Also, thanks are offered to the many people with such a wealth of knowledge from historians and those whose lives are devoted to properties both large and small, and to the archivists, who have provided a wealth of data. A single question asked has produced an inordinate amount of relevant and salient facts, frequently providing suggestions from where further information can be obtained. All proving the devotion to their work or hobbies of these guardians of the Nation's history.

The County Council Library Services, particularly that of the county of Somerset, with others which have been involved, have been invaluable in searching for required books and for supplying many papers on specialized subjects, and to that service acknowledgement is gladly made.

Preface

An eminent broadcaster once suggested that an organization such as the National Trust required only one guide book to satisfy all the properties within its care, as they all contained the drawing room, the saloon, the library, the great staircase, the red bedroom (or whatever other colour), the bed on which someone of note once slept – usually Queen Elizabeth I, et cetera. A cursory glance may lead one to believe that there could be some truth in this unqualified remark. The broadcaster continued by saying that a standard guide of reference merely required changes of detail such as dates, names of architect, artist or owner, and so forth, to cover all those properties open to the public.

More detailed investigation shows how completely untrue this view is; it is reading between the lines of the written word in the abbreviated guide book which is of real fascination, at least to those sufficiently interested to read between the lines.

The quoted broadcaster's comments may indeed appear to be somewhat facetious but quoting the nineteenth-century French novelist Balzac '...every great fortune starts with a crime', may be considered of similar ilk – until reading one or two of the sections in this book.

Properties, whether buildings of any size or the smaller lesser-known properties, or the great tracts of land protected by a number of different organizations for future generations to enjoy and learn from, represent part of the present-day export trade. It is one of the great industries of the British Isles and satisfying an export without which the economy of the country would be in an even more parlous state. Perhaps the term should be invisible export, but nevertheless a very real export.

This book does not delve into the details relating to estate architecture or the pros and cons of their existence; there are many learned authorities who have produced tomes which cover this aspect should these details be sought. This book does attempt to relate some stories which can be gleaned from years of research and cross-referencing into many of the written words about people whose lives produced the properties as they can be seen today. Some of the material emanates from individual guide books and without those there would be a lack of background, other material has been found in the many individual writings of each property or person. At the same time that this book is based on facts it is hoped that even the hard, cold facts give an insight into the circumstances prevailing at the time and also the interrelationship between the various people involved in each story. Persistent research results in each story becoming wider in its ramifications and inevitably this in turn leads to overlapping of interest within the story and the historical interrelationships become even broader.

Investigations into the many, although in fact only a very small percentage, of the writings of nineteenth- and twentieth-century authors have already shown that caution is required whenever quoting dates, ages and even names. Some may be errors of one kind or another but some contradictions may be as a result of more up-to-date research and investigation proving the original statement as being inaccurate.

Whenever facts and dates have been quoted here caution has been applied. Those facts used have, in many instances, been obtained from more than one source and towards the end of the book there is a comprehensive Bibliography indicating published works reviewed. However, there are no doubt further publications on specific subjects which may not have been used, and to avoid endless doubt, and in some cases further contradictions being discovered, restrictions have been made to the number of sources used.

Introduction

People of Property, the emphasis being on people rather than the properties, if completed could, with research, be such a vast subject that only the periphery can be covered in one book. Immediately a problem then arises as to which properties and its people should be included and which should be abandoned through lack of space. As the aim is to give an insight into the people of great estates, rather than smallholdings, those with what could be called intriguing stories and backgrounds have been chosen, at the same time how those estates in the grandiose manner have been amassed and developed over the years is almost a by-product.

To add to the interest one deviation of purpose has been made by the inclusion of a section with the main theme being the builders and con-structors rather than the owners of the properties; this is entitled Brown and Holland which embraces a considerable number of properties and lists a large number of owners, many of whom are famous names by virtue of both history and trade. Many sections illustrate the number of properties a single family has, or still has involvement with to some extent. Little is written on the subject of vernacular buildings, of which there are so many, but an exception has been made for ice-houses, tithe barns and dovecotes, to widen the interest.

As an introduction it may be of interest to ask the question how and why relatively few families owned and controlled the largest proportion of the land, but in answer it would be an advantage to turn the clock back a few hundred years and consider the countryside as an open area with basically three types of owners. Obviously this is dependent on how far back the clock has been turned.

The three divisions, by no means equal, can be summarized as the church, the crown and the commoners. Possibly the most frequent and well-known change was between the crown or monarchs and their sub-ordinates who, by either being in favour or performing a favour, were awarded lands. Land, certainly as late as the eighteenth century, produced wealth – and wealth produced further wealth – with the result that, unless

1

the favoured was unfortunate and ended life at one of the ceaseless battles, which so many did at an early age, the patron would continue to patronize. There were of course frequently the dangers of political change when much could be lost, or gained, in a relatively short period of time. The Tudor period, one of the most familiar periods, was also one of the greatest for change of ownership of land, but this is a perpetual state of affairs, more in the past than in modern times. One simple example of this, for interest, is that most notable example of Jacobean architecture, Hatfield House in Hertfordshire, seat of the Cecils since 1603, but what of the ownership of the estate before the 'pile' was built by 1611 on the instructions of Robert Cecil, 1st Earl of Salisbury? James I gave it to the Cecils in exchange for Burghley's palace at Theobald's, near Waltham Cross; Theobald's (pron. Tibbalds), a property demolished in the mid-eighteenth century. James obtained Hatfield estate from Elizabeth I who had held her first Council in the original manor; it was conveyed to Elizabeth by Edward VI who had occasionally lived there, Edward inheriting this manor from Henry VIII. All normal progression through the monarchy, but Henry obtained it by conveyance granted by the Bishops of Ely who agreed to exchange it for lands in Cambridgeshire, Essex and Norfolk. Prior to Henry the Benedictine monks of Ely had, in the first century, been awarded the lands by the King of Mercia, Edgar, and here the monks built the great palace for the Bishops of Ely. In brief, therefore, the estate could have been classified as royal until the first century, then to the church until the sixteenth for a short period when it returned to royal before into private ownership as a favour.

Any lands do not remain static over the centuries and the British Isles, by virtue of being islands, have many comprehensive records of changes made by both nature and man. This applies particularly to ownership and land use, and the consequential effect on the population. An example can be seen during the Middle Ages when the monastic estates were responsible for the removal of large numbers of long-established villages regardless of the hardships incurred on the local peasant communities. It should be no surprise that little is recorded on the subject of commoners acting in defence of the church and the abbeys when the destruction of the great edifices took place in the sixteenth century. The labourers had suffered greatly during the founding of the places of God and the monks' searches for places of solitude for contemplation. No doubt much wasteland was reclaimed by the monks to be productive, but solitude, secrecy and the obtaining of vast lands, not always by honest means, was paramount. It was the secrecy, almost mystique, which introduced the fear to the people thus removing the possibility of serious or organized objection. Having obtained the lands they had to be economical and it soon became evident that a greater profit could be obtained from open farming and the production of wool from sheep than the labour-intensive ploughing of land for grain. More village removals took place as the method of transporting the bulky but light commodity of wool developed and export to foreign lands became possible.

There has without doubt been problems between the upper and lower classes since time began and much of the problem in bygone days related to the use and ownership of the countryside. The following few notes give, in very brief terms and roughly chronologically, generalization throughout the periods, but first a comment on movement of labour.

There were many reasons why inhabited areas moved, or indeed disappeared completely, and today there is ample evidence, well documented, of more than 200 villages which no longer exist; there were obviously countless others of which there is no real evidence. Many of these habitations vanished because of medieval problems such as periods of plagues or the church and hierarchy, which must include more modern gentry emparkments; in some areas the local trade became exhausted, there was the clearance for increased animal breeding, there was coastal erosion, and, in very modern years, the clearances for military purposes.

The fourteenth-century plague had considerable repercussions throughout the land and subsequent reduction in the labour force resulted in the reduced number of workers who expected higher wages. The landowners required more security for their income and many, including the ecclesiastical landlords, took action by way of increasing their control of land and, by some not too honest means, enclosed even more of the former common lands. Circumstances which, together with the introduction of yet another increase in the poll tax – this time to a shilling a head – resulted in riots and revolts in many parts of the country.

In the sixteenth century, with the Dissolution of the Monasteries, when landowners' attitudes to owning estates was solely for exploitation and producing quick profits, not as a valued possession for the whole communities, two thirds of all peers were granted or purchased the former monastic estates.

In the seventeenth century riots continued amongst the country people as their rights of use of common lands was being lost because of enclosures by the gentry; in addition to which vast areas of the fens were being drained to increase the acreage of the nobles, regardless of the threat of a way of a livelihood enjoyed by many for centuries. Originally an area of 2,500 square miles constituted The Fens, today there are little more than 700 acres. The Fen Country is included as a separate chapter of this book. Blatantly, during this century, was the Elizabethan law whereby new cottages built for farm labourers had to include a minimum of four acres from which they could survive, but was ignored.

Clearances, for so long associated with north of the border because of the abundance of the written word on the subject, was not confined to Scotland, although much more has been recorded on that area which produced some of the most harsh suffering to the lower classes, but the church and gentry in England also compounded the system. Counties as far south as Wiltshire also took part in placing sheep before man. Clearances, particularly the Scottish 1782–1820 and 1840–54 periods basically refers to the removal of man's habitation to allow open areas for sheep; useful though the croft walls were to protect the animals from the winds and rain, man was not required. Enclosures on the other hand were purely a means of enlarging the owners' acreage and mainly an English problem rather than being experienced in Scotland or Ireland.

As recently as 1830 there were more serious riots largely as a result of enclosures and the loss of rights of the lower classes to benefit from the use of previously common land, whether it be for the feeding and breeding of their livestock or for the growing of foodstuffs. Many small owner-occupiers of mini estates were being lost within the great tracts of enclosed land; a number of the lesser yeomen lost their total estates this way. The Tolpuddle chapter of this book gives a detailed account of this problem in the nineteenth century.

The reader will gather that the practice of enclosing land has continued for a long time and even during the seventeenth or eighteenth centuries there was a general outcry from the populace; as there was in Tudor times. Turning the clock back even further – the Statute of Merton dated 1235 allowed enclosure, providing there was sufficient land not enclosed to meet the rights of the commoners. A procedure whereby enclosure was permitted but each case had to be processed by individual special Acts of Parliament was introduced about the year 1700; this allowed the land to be distributed between the lord of the manor and a number of persons who had right to it. Between the introduction of this Act and 1845 about 4,000 Acts agreed to approximately 5,000,000 acres of land being enclosed. Over the centuries various 'half-hearted' official bodies attempted to control the matter but, not until an Act of 1876, was the practice stopped.

Unrest was not unusual, indeed at the end of the eighteenth century Pitt's parliament temporarily suspended the Habeas Corpus Act as a desperate measure. It was not as a direct result of enclosures but an accumulation of deteriorating conditions suffered by the labour force, including general loss of access to common land, poor habitation and working conditions, poor wages and a series of poor harvests.

By the twentieth century land transfer systems had changed dramatically and perhaps a nice example of this can be the circumstances surrounding the purchase of a new home by one of the greatest history-makers of the era. This is the subject for the first chapter of this book entitled 'Churchills'.

Although the introductory instigation of each of the chapters of this book was by scrutinizing a property, the stories relate to the associated people. There is no underlining theme such as period, architecture or owner, nor is one particular conservation body, whether it be the National Trust, English Heritage or those assisted by Historic Houses Association, given preference. The National Trust as the largest conservation body of its type in the world is inevitably referred to frequently, but deliberately no preference is indicated.

Chapter I

Churchills

The name Churchill must be recollected by most of the mature people of the civilized world, in fact there can be few people throughout the world who have not been affected, directly or indirectly, by the history-maker Churchill during the twentieth century. Many with little knowledge of the family will draw association with Marlborough, Blenheim and Queen Anne, and in more modern times Chartwell, but a small amount of reading discloses a far greater history of the family than that; indeed the Churchills can be traced in the West Country to the twelfth century. In that century at Broad Clyst in Devon and in the fifteenth century in the area of Minterne Magna and Bradford Peverell just north of Dorchester in Dorset, John Churchill leased from Winchester College, a house and farms at Minterne; John married Sarah, daughter of Sir Henry Winston, a name perpetuated through to the twentieth century.

There is interest in the associations the family had with other famous names; such as James, Duke of York, whose mistress was Arabella, granddaughter of John; the first Duke of Buckingham, his sister becoming mother of Sir John Drake; and the Blandfords and the Bridgewaters, later the family founding the Earls of Spencer. Perhaps the most famous name is that of the Dukes of Marlborough, a dynasty founded by a member of the family of which more will be recorded later.

Equally of interest is the fact that there has been not one Winston Churchill but two, both of whom have changed the course of history. The earlier of the two was Winston born in the West Country in 1620, and the latter Winston Leonard Spencer born at Woodstock in 1874. It can also be learned that the two had many similarities both in personalities and in the circumstances which prevailed during their lifetime. The former was involved with land redistributed after the upheaval of the Civil War, and the latter, less than 300 years later, land redistributed after the much more devastating world war during the twentieth century.

The two men, whilst following similar lifestyles in some things, for example, both wrote books although the former wrote mainly on the subject of monarchical history whereas the latter in modern times wrote much more widely on the history of English-speaking people. Further, the twentieth-century Winston took great interest in the sciences but the seventeenth-century man had a complete lack of interest in the subject despite the Restoration period being the time during which the Royal Society was formed and the new sciences were uppermost in the minds of many in public office. Another subject common to both was the multifarious problems of Ireland, a topic on which the modern man had many views, and a problem on which the earlier man had first-hand knowledge by spending time in that country on official business; a post neither he nor his family relished.

It would be logical to base this chapter on the first of these two great men and mention one or two variances between them. The first Winston was a true monarchist and Protestant, the name Winston being used out of respect for his grandfather, Sir Henry Winston of Gloucestershire. Winston's father John wisely married into a class above himself, his wife being a minor heiress, and Winston also married well to Elizabeth the daughter of Sir John Drake of Ashe House. This marriage into one of the leading families in Devon took place in 1643, about seven years after Sir John had died, so the Civil War was already taking place and Winston as Captain of Horse fought in a number of skirmishes.

Ashe House, off the Seaton road from Axminster, may not be one of the West Country's great houses, but a building still exists, privately owned, on the site of the original house, although today there is a relatively new house built early this century. The old house was a large, fine, Elizabethan 'E' shaped building which provided an important function during the seventeenth-century unrest becoming the centre for many of the Civil War intrigues with plots and counter plots, experiencing the trauma of siege more than once. The fines imposed on the Churchills for their part in the war meant that the house and the estate had to be sold, and at this stage Lady Drake, although a staunch Puritan and Parliamentarian and therefore an opponent of Winston, would have helped as family affairs now returned to being important. But Ashe had been pillaged and partially burned during the height of the war, an act performed by a member of another great West Country family, the Pauletts, and as even Lady Drake's wealth had suffered badly, although she did eventually receive some compensation from the Paulett estate, it was many years before the house could be repaired.

Winston's life lasted about sixty-eight years and he lived through some very difficult periods including the reoccurrence of the plague, the Civil

War during which Churchills took part in maintaining the Royalist cause in Devon, and the great fire of London. Whilst living at Minterne Magna in Dorset he was MP for Weymouth, a post he held for eighteen years, holding many positions from legal to financial, and immediately after the 1660 Restoration of Charles II he was involved in the vexed question of ownership of lands which had changed hands either by way of confiscation or sold to raise funds to meet fines imposed during the disruptive 'Commonwealth' years. He was consultant on many points whether legal, ecclesiastical or constitutional; all matters in need of clarification after the Restoration. It was not until four years later that he received Court office, and a knighthood, which turned the tide for monetary prospects and by 1669 building work by way of improvements was taking place at Minterne. Less than 300 years later the twentieth-century Winston was involved with similar land distribution problems, this time between countries, resulting from the much more devastating and international war.

Unrest in Europe during the seventeenth century was rife, particularly with Louis XIV not only maintaining the largest army in Europe but known to be amassing a navy to overshadow the English, subjects Winston was deeply engrossed in with debates to counter this state of affairs. Consultant perhaps and orator many times but not in the top echelon – more a straight-forward, uncomplicated edict-maker without frills. Winston was unfortunately frequently outspoken and not always entirely in the King's favour; perhaps the reason why no further promotion was received despite so much support having been given to the Stuart dynasty.

After the end of the Civil War Winston and Elizabeth produced a large family although only a few of the children survived. The second son, John, was to be the most famous and thanks to his mentor, James, providing the opportunities for military life at a very early age, rose from being a royal page to the hero of the country within a relatively short period of time. The first son, called Winston after his father, did not survive infancy. John, born at Ashe House, was page to James, Duke of York, and he took army command for James II, then allegiance to William of Orange whence he was created Lord Churchill two years after Anne succeeded to the crown. He won the Battle of Blenheim as Duke, further fame being confirmed by winning the Battle of Ramillies. John whose life proved to be a more sad affair than generally realized, married a headstrong girl, Sarah, ten years his junior, daughter of Richard Jennings of Sandridge, Hertfordshire. She was maid-in-waiting to the Duchess of York, and friend of the young Princess Anne. With Anne's accession to the crown Sarah received high favours; she became a staunch Whig, but she had an uncontrollable temper, and she was dismissed from Court in 1710.

John and Sarah in their early years lived at Minterne with his parents and later, with John's rapid promotion, his brother Charles, whom John promoted to Brigadier on the capturing of Cork, and then to General, the two brothers working side by side in many battles, took over the property. One of the children of John and Sarah's union, Anne, married Charles Spencer, 3rd Earl of Sunderland, and from this line the Earls Spencer descended, the name Spencer being perpetuated by Winston of the nineteenth and twentieth centuries. This rapidly promoted John Churchill, with his connections with Blenheim and the title Marlborough, is sufficiently well known and his exploits documented by many learned writers that they will not be reiterated here. Let it suffice to continue with the story of the two Winstons by mentioning that the glory of John's life during the first years of the eighteenth century resulted in the birthplace of the twentieth-century Winston being built.

With the Battle of Blenheim and other battles won, Queen Anne conferred on the First Duke of Marlborough, now Captain General of her forces, a new palace of suitable proportions; as none existed one had to be built. The impetus for building, and building in a grand manner, could be said to stem from the end of the Civil War, and the reallocation of lands resulting from that period, followed by the great fire of London and the subsequent increase in the well-educated taking an interest in architecture; and what could be more fitting than the building of a country palace for the hero of the day?

John Vanbrugh, fourteen years senior in age to Marlborough, was selected by the Duke to design such a house. Why Vanbrugh? His only claim to fame architecturally was Castle Howard in Yorkshire for the third Earl of Carlisle, an incomplete building at that time, started only four years previously. Vanbrugh, who was brought up with no apprenticeship, trade or profession, at the age of thirty-five started to take an interest in architecture. Prior to that he had been a soldier, even spending two years in French prisons allegedly for being a spy, but he had been raised as a gentleman, so it is recorded, and presumably that was his great advantage. He certainly achieved a great amount – Castle Howard his first, and remains his greatest masterpiece. He became a prominent Whig, his undoing a few years later when he became entangled with Marlborough's controversy with the party. Vanbrugh had many connections and was appointed as Controller of the Royal Works by 1702, about the time of his liaison with Lord Carlisle.

The palace at Woodstock in Oxfordshire was started in 1705; during the building Vanbrugh had many conflicts with the Duchess, who always opposed the palace building, indeed she had not been overjoyed when her husband was raised to the peerage. Marlborough's dismissal from the Tory party in 1711 resulted in Vanbrugh with his Whig leanings being eventually excluded from his own masterpiece which was completed by Hawksmoor about 1724. Regrettably during the controversial political events of 1711 the Duke was accused of misappropriating public funds, an accusation never either proved or disproved, and he retired abroad, but, on the accession of George I, he was recalled to office. Within a couple of years he suffered an apoplectic stroke and died in 1722. Nevertheless he was still considered to be one of the greatest masters of the art of war.

Nicholas Hawksmoor, of comparable age to Vanbrugh, and their paths crossed many times, was born in Nottingham and started life as clerk to a Yorkshire justice. At eighteen years of age he moved to London and by twenty-one he was assisting Sir Christopher Wren; some years later he became Deputy Controller to Vanbrugh. Described as dowdy and modest – not born a gentleman – too modest to come to the fore. At Castle Howard he assisted Vanbrugh, and at Blenheim; and later, after Vanbrugh's problems with political issues as previously mentioned and his subsequent departure from the site, Hawksmoor completed the building work about a year or so before Vanbrugh's death. It is always difficult to establish which part of a building originated from which architect but in the case of Blenheim – and of course Castle Howard – it is true to state that the overall concept was that of Vanbrugh.

The property at Minterne Magna has been mentioned a number of times and it was here that many of the family events took place, and indeed where a number of the early Churchills lived. Minterne is in the area of the legendary hunting forest of Henry III of the thirteenth century. The Churchills in the early seventeenth century were involved in disputed land enclosure to establish their emparkment. The Parish Church in this woodland countryside by the Cerne road contains some interesting memorials to the family of the first Winston Churchill. It is here that his father was buried and when Winston died in 1688, considerably in debt – the £2,000 lent to Charles II during harder times was never repaid – it was at Minterne. Charles, Winston's fourth surviving child, who was appointed heir and beneficiary under the terms of his mother's Will, here spent his retiring years and having married another heiress, Mary Gould of Dorchester, was able to complete the building work started by his father.

Previously within the paragraph referring to John Churchill, Blenheim and Marlborough is the comment that there are already in existence sufficient recorded works of reference on the subject therefore there is no justification for enlarging on the details in this chapter. This thought is even more appropriate whilst dealing with this final part of the subject when considering the modern Winston Churchill. Many authoritative writers have produced a large number of books and biographies and this subject will be terminated by relating a few facts appertaining to the country house of Chartwell near Westerham in Kent.

In the year 1921 Winston was seeking a country estate for family use and discovered the previous home of the Campbell Colquhouns since the middle of the nineteenth century was for sale; it had already been empty for nine years and in this year it had been offered at auction but failed to meet the reserve price of £6,500. Winston and his beloved Clementine viewed the house, he interested, she appalled by the grey Victorian mansion built on and round a much older house, damp, dreary and ugly within eighty yards of the road and a public footpath giving access through the grounds. The following year Winston bought it for £5,000. Mrs Churchill was not pleased, being very much more aware of the costs and the difficulties of modernizing, maintaining and trying to eradicate the dry rot in the original fabric; she was proved to be right and by 1926 economies had to be made, but they managed and the family thought it great fun. Somewhere in the region of £18,000 was spent, much on modernizing and modifying the building to take advantage of the views of the attractive parkland surrounding the house.

The Wall Street crash of 1929 had serious financial implications for Winston, but the family still managed, and the great joining of family and friends for Christmas 1934 was the zenith of life at Chartwell. By 1937 Winston was thinking that perhaps they may have to sell, and a price of £25,000 was in mind, but circumstances interfered by the outbreak of war; during that period the house remained empty on advice as the site was considered to be an easy target for enemy action. This war period sadness was compounded by the Conservatives losing the election in 1945 and that was the point for a decision to be made for the estate to be sold; this time the price was £20,000. However, a group of friends and admirers of the Churchills, including presidents, heads of foreign governments and other leaders of countries from around the world made a gesture by buying the whole estate with the proviso that it would be given to the National Trust for permanent preservation at the time the Churchills no longer wished to live there.

This second of the Winston Churchills was knighted in 1952 and died in 1965. His wife, Clementine, decided on an early handover of the property to the National Trust, donating much of the furniture and pictures enabling the property to look as though lived in by the last private owners. Many thousands of visitors arrive each year, a large number to pay homage to the painter of so many of those pictures seen today – Winston Leonard Spencer Churchill.

Chapter II

Brownsea Island

How many of us have dreamed at some stage in our lives of owning and living on our own private island? To some it may have been a fantasy during childhood – perhaps in those early days imagination was more adventurous and our island would be complete with a castle so the unwanted visitor or the enemy could be repelled. Perhaps our dreams even included a defensible castle complete with drawbridge so our secret place could be defended to the bitter end. Later, childhood thoughts fortunately, or unfortunately, become more realistic and there are those who have been able to experience, not perhaps the childhood fantasy, but practical living on an island because circumstances made it possible or wealth allowed a whim to be brought to fruition.

In Dorset there is situated within the second largest natural harbour in the world the 500-acre island of Brownsea, preserved by the National Trust since 1962. The harbour is Poole Harbour (the larger natural harbour is Sydney in Australia) and the very varied history of Brownsea can be traced over many hundreds of years. Today this island, only accessible by ferry, is visited and enjoyed by thousands of folk, some local but many more holiday visitors, but only just over thirty years ago ownership was zealously guarded and visitors were the select few, and then by special invitation.

Historically the island has seen many changes from the days of sanctuary whilst owned by the church, to the days of private individual owners, to more liberal days of walkers and the introduction of the Boy Scout movement (a section of the island is still reserved for use by scouts and guides), to the present day of holidaymakers' visits and providing sanctuary for birds as well as people. Brownsea may not be the island of childhood dreams, being too large and too flat for our raised defensible castle, certainly not with a drawbridge, but in reality it has indeed been defended and has played a role in the national defence of the South Coast for a very long time, as recently as the Second World War. This harbour like so much of this country's topography was formed by the great ice-age and Brownsea no doubt a depository of silt washed down by the flow of melting ice on the journey to the Solent, a fact substantiated by the type of deposits now making up the island deposits of sand, gravel and clay producing the distinctive heathland terrain.

Home to Roman Legions for many years, this region of England was persecuted by the Danes with their spasmodic raping, burning and pillaging until good King Alfred intervened about the year AD 876. Nearby Wareham town on the mainland, once a thriving port, must surely have experienced many frightening periods of invasion. The great Abbey of Cerne (pron: SERN) had a satellite chapel on the island, possibly founded in the sixth century, this island of fishermen, hence the chapel being dedicated to their patron saint of St Andrews, until 1015 when the Abbey and Brownsea chapel were sacked by the Vikings with Canute. Interestingly, although the island was of sufficient note to be invaded many times, by the time of the Normans and the writing of Domesday Book (1086) Brownsea, or whichever of its half dozen other names referred to – even as late as 1857 it was written on a map as Branksea – was not even included in the listing. It is known that William of Normandy gave Studland, which included Brownsea, to Robert de Mortain, his half brother, but Robert was banished by William Rufus for treachery, so Brownsea reverted to the Crown. Notwithstanding this transfer of ownership there is evidence that charters existed in favour of the monks of Cerne up to the time of the Dissolution by Henry VIII. The island did become one of the sites for Henry's line of defensive blockhouses to protect the south coast against the French, and later the Spanish, and these defences were maintained and manned into the latter part of the sixteenth century.

Queen Elizabeth I, known for her habit of rewarding those in favour, albeit only at the time, gave neighbouring Corfe Castle to her favourite of the day, Christopher Hatton; by tradition the owner of Corfe Castle automatically became governor of Brownsea Castle. Hatton was knighted, became Lord Chancellor, invested with the Order of the Garter, given many gifts of land throughout the country, and was in royal favour for two decades, perhaps for his foresight in generously investing in Drake's circumnavigation of the world; after all Drake was even more a favourite of the Queen so Hatton's investment produced a very good return.

Mid-seventeenth century during the Civil War, Henry's royal defence was a Parliamentarian stronghold against the Royalists; thankfully Henry died a hundred years previously as he would not have been amused!

The eighteenth century saw great changes to the island perhaps principally because two men spent money on both the planting and cultivating of the vegetation, particularly the trees. The blockhouse was also converted from a block for defence to a residence. William Benson was an MP, philosopher, poet and patron of the arts, formerly holder of the post of Surveyor of Works in succession to Sir Christopher Wren. An eccentric perhaps but an advocate of botany in many ways; unfortunately not a lover of his neighbours in Poole. It may be that the people of Poole did not favour Mr Benson who, as an active Whig persuaded the Government to replace Wren, who was in his eighties at the time, in favour of himself as Surveyor of Works. Benson did not hold the post above a year before enforced resignation because, so it was said, he received more from his one year of office than Wren received in forty years of honest endeavours. Benson did, however, instigate the converting of Brownsea Castle to a residence.

In 1765 Sir Humphrey Sturt of Moor Crichel, described as one of the leading Dorset landowners and an MP for the county, took over the island. He enhanced both castle and garden, the one into a large elegant residence, the other into fashionable grounds complete with glasshouses. Also, being aware of the latest methods in horticulture and agriculture he introduced and imported fertilizers and used the latest in the rotation of crops. The newly discovered methods of controlling water by use of sluices and gates was also installed; actually the Romans had been aware of such controls a thousand years previously. At about the same time Sturt was converting Brownsea Island to a summer home he was also lavishing money on the rebuilding of the family seat, Crichel House, which was of sufficient grandeur for the Prince Regent to rent at a later date. The 'media' were equally invasive in the eighteenth century as in the twentieth and during a number of the Prince Regent's periods of indiscretions Crichel House at Moor Crichel, some five miles from Wimborne, was used by His Highness as a retreat, even if only partly successful. On Sturt's death in 1786 Sir Humphrey's son, Charles, MP for Bridport inherited the island and made it his home. It was Charles's son, Henry who much preferred the splendour of Crichel, and took the Prince Regent in 1818 on a visit to the newly developed Brownsea. That same year Sturt sold the island to Sir Charles Chad who continued the Sturt improvements adding even more modern pineries, greenhouses and, to complete the eighteenth-century image, introduced a herd of deer.

By this date the island had survived many differing types of invasion and uses, but the position of this island on the south coast and being accessible only by water made it ideal and very susceptible for use by privateers of one form or another. This to such a degree that a special force was created and armed to serve under the Preventive Service, later renamed the coastguard. Charles Sturt was appointed Captain of the 150-strong group and buildings exist to show the accommodation for this force.

Following Sir Charles Chad's ownership, for a brief period before he committed suicide, was a retired diplomat Sir Augustus Forster.

The second half of the nineteenth century saw the one period of the island as a great commercial exercise. An Indian Army Colonel named Waugh and his wife decided that the large deposits of clay were of sufficient quality to be used in the finest chinaware. Even an expert confirmed this and the estimated value of the material was put at about one million pounds. With this information large sums of money were borrowed and a mass production line installed; sadly the clay was not of good quality and the value of goods produced was low. Financial litigation followed for years and eventually Waugh fled to Spain.

The Honourable George Cavendish-Bentinck bought the island but the pottery business finally closed in 1887. Cavendish-Bentinck's real interest was not production of pottery but he was, in addition to being an MP, a connoisseur and collector of fine art. The last decade of the nineteenth century changed the whole course of the island's productivity yet again. Cavendish-Bentinck's death in 1891 resulted in another change of ownership, this time the island was bought by yet another member of a political family, Major Kenneth Balfour.

Within five years a disastrous fire destroyed both the castle and thousands of pounds worth of works of art. Again, the ownership of Brownsea proved to be short-lived as, although rebuilding took place between 1897 and 1901, Balfour sold the island to a couple who bought the island and they changed the image to what can only be described as a period of extreme elegance. The country was in mourning, the Queen was dead, the country was about to be introduced into the period of transition from Victorian to Edwardian and Brownsea Island was about to be resurrected to the standard an island should be – by someone with the means necessary.

Florence and Charles van Raalte, whose fortune had come from jute and tobacco, were so accepted by the people of Poole, unlike various previous owners of the island, that Charles, without even serving on the council, was elected Mayor. The island was now inhabited by over 200 people, including the castle staff said to be thirty, plus ten gardeners and a silver band of twenty players; this all contrary to a few years previously when the population was about twelve. The island was now ready for grand entertaining and that is exactly what took place. The guests ranged from those of European minor royal households, to society people who were worth inviting, all of whom could take advantage of the new golf course, the fishing and hunting, and eating the produce from what was by this time almost a self-supporting island, including many exotic fruits. Although Charles died in 1908 a new industry of daffodil growing was introduced shortly after, based on the Scilly Isles knowledge. However, the year before the death of Charles a new innovation was attempted by a friend of the van Raaltes, Major General Baden-Powell.

It was on this island that the first camp for boys was organized and the result so successful that the week's camp was extended to ten days. Twenty boys from a complete cross-section of the social spectrum were given the opportunity to be self-sufficient and enjoy the normal summer holiday activities, but, at the same time learn of such unknown crafts as tenting, cooking, tracking, stalking wild animals, map reading and so forth. All unknown to the city dweller, but from this experiment the worldwide scouting and guide movements developed. The Scout and Guide movements alone are permitted to camp on the island. Mrs van Raalte continued to maintain the estate, and to entertain, but in 1925 she left the island.

The nearby Haven Hotel, which was used by Marconi for his wireless experiments, bought the island with a view to developing it further for rich clientele to use as a golfing and yachting playground. When the local council refused planning permission the whole island, castle and treasures became subject of an auction sale which lasted three weeks.

The next, and final private owner of Brownsea Island was Mrs Mary Bonham-Christie and it is thanks to her near obsession for privacy and love of solitude that the island was returned into a natural paradise. The inhabitants left for the mainland, the run-down flora became the natural wild flora, and visitors were very far from welcome, and that applied to even the local fishermen. So the island population changed yet again, now from the 200 or so in the days of the van Raaltes to Mrs Christie, one gamekeeper and a blonde female described as a powerful Scandinavian 'PT' instructor employed to keep out intruders. An out-of-control fire raged over two-thirds of the island for seven days in 1934 and that resulted in even larger areas reverting to the natural state. The Second World War years, did, however see the island being virtually commandeered for security purposes and the very site on which Henry VIII had raised his blockhouse was used for the installation of a battery of six–inch guns for national defence.

Mrs Bonham-Christie died in 1961 and Brownsea Island was accepted by the Treasury in lieu of death duties, thus being taken into the care of the National Trust, thanks to contributions from many organizations and trusts towards the endowment. Similar to other National Trust areas the management is assisted by other conservation bodies.

If only three people inhabited the island during the lengthy period of Mrs Christie's ownership – excluding the war years – life has since changed; now visitors can total up to 70,000 in a year. The castle was at one time leased to the John Lewis Partnership as a holiday centre for their staff. Perhaps they appreciate this as one of the few places in the British Isles where the red squirrel can still be seen in its natural habitat. Even with the large number of visitors the island remains a haven, a sanctuary, whilst Poole Harbour suffers more and more from boat building, oil exploration, the ferries becoming larger and larger, the mainland holiday camps and the nearby urban developments, but the island remains an island and long may it continue.

Chapter III

Writers by the Lakes

The research conducted to produce this chapter of *People of Property* became more diversified than other chapters purely because of the fascinating diverse people who can be included in the criteria Lake District and literature. Few other areas of the British Isles can boast such concentrated affiliation with literary personnel as the southern Lake District, considering that no less than nineteen men and women of letters became, at one time or another connected with at least fifty-two different properties, (not including all the different districts, hills, vales, et cetera) each of which is within twenty miles of the other. In the north is Grasmere, in the south Haverthwaite, the east Levens Hall, and in the west Lowick.

Many of these writers became, like the Wordsworths, associated with a number of different properties, sometimes moving out of the district only to return years later. Some paid only a fleeting glimpse on holiday like Charlotte Brontë who stayed with the Kay-Shuttleworths at Briery Close near Ambleside. Lady Shuttleworth was the heiress of Robert of Gawthorpe Hall, Burnley, Lancashire, which is a house, originally early seventeenth century, restored in the mid-nineteenth century by Sir Charles Barry and now a National Trust property which accommodates a textile collection. Here Charlotte met Mrs Gaskell, who had married the great Unitarian Minister and Professor of English; during this visit and years later Mrs Gaskell produced *The Life of Charlotte Brontë*. Others associated with Ambleside include Harriet Martineau, the nineteenth-century novelist and political economist from Norwich, whom Charlotte Brontë also visited. Harriet lived in the area from 1845 until her death over thirty years later; she wrote *The Complete Guide to the Lake District* which was published in 1855; Wordsworth's *Guide Through the Lakes* had been produced only twenty years previously.

Another Ambleside visitor was Henry Crabb Robinson originally from Bury St Edmunds. He was a journalist, diarist and letter writer, and an advocate for the foundation of University College, London. His employment involved the legal profession but on inheriting money he became more involved with letter writing, journalism and travelling. Matthew Arnold, the eldest son of the very famous father who became headmaster of Rugby was basically a poet and critic and he spent holidays in Ambleside. For over thirty years he was Inspector of Schools; his writings were very influenced by Wordsworth. Ambleside cannot be abandoned without mention that nearby is Rydal Mount, Wordsworth's home from 1813 to 1850, prior to which he was at Dove Cottage.

The Manchester-born essayist and author of great character, Thomas De Quincey in the early years of the nineteenth century started travelling, and after a couple of years of voluntarily being homeless in London, despite his education and intellect, went to Nab Farm, or Cottage, near Grasmere with his future wife. In the same year he met Coleridge in Bridgwater and was very influenced by him to such an extent that he assisted Coleridge financially; Wordsworth was another influence, that is until they fell out. In addition Thomas stayed in Grasmere, after which he rented Dove Cottage for over twenty years as his headquarters after Wordsworth had left it; he was married in Grasmere 1817. After a time in London, he owned Nab Farm from 1829 for about four years. Finally he spent his latter years over the border in Scotland where he died. Grasmere was also very synonymous with the Wordsworths and Coleridges, the churchyard containing the graves of William, his wife, their daughter and Hartley, the son of Coleridge. Dove Cottage previously mentioned was Wordsworth's home from 1799 for about nine years. It is now almost a shrine to the great man and is complete with museum and exhibitions.

The popular holiday area for so many people in modern times, Windermere, is associated with a number of writers including John Wilson of Elleray in Windermere who entertained Sir Walter Scott and J.G. Lockhart the novelist and biographer of Scott. John Wilson, known by his pen-name Christopher North during the first half of the nineteenth century, was a poet, essayist and critic from Paisley and lived in the Lake District in 1807–12, but the loss of his fortune resulted in his return to Scotland to work at a university. During the period in Windermere he became involved with Lockhart and jointly they were the mainstay of Blackwood's *Edinburgh Monthly* magazine, established as a Tory rival; other contributors being Sir Walter Scott, De Quincey and Anthony Trollope.

Coniston brings to mind a number of famous names particularly John Ruskin, the great writer on art and social subjects, who bought Brantwood on a bank above Lake Coniston without seeing it, and then spent a small fortune in restoration work. For nearly thirty years until his death this was his home, a site which Ruskin considered to be the finest he knew in Cumberland or Lancashire, a thought substantiated by one authority who considered that Brantwood is the most beautifully situated in the Lake District. Ruskin was a prodigious writer, his radical thinking creating disturbance for many; he had associations with a number of eminent people such as Tolstoy, Mahatma Gandhi, Proust and William Morris, to name but a few. Brantwood is at present used as an adult residential centre in the hands of the Brantwood Educational Trust. The first Baron Alfred Tennyson, one-time Poet Laureate, made a visit to Coniston whilst on his honeymoon.

Coniston was also the holiday destination in the early twentieth century for the writer of books for children, Arthur Ransome, perhaps his most remembered book, and his favourite, being *Swallows and Amazons*. Ransome lived at Cartmel Fell at the south end of Windermere from 1925 for ten years; the Fell is also featured in the novel by Mrs Humphrey Ward entitled *Helbeck of Bannisdale*. Lowick Hall, a manorial hall dating from Norman times, a few miles south of Coniston Water, was the home of Ransome for only two or three years after the Second World War, but during that short residence he made great improvements to the standard of the property. His last years were spent at Hill Top at Haverthwaite near Newby Bridge, a house – now a kennels – one and a half miles north-west of the village. Mrs Humphrey Ward was the granddaughter of Thomas Arnold of Rugby, and she stayed at the privately owned Elizabethan mansion of Levens Hall, most famous for the seventeenth-century topiary garden, using the hall and nearby Sizergh Castle, the National Trust property with an impressive fourteenth-century Pele Tower, as well as Cartmel Fell, in her writings.

On the shore of Esthwaite Water is the Georgian house of Esthwaite Lodge and here, for about five summers, Francis Brett Young spent his holidays before the last war, and he was joined by Hugh Walpole for some of the time.

And so the list could continue but there is yet another cluster of properties associated with equally prominent literary persons some fifteen miles north, adding a further four men and fifteen properties to this impressive list. This group more dispersed than that previously mentioned, is Penrith, Keswick, Crosthwaite, Cockermouth, and the most northerly Bridekirk. In these locations the associations are perhaps with some of the most familiar names such as William Wordsworth, whose origin stems from Cockermouth, he and his sister Dorothy being connected with many of the properties throughout Cumbria; the Globe Hotel in Cockermouth was visited by the great Scottish poet, essayist and novelist Robert Lewis Stevenson. Penrith, and Broughton Castle ruins, were home and playground to William Wordsworth after his father died as it was in this town that his mother lived before marrying John Wordsworth, and time was spent with the grandparents; later sister Dorothy joined him.

Keswick and district with nearby Greta Hall, Shelley's Cottage and Fitz Park can claim fame many times over from the list of notable visitors and affiliations from Coleridge and Thomas Gray, to Shelley and Southey; Sir Hugh Walpole is buried in St John's churchyard. At nearby Mirehouse the connections are with Thomas Carlyle and Tennyson.

Crosthwaite has in its graveyard the resting place of Robert Southey who wrote of *The History of Brazil*; in memory of this the Brazilian Government paid for the restoration of the tombstone in recent times.

Bridekirk, on the other hand, may indeed not be so familiar to many, but at the vicarage of this small village some two miles from Cockermouth was born during the seventeenth century the poet Thomas Tickell. By no means one of the earliest English poets, but let it suffice in this volume to consider writers from the late seventeenth century onwards, rather than earlier and back to medieval times, a subject on which much has previously been published. Tickell was certainly one of the early literary people emanating from the Lake District. A Whig politician who had great enthusiasm for the Wiltshire poet, essayist and statesman Joseph Addison for whom Tickell acted as editor for some of his work, and on Addison's death wrote a great elegy. During his life time, apart from this elegy, his main claim to fame was the translation of part one of the *Iliad* but, unfortunately, according to one authority, this was published on the same day as the first volume of the translation by that great London contemporary, also a poet, and former friend of Addison, Alexander Pope.

Why, one could ask, did the Lake District became such a magnet to this group? Perhaps the quiet and solitude, or perhaps the sheer awesome beauty, but whatever the individual reasons, even today in a world of noise, bustle and technology, a visit to the area can produce the atmosphere, the solitude sought by writers, artists and visionaries alike, all of which can be felt and appreciated.

This subject has by no means been exhausted, very much to the contrary, but by retracing steps to Crosthwaite brings contact with a famous Vicar of the Parish who, although not perhaps a member of the literary world in the accepted sense, he certainly did write copiously including many sonnets whenever a subject justified his attention. This was Canon Hardwicke Rawnsley, Canon of Carlisle and Honorary Secretary for the first quarter century of the newly formed National Trust, being one of the three who instigated the association in 1895. He was also a great friend and supporter – mentor may be a more appropriate word – to the person who is prime subject of this chapter of this book: a lady, although not as yet mentioned above, can be described as the greatest donor of properties into the care of the National Trust, and thus permanently preserved for the Nation, in the Lake District, namely Miss Beatrix Potter.

There can be few people today who cannot relate in some way to the writer and illustrator of children's stories who died more than a quarter of a century ago. To many she will evoke childhood memories, to others their children and children's children will enjoy the sheer delight and pleasure from the fascinating and lovingly written words, as refreshing as if they had been written only yesterday. And yet, why or how did the young lady who spent the first thirty years of her life in an atmosphere of Victorian servitude, survive and blossom to become one of the great literary names throughout the world? During the latter part of the twentieth century her words have been used to teach English to the Japanese, in addition to other countries and her first purchase of the property 'Hill Top' has developed into a place of pilgrimage. How refreshing, as Beatrix as a girl was brought up on the readings of Scott's *Waverley Novels*. Could the answer be that what distinguished her, in particular, was her prime world involving animals not humans who in the main were unnecessary and even intrusive? Her stories were by illustrations, for Beatrix was a self-taught artist, and the words, although complementary to the pictures, were secondary.

Queen Victoria had already reigned some twenty-eight years when Beatrix was born and Prince Albert had died five years previously; this perhaps was a contributory factor to the sober lifestyle into which the child was born. Queen Victoria during her lonely childhood at Kensington Palace made dolls in the likeness of adults; Beatrix during her lonely early years at 2 Bolton Gardens, South Kensington in London, studied, dissected and drew any item of nature she could obtain from fungus, insects to small mammals, some of which were found in the house cellars, but a greater collection whilst on the annual family holidays. Her company in those days was not human but a dilapidated, well-worn, black, wooden doll called Topsy; a name to reappear years later.

In this day and age it is difficult to visualize the lifestyle and atmosphere in a large, dark, stuffy house, complete with aspidistras, in South Kensington, London, owned and disciplined by a couple of wealthy, conventional, middle-class Victorians, dominating their children as strictly as they treated the servants. Bolton Gardens, which Beatrix referred to in later life as her unloved birthplace, no doubt a reflection on the third floor where she had spent so much of her childhood in her lonely incarceration, was demolished by a bomb during 1940, the year of the Battle of Britain.

Master of the house, Mr Rupert Potter and his wife, both of whom inherited fortunes from Lancashire cotton mills, rigidly adhered to the appropriate standard of living as expected during the middle and latter part of the nineteenth century. The fortunes were large enough for them to be divorced from the stigma of being associated with work or trade; he was best described as a non-practicing barrister – a gentlemanly profession even if not exercised. There was, however, annual relief for the children from the domination of the parents and that was the holidays; Easter heralded by the preparing for travel of parents, children, servants and countless trunks and portmanteaus; the visit to the seaside for some weeks, enough time for the staff to spring-clean the winter residence. The summer produced a similar exodus, albeit this time for some months, when the whole household moved to various rented properties to repeat the daily routines as experienced in London. The main variations in the routine between abiding in London or the summer holiday addresses was that in London Rupert Potter spent time at his club, whereas on holiday leisure time was filled by shooting, fishing and entertaining.

Until 1881 all were transported to rented houses in Scotland, but from the following year moving affections to other rented accommodations in the Lake District. One of the Lakeland properties was Wray Castle, a neo-Tudor pile, with terraces, typical nineteenth century, on the west shore of Lake Windermere; given to the National Trust in 1929 by Sir Noton & Lady Barclay. It is now privately let.

Perhaps to have insight into the character of the girl herself and from where she inherited her great determination to be her own person can be understood by looking at the life of her ancestors.

Her mother was descended from the Cromptons, who certainly can be traced through six generations. Originally they were rich yeomen, farmers, merchants and cotton spinners and it was Abraham, described as a banker, who bought the great estate of Chorley Hall, with its ninety-acre park, in Lancashire from the Crown for the sum of £5,550. This was formerly the home of Chorley who was beheaded at Preston in 1716 for his part in the Stuart uprisings. As Abraham Crompton bought the Hall about 1718 he must have been the owner when the Younger Pretender visited the property during the further incursions of 1745 but he may have been conveniently absent as he is not cited as being involved in this affray. The previously important Chorley family whose existence can be traced to pre-Conquest days, and one of the most respected and honoured of the families in Lancashire, faded into obscurity. Interestingly one of the Chorleys is recorded as being married in the seventeenth century under one of the edicts by Cromwell's Nominated Assembly whereby the ancient religious ceremony of marriage was abolished. Unity in matrimony was performed by a Justice of the Peace and not by a priest or minister. There are few records of a marriage taking place in these circumstances.

Beatrix's maternal great-grandfather, another Abraham, great-grandson of the banker, inherited Chorley Hall and whilst there is no evidence of the banker's direct involvement with the attempted uprising it is known that the young Abraham had sympathies with the revolutionary movement in the nineteenth century in which such people as Thistlewood were involved, one of the leaders of the Cato Street Conspiracy for which he and others were ultimately hanged. A visit to see Thistlewood in prison resulted in Abraham being removed from the bench on which he served, and being out of favour he sold the Hall to a R.T. Parker who demolished the building in 1817; the Cromptons moved to Lune Villa. There now remains only a farmhouse bearing the name Chorley Old Hall, this the last indication of the great ancestral mansion; albeit that part of the old stables could be part of that eighteenth-century date and a number of street names in the area perpetuate the estate's existence.

Grandmother Crompton, Jessy, who let no one forget that she was a Crompton, was from a family of twelve children, married Edmund Potter who was the builder of Camfield Place, Essendon in Hertfordshire where Beatrix stayed with her grandparents during her younger days. Jessy and Beatrix spent many hours together, Jessy relating many tales of the 'good old days'; this at the stage when Beatrix was ten and Jessy seventy-five years of age. Beatrix, whilst listening to the interesting and somewhat fanciful stories of the Crompton family lifestyle, tales many times embroidered by Grandma who lived to the age of ninety years, would doodle by drawing butterflies and, like the Brontë sisters and Samuel Pepys, made notes and diary-type entries in her own minute, self-devised shorthand, not discernible to unwelcome prying eyes. Camfield Place is now a privately owned residence of a famous modern authoress.

Beatrix's father Rupert Potter, apart from his support by his almost daily attendance at the Athenaeum Club in London, had few hobbies but one interest appears to have been photography for which he became quite well known and this lead to his association with Millais whose studio he visited to make use of the artist's models for furtherance of his new-fangled art. He also devoted much time to genealogy, particularly to the Cromptons. Grandfather Potter, Edmund, Manchester born 1802 of poor parents, became a self-educated and self-made man and by middle age the owner of Dinting Vale Works at Glossop, but calico printing declined and in his thirties – about the time when Rupert Potter was born – he was bankrupt. Within ten years debts had been paid and another fortune made; he became Liberal MP for Carlisle and had Camfield Place built, complete with marble busts of Gladstone, Cobden, Bright and Peel. Was the interest in genealogy which showed the Crompton Lancashire connection and the holidays for the Potters curtailed from Scotland to the Lakes a matter of Rupert following in father-in-law's footsteps?

Bolton Gardens was little used for entertaining but the various holiday homes provided for parties, shooting and fishing. A number of Unitarian Ministers such as Mr Gaskell whose wife had died some years previously, and John Bright the devout fisherman, were frequent visitors.

Holidays, both in the early days in Scotland and those later in the Lake District, were, for the children Beatrix and Bertram, five years her junior, occupied almost entirely by study as they were somewhat besotted with analysis, drawing and recording of nature from fungi to all small living creatures. Many specimens were transferred to London, providing all livestock was kept well out of sight of adults, for further dissection and study whilst Bertram was away at school. Even whilst visiting relations and countless cousins, sometimes Beatrix on her own continued her investigations into all living things. There were many opportunities as apart from Scotland and the Lake District visits included Camfield Place to grandparents, an aunt in Putney, Hastings for Easter – that a family affair – to Sidmouth and an uncle in Wales; other relation visits are mentioned later. Bertram in his late teens, having finished at Charterhouse, persuaded his parents the acceptability of an interest in art, particularly landscape painting in Scotland. This provided the means for escape. There were few places Beatrix was allowed to go to in London, certainly without a chaperone, but the Victoria and Albert museum and the South Kensington museum were allowed. It was from these visits that illustrations of period costume designs were made and used years later for the considerably imaginative adornment of the little folk by dressing them in mufflers, bonnets, parasols and the like. At this stage a large collection of fine watercolours and sketches was being amassed, many of the drawings entered in home-made books of scrap paper.

Beatrix's private education was terminated in fairly early days when the private tutor had imparted all she could; further education was on one or two specialized subjects only. She maintained contact with her German teacher who was the mother of the little boy, Noel, whose illness was the reason for the letter with illustrations about Peter Rabbit. This letter was the story of Peter with Flopsy, Mopsy and Cottontail, plus the infamous Mr McGregor. It was dated 4 September 1893 with the address Eastwood, Dunkeld. Eight years later it was borrowed back from Noel to become the basis of the first book, *The Tale of Peter Rabbit*; rejected by six publishers then published privately. Later the publishers Warnes agreed to take over the publication, almost making a condition that it have colour drawings. They continued to be Beatrix Potter's publishers for the following twenty-six books into the 1940s. A few others were published by an American firm without consent.

Whilst this narrative does not purport to chronologically relate to each and every stage in the life of Beatrix Potter, which would in any case prove abortive as there are periods during which little is known or recorded, such a period is that between the end of her time scheduled for private education and her mid-thirties. Years later writings and drawings on the subject so dear to her, the details of the natural world were to be found, proving this actually occupied much of her time and so the end of the nineteenth century sees great changes when book production begins to dominate and continues to do so for the next decade and a half.

One of the greatest encouragers of Beatrix's most pleasurable hobbies – it was still a hobby and not thought of seriously – was Canon Rawnsley, who fortuitously was in the midst of his long crusade against any form of development in the Lake District, whether installation or the building for holiday accommodation for the general populace of Lancashire, or the building of a suggested railway round the lake; this about the same time as Beatrix Potter's early days of writing stories. The Canon was well known to the Potters and a number of photographs taken by Rupert of the Canon and others are still in existence. It was about 1878, Canon Rawnsley was Vicar of the Parish of Wray and within a few years Potter discovered the old castle which was to let for summer holidays. The friendship between them grew, and this great defender of the environment, writer of poems, naturalist and friend of Tennyson, continued when the Canon became Vicar of Crosthwaite near Keswick. It was not however until 1895 that Rawnsley joined others and became founders of the National Trust. Rupert was one of the early life members of this new Trust.

The writings were now to be placed on a business footing with her publishers since they had had second thoughts about committing themselves and even then their lukewarm reception was tempered by them dictating details of presentation. Beatrix Potter coped with the incarceration of Bolton Gardens between holidays by continuing mentally fulfilling her imagination with the study of little folk. Her brother Bertram had no such safety valve. In younger life he escaped from the confinement by being away at school but with no such retreat being available he now made his own escape. With no conviction that art was to be his future forte and when he became of age he arrived in Roxbroughshire and took over a farm. Brother and sister started a new life style with the introduction of the Scottish farm, he discarding the yoke of parental control, she taking advantage for an even closer study of nature, and some of the enchantment to appear in future writings was born during this partial life of freedom.

If the reader has the impression that Beatrix wrote books from preformatted ideas in her head and wrote them at one sitting, as so many authoresses of novels appear to do, this was not true. Beatrix's ideas stemmed from very many isolated instances and the finished work was only achieved after many alterations, additions, editing and considerable work, together with many stage by stage discussions with her publisher. The second and third published books, *The Tailor* and *Squirrel Nutkin* respectively, illustrate this point.

Almost against the wishes of her mother, who considered Beatrix too frail even at the age of twenty-six to endure much travelling – despite all the toing and froing between London and holiday destinations – Beatrix made a visit to Harescombe Grange near Stroud in Gloucestershire with her cousin Caroline Hutton. Here Beatrix heard a curious story referring to a tailor in Gloucester and this provided the basis, and the drawings, after a personal visit to the tailor's shop, for a story to be sent to Noel's sister Freda whilst she was poorly. Similar to Peter Rabbit, because of the authoress's lack of confidence, it was initially printed privately and later in modified form officially published by Warnes; hence the birth of one of Beatrix's favourite stories, *The Tailor of Gloucester*, published the year after Peter Rabbit.

Here it should be mentioned that an even earlier letter had been written to a child, possibly in the 1890s, this to Noel and Freda's brother Eric; the subject was Jeremy Fisher although the idea existed so long ago it was not published in book form until four years after Peter Rabbit, and became entitled *The Tale of Jeremy Fisher*.

The next published book was *The Tale of Squirrel Nutkin* the original idea for which stemmed from a visit to yet another cousin, this time the Hyde-Parkers of Melford Hall in Suffolk, where many almost tame squirrels roamed. The eventual drawings, however, particularly of the squirrels rafting across water to Owl Island, were not devised until the next visit to the Lake District. Owl Island in fact being St Herbert's Island.

Even at this stage Beatrix was still being restricted particularly by her mother who considered the writings disrupted the family life. Many ideas were curbed when holidays took preference to business negotiations with publishers; Mr Potter did take an interest in the legal side of contracts but at a distance. Beatrix openly confessed, more than once, at the disquiet of her parents' feelings, nevertheless she did test her style of writing on some of her children's friends and this influenced her style and presentation of future writings. In one of her frequent letters to Norman Warne, this one from Fawe Park, Keswick during a three-month stay with her parents, she referred to holidays as 'a weary business'.

The necessity to discuss with the publishers Beatrix's next few books introduced her to a completely different lifestyle. From the formality of the Potter household at Bolton Gardens she now became intimately involved with the members of the Warne family and their informality at the large house of 8 Bedford Square. At this address the widow of Frederick, the founder of the publishing business, lived with two of her children, Norman and Millie. Harold, now head of the firm, Fruing and Edith lived elsewhere but frequently descended on the house for business and pleasurable get-togethers, many times accompanied by their children.

The books now under discussion in great detail included *The Tailor*, *Benjamin Bunny*, *Two Bad Mice*, and *Mrs Tiggy-Winkle* which was based on Beatrix's pet hedgehog which had been adored for many years, and had travelled, duly secreted from parental eyes, hundreds of miles, but finally succumbed to age to be tearfully buried in the back garden of Bolton Gardens, thus joining in the resting place of other doted-upon pets.

The long and intense association with Norman Warne over the last four years was producing a deep relationship and as temperaments were similar and both were nearly forty years of age, Norman amicably made a proposal of marriage and was warmly accepted. Joy was felt throughout the Warne household; unfortunately to the Potters at Bolton Gardens the feeling was one of complete condemnation and the daughter of the house, despite her age, would no way be allowed to marry into trade, even if the Potters' fortune emanated from trade. For a time Beatrix experienced the freedom of Bedford Square whenever possible, even wearing an engagement ring in defiance of her parents' thoughts, but alas the new-found joy was to be short-lived as Norman, who had always had a far from strong constitution, died from pernicious anaemia just before Christmas of that year. The loss of a dear one for the first time in normal family circumstances is heart-rending enough, but when the family had been against the liaison in the first instance it must have been even harder. Fortunately Beatrix had a confidant in Norman's sister Millie and it was with her a close friendship blossomed and continued for many years. The rounds of London – holidays – London continued with little interest for Beatrix; a few visits were made with an aunt, Lady Roscoe, in Bath, whilst her husband Sir Harry the distinguished chemist, was taking the waters.

With the following year there came the opportunity to provide the required safety valve. Of all the different places Beatrix visited, almost always with her parents, and for a time with her brother, the one place dearest to Beatrix's heart, and the area in which her later and final life was spent, was the complete opposite to where she had spent her childhood in London. Not the delights of Scotland, although enjoyment had been experienced there sometimes, and where her brother had chosen to escape, but to the area of north-west England not far from where her parents had descended and a short distance north of the area where the family fortunes had been made so many years before. To be precise it was the area which was formerly called Furness, being a district of Lancashire and between Westmoreland and the sea; a district in modern times designated Cumbria which embraces the Lake District.

By now in a comfortable financial position with the royalties from Peter Rabbit and a legacy which had been received from an aunt, Beatrix made her first property purchase, this being the seventeenth century farm of Hill Top. To her parents this indicated a wish for the not understood independence, and thus explanations were required. Investment was the excuse given, and never can there have been more truth in one word as was proved in the years to follow. The idea of investment in any form would certainly have had approval of the money-conscious Rupert Potter. So brother and sister had by now both become involved in farming but not quite in the same manner. Beatrix as an unmarried daughter still had a duty to her parents so a manager/tenant had to be found. Fortunately the farm already had a tenant and within a short time agreement was reached between owner and tenant, a John Cannon and family, the existing occupiers remaining in office, an arrangement which lasted for about twelve happy years.

Whenever the Potters spent holidays in Keswick Beatrix now had a legitimate excuse to have freedom from the family; the farm had been moderately extended to allow separate homes, one for Beatrix and one for the Cannons. With the ownership of Hill Top Beatrix now had even more mental stimulus for her writings, many of the illustrations emanating from the contents of the farmhouse, and indeed from the farm itself. Some of her sketches of animals were drawn from the animals in real life, such as the farm rats, of which there appears to have been a plague, some of the drawings being used in the story of *The Roly-Poly Pudding* and *The Tale of Tom Kitten.* Books were now being produced apace.

Family visits still had to be endured, even to Uncle Frederick Burton at Gwaynyog near Denbigh, this large house and estate resulting from another member of the family having a cotton mill fortune. During this period the Potters were thankfully spending more and more visits to the Lake District, during which Beatrix could at least spend some time, even if only too short a week or two at Hill Top. During the first eight years following the purchase of Hill Top Beatrix Potter's best works were written by the completion of thirteen books, most having direct association with the little farmhouse, the interior fittings, the exterior position, the farm buildings, and most importantly the animals. The village and surrounding district of Sawrey were also being major contributing factors to the books' contents, as indeed were some of the local residents, who by this time were becoming well known to Beatrix as she was becoming well known to them.

Although more months of the year still had to be endured in London than in the beloved Sawrey area Beatrix was by 1910 continuing to buy more and more animal stock for the farm and purchased a number of cottages and farms as they became available. Within a few years her ownership extended to half the valley of Sawrey. During the first decade of the twentieth century, Beatrix's time in London with her parents was not entirely wasted: there was business to be dealt with. The writings and publications were big business and had sufficient fame for more commercialism to be considered. There were however problems with the idea of producing toys based on the characters within the books as international free-trade policy within the Government resulted in there being virtually no copyright protection. As far back as the first book of Peter Rabbit an American publisher had produced the book for their home market; Germany, never being slow to commercialize from other people's ideas, was producing toys in the guise of Peter Rabbit and Squirrel Nutkin; the latter with the actual name of Nutkin, and these cheap goods were being imported into England. Unfortunately the time for producing such toys in England was when the British toy trade was in decline, many of the factories having closed because of the import of cheap copies.

It may be difficult to imagine Beatrix who would chose to spend her life in the apparel of a country farmer in her beloved Lake District actually becoming involved in politics but on the periphery this is exactly what she did during the period of the 1910 government elections. With no votes for women letters and posters were produced and distributed in her area of South Kensington giving force to the need for tariff reform as opposed to free trade. More commercialism was considered by Beatrix's publishers, contacting the firm of Sandersons to produce nursery wallpaper with Beatrix's characters and this was partly successful by being produced as a nursery frieze, the royalties received being added to the revenue of Hill Top.

A property purchased in 1909 proved to be of considerable significance in a number of ways. The property was called Castle Farm which was situated in very close proximity to Hill Top, and in addition to the farmhouse, a cottage adjoined; the fields of Hill Top and Castle Farm could conveniently be joined as one.

The solicitors dealing with the Castle Farm transaction were the long-established family firm of William Heelis & Sons; the Partner who dealt with Miss Potter was of the younger generation of the firm, that being William Heelis. The next few years again saw unhappiness and disagreement within the Potter family, similar to that period the best part of ten years previously when Norman Warne and Beatrix became betrothed, only this time the suitor was a solicitor in the form of William Heelis. Ages and temperament were similar but now Beatrix was not only in the latter half of her forties but she was also suffering from far from robust health, including a suspected weakness of the heart. It will never be known what type of suitor would have been acceptable for this daughter but certainly the Junior Partner of a country solicitors' practice was not, after all she was the daughter of a barrister even if he had never practised in his life. With the constraints enforced by the Potters on Beatrix's acquaintances it was extremely unlikely she would ever meet a suitable male companion, if ever one was likely to exist.

During Beatrix's lengthy recuperation at Bolton Gardens her brother Bertram paid one of his rare visits and he not only supported his sister in her intentions to marry but he announced his marriage to a farmer's daughter years previously; and happy years they had been. Bertram had taken the disagreeable step of marrying without informing his parents knowing that they would have vigorously opposed such a union. Beatrix's marriage did take place at the Parish Church of St Mary Abbot's, Kensington on 15 October 1913, with the honeymoon at a rented cottage near Castle Farm. Castle Farm house at this stage was in the course of being modified and enlarged and water supply being connected. Hill Top would not have been suitable for the newly weds, being too small and already the home of a manager and family, and, by no means least, being sacrosanct to Beatrix as the birthplace of so many stories, so it was not to be violated.

Father, Rupert Potter died at the age of eighty-one within a matter of months of Beatrix's wedding.

This in reality brought to an end another stage of Beatrix's life. During the unnatural confinement and incarceration in a London Victorian environment had materialized a mass of children's stories inseparable from drawings and paintings of nature, the latter stemming from the advantage taken of every opportunity to relate with nature, a nature not experienced in the confines of a built-up area but during the extended holidays taken in country districts – albeit some drawings emanated from the city museums. How much had been achieved. The first letter in story form sent to a sick child was dated 1893, was subsequently enlarged into book form and limited publication privately produced seven years later; professionally published two years after that. The last of the series was published in the year of Beatrix's marriage to William, but from the mass of ideas, further stories and illustrations which had been accumulated over the years a further nine books appeared, in addition to three children's painting books. The following years produced much international recognition and Beatrix received a great amount of appraisal from many people from various parts of the world, particularly America.

The new life Beatrix now experienced, and with the happiness of her husband, must have seemed like heaven compared to the condition of her upbringing, and their home at Castle Cottage became the centre for William's legal dealings on the one hand, and Beatrix's bits and pieces for her participating in country and village life on the other.

Mrs Potter moved to a small rented house in Sawrey which she shared with her only surviving sister-in-law, thus avoiding the dangers of Zeppelins over London. Mrs Potter after the war did not return to London but moved to Lindeth How being a large Victorian house on the other side of Lake Windermere, not far from Bowness, which had on occasions been one of the Potter rented holiday homes. Much furniture (and servants) were duly installed from Bolton Gardens and life routinely continued for the secluded widow pursuing her interest in her canaries and needlework.

Unlike her daughter she did not have sight problems and she also had the companionship of her little dog. And so life continued in the big granite house until at the age of ninety-three Mrs Potter joined her husband after nearly twenty years of widowhood.

War years were busy for William, continuing to run his legal office and Beatrix maintaining the farm production; both operations being run with shortage of manpower. In 1918, a few months after the armistice, Beatrix's brother Bertram unexpectedly died peacefully in Scotland.

With the death of Rupert Potter Beatrix had become a comparatively wealthy woman to such an extent when the large and lonely fell farm, Trout Beck, with its over 2,000 acres and solitary farmhouse and many hundreds of home-bred sheep, came on the market in 1923 Beatrix bought it. This was perhaps the most idyllic of all the places in Beatrix's life. This purchase was the introduction to the Herdwick sheep that she got to know and love so well, the breed for which she became a leading authority and her knowledge so accepted by the hill farmers, who did not view the amateur, and certainly not a female, kindly, but Beatrix was paid respect by being the first woman to be appointed Chairman of the Herdwick Breeders' Association. Hours and days were spent by Beatrix walking the sometimes cruel fells within her Trout Beck estate and the solitary figure wandered for miles, but was by no means solitary.

The National Trust for Places of Historic Interest or Natural Beauty was officially formalized in 1895 but there had been much talk and publicity about such an organization for many years prior to this date. It is not therefore surprising that Beatrix could now envisage as an end product, a goal, a reason for completing as many purchases as possible, knowing that with title ultimately being conveyed to this new protected, by Act of Parliament, Trust, the safety of the properties would, with inalienability, perpetuate. The great difference being the Trust's permanency thus avoiding the inevitability of private ownership which changes with differing generations and can be subject to risk with changes in financial status. The Trust of course was at an enormous advantage in that it did not suffer like the private landowner from the scourges of Income Tax nor Death Duties, whatever it may be called at the time. It is not possible to know the workings of Beatrix's mind but it may in all fairness be guessed that her earliest purchases were for her enjoyment and satisfaction, but as the years progressed she was convinced that the National Trust could continue her devout wish for preservation long after her death. With this in mind the speed at which properties were purchased accelerated resulting in her becoming one of the greatest contributors of properties to the Trust in the Lake District. Ultimately on her death she left a legacy of fourteen traditional farms plus 4,000 acres to the care of the National Trust.

The Second World War had more effect on the Lake District than most people realize. There was the inevitable influx of evacuees, and a surprising amount of building damage from enemy planes either releasing their surplus bombs or damaged planes being jettisoned; in addition there was, as elsewhere, a shortage of manpower, food to be produced from the land, and a shortage of many commodities. The Lakes were in no way a haven excepting that there were more open spaces to run to. William Heelis continued his work as a solicitor in addition to being Clerk to the Justices and officiated on the County War Agricultural Committee. Beatrix by now suffering as an old lady, continued her normal country pursuits as best she could without complaint and carried on with farm work when most at her age and in her poor health would have surrendered into ease. With her affairs put in order, even instructing exactly where some ornaments should be displayed, she departed this life on 22 December 1943 at the age of seventy-seven.

The tales, or stories, of Beatrix Potter would be continued and be as many and as varied as the sketches, the colour-washed drawings, and the children's stories she produced, but let the reader accept that there is much in the way of further reading to be searched for and enjoyed.

Chapter IV

Fen Country

Essentially a unique area of the flat eastern counties of England the Fens have almost disappeared compared to their original acreage, but thanks to the National Trust who with great diligence have preserved what is in fact a small remaining area called Wicken Fen. Also, thanks to the research and great devotion of Sir Peter Roberts Bt., there is a reconstruction of a village as it may have looked when the Iceni tribe inhabited part of the northern fens at Cockley Cley near Swaffham nearly 2,000 years ago. These two outstanding pieces of conservation provide the means for appreciating both the type of terrain and the lifestyle of the inhabitants during the period of the first century.

Wicken Fen, a mere 600 acres managed by the Trust, has been acquired by purchase and gifts since 1899. Although there are about 730 acres of true wetland in the area, Wicken is a maintained wetland, considered to be one of the most important in Europe which shows the type of ground which existed over an area of about 2,500 square miles, from Lincolnshire to Suffolk, including parts of Norfolk, Cambridgeshire, Bedfordshire and Essex, in the first century and before. It is not only a record of the type of country but provides habitat for a large variety of insects (over 5,000 species) and birds, some of which have not been recorded in any other district of England, together with over 300 species of flowering plants. In order to maintain the water level a restored wind-pump is kept in working order; the difference is that whilst the original pumps drained the land, the motor of this one has been reversed to pump water onto the land to ensure its wet status. Today this part of the Fens – a word which is Anglo-Saxon for marshy or boggy land – is well supported as part of Britain's Ecological history, involving schools and educational organizations.

Historians suggest that originally the whole of the flat Fen district was one large bay which over the years silted up and the Wash is the only remaining part of that bay. It is well recorded that from Roman times systematic drainage has taken place. In the seventeenth century, much to the resentment of locals, a number of earls, the Dukes of Bedford and others, involved Dutch drainage experts and spent considerable time, effort and money on reclaiming the land. The most successful attempts took place during the eighteenth and very early nineteenth centuries. Perhaps one of the most famous was 'Turnip Townshend', or correctly titled Charles Townshend, 2nd Viscount, the British politician who spent time in the Netherlands as a diplomat where he learned of land drainage. His nickname stems from his interest in agriculture and the introduction of turnips and other root crops which were not grown in England before the seventeenth century.

From this very distinct area a lot can be learned of the people who survived from land which was poor in the production of any foodstuffs, and an area which in the days of the Romans and the Normans was populated by differing tribes. Lessons can be learned not only about those people but about attitudes between the residents and the invaders.

In the year c.55 BC the Romans invaded to obtain greater wealth by increasing the size of the Roman Empire and they discovered resources in the British Isles were rich in both minerals and timber. If only they had realized that the people, being an isolated independent race, were very different from the Romans themselves and other Europeans, history may have been different.

During this Roman period the area now called the Fens was inhabited by various tribes in the north of what is now called Norfolk, the main tribe being the Iceni, a tribe which had migrated from the northern shores of the European continent about 200 BC. Further south in an area northeast of the River Thames was the Trinovante tribe, which arrived in Britain about a hundred years after the Icenis. The indications are that the two tribes were very different from each other, in fact almost opposite in attitude and material possessions. The Iceni in the north were more content with their lot, having a poor standard of living but being peace loving and satisfied with the goods they could forage. Having said that they did indeed, like all the people of the period, make wars against each other but only if they found it necessary to do so in order to survive. They also, when roused, would act like normal ancient man and cut the heads off captured enemy or throw them in the snake pit to be bitten and subsequently starve to death. Their near pacifism resulted in there being less weapons and tools, whether made from iron or flint.

The Trinovantes much preferred to be permanently at war. There was another warlike tribe which arrived at about the same time as the Trinovantes called Belgae. Perhaps they were more warlike because they lived just north of the River Thames in an area the Romans were using as a port – that is London. There was a formidable amount of antagonism between the invaders and the Trinovantes which may have resulted from the fact that the Romans taxed the Trinovantes to an unreasonable degree. They were nevertheless a belligerent tribe, and they did possess warlike weapons, largely flint daggers and spears.

The Icenis meanwhile had remained peacefully in the north, quietly keeping out of the way of the Romans hence not being charged taxes or having interference from the newcomers. The King of the Iceni was an old man called Prasutagus who wished for the peace to be maintained and before his death, which took place in either AD 59 or 60 when he was aged sixty-two, he agreed with the Emperor of Rome, Nero (an agreement signed by Claudius) that on payment of half the Iceni kingdom being given to the Romans, and the other half to his wife Boadicea and their daughters, peace would reign.

Unfortunately Rome was in financial difficulty because of the high cost of invading and controlling different lands, a change in financial circumstances which meant a difference in attitudes in the conquered Britain and the Iceni tribe was also charged high taxes by the new Empire. This was not accepted, and Queen Boadicea herself travelled to the Roman headquarters to protest, for which she was flogged, and subsequently her daughters were raped. This was the end of the peace between Iceni and Romans.

It is a much-written story of Queen Boadicea (variously spelled Boudicca – allegedly the correct old-type spelling – or Boudicea, and a number of permutations thereof) and it was at this stage in history, AD 61, that the Iceni tribe joined their previous enemies the Trinovantes to create battle with the enemy. During this exercise Colchester and other cities were burned, but the Romans won the day and the saga ended with the Queen committing suicide by poison in about the year 63.

The Romans with their over-extended empire, could not justify the drain on their resources and departed the country, leaving the tribes to revert to their old habits of pillaging each other's camps – but not for long before the Normans arrived on the scene.

During the period after that most famous of battles – 1066 and Hastings – the area of the Fens again became the most difficult for the invaders to handle and was the last area of England to hold out against them. At the strongholds which existed there were inevitably to be tales of defiance whether based on fact or myth. These tales would bring to the fore names of people who can be proved to have existed but were much surrounded by myth and well-embroidered stories in such a way that separating fact from fiction is nearly impossible. Embroidered stories could be said to exist for the period of Queen Boadicea and yet there is another whose name may be known to many but as a real person or a myth is questionable.

There is evidence that a man called Hereward was born in Bourne in Lincolnshire and survived with his small following of guerrilla-type force. Remembering that it was very possible for such a small band to reek chaos at defence posts of the invaders and then retreat and disappear along the almost unknown tracks through the swampland of the Fens, they in their secret undetected camp sites took refuge whilst resting, recuperating, rearming and regrouping before the next incursion into enemy territory.

Hereward has been described as being 'larger than life', of extraordinary strength of body but perhaps not so strong of mind, yet he nevertheless had power, and whether by charismatic means or brute superiority of strength, he could form a group of adventurers associated with those who disliked the Norman rulers. The entry in the Domesday Book shows that a Hereward existed and had lands near Bourne. It has also been proved that this Hereward died sometime before 1109 and married at least twice. Even Hereward's death or last stand of defiance is veiled in myth and mystery, but a place in Bedford has been cited as being possibly, or probably, his last resting place. Leading genealogists provide much controversial argument whether he was, as some claim, son of Leofric of Bourne, others support he owned lands in Warwickshire. Some would say this infamous outlaw was a most noble knight, founded in Saxon times. The title 'the Wake' originated in the thirteenth century.

Hereward is one of those named as being involved with the burning of Peterborough Abbey, and there could be truth in that. About the year 1070 news was received by the monks that the King was to appoint a Norman as Abbot, a state of affairs not to be accepted. A Norman Abbot in a land so steeped in conformity raised objection, and this was in itself enough to cause strife, but when it was heard that an officer of the Church removed the valuables during the night and took them to the Norman for supposed protection, action had to be taken. The leader was said to be English who was joined by people from throughout the lands in support and the outlaws forced entry into the monastery, set it on fire as with other buildings in the town and left by boat. Perhaps justification for revolt if the Normans were taking over the Abbey. This action may give credence to the tale that it was the monks who made it possible for the rebels to be found by the Normans in this labyrinth of bogs, as these men of the Church were familiar with the concealed pathways.

The demise of this noble hero is in doubt but the story continues, saying that Hereward narrowly escaped capture when William arrived in the Isle of Ely. Whether real or imaginary makes good reading and a story to be remembered from schooldays. The evidence remains and it can easily be imagined a Hereward being able to disappear in land such as the Fens.

Comparison could be made with King Arthur of the West Country; whereas Arthur was immortalized by such as Tennyson, Hereward was immortalised by Kingsley, who spent some years of his childhood in the Fen country. Did Kingsley light the spark for the Victorian awakening and interest in the hero? The Victorians were very fond of idolizing heroes. What is known is that the hero figure could have existed and stood fast against the invaders, and the type of terrain in which the alleged skirmishes took place did exist, and in a small way still do, thanks to the interests in conservation of the Fen country.

Chapter V

Hanbury Hall

Hanbury Hall, is one of the many great stately houses owned by the National Trust, but in this instance a very different image in a number of ways. There is no great portico as the entrance, in fact a rather plain entrance that almost appears to be incomplete. It is not an estate built from money earned by giving service to the Crown, nor from money obtained by paying homage to the royal court, but an estate enlarged and beautified with money received by association with the legal profession. Nevertheless, it is an estate which today illustrates how the gentry, even if not of the top echelon, lived in comfort and followed the fashions of the day from the baroque art within the building, to the modernizing of the park from labour-intensive Dutch or French style compartments in vogue in the late eighteenth century to the open naturalistic park.

In times gone by, Hanbury, with its old deer park, was within the ancient Royal Forest of Feckenham, and in Domesday was owned by the Church of Worcester; later belonging to the Bishops of Worcester until appropriated by Queen Elizabeth I in 1558. Elizabeth Knollys, a kins-women of the Queen, had married into the Leighton family and to that family the Queen granted Hanbury.

This Worcestershire estate is one of the most impressive of the great houses in the Midlands, not only as a fine example of a square, red-brick estate house – sometimes referred to as William and Mary style – built for the wealthy, but it also provides interest inside with one of the great painted staircases being the work of one of the trio of eighteenth-century painters. In this instance it was Thornhill who was commissioned by Thomas Vernon the builder of the present house about 1710, credit for which was given to another artist by an eminent historian.

According to the carved date above the front door, the house was built in 1701, although this probably indicated the date of completion of the building; the cupola was rebuilt and the clock added in 1809. The architect of this old-fashioned building with hipped roof and dormers is unknown but there are a number of similarities with both Ragley Hall, built about

1680 by Robert Hooke some eight miles distance away in Warwickshire, and with William Talman's Thoresby Hall of like period, formerly built for William, 4th Earl of Kingston, in The Dukeries, East Midlands.

The details of the history and the architectural story can be read in many publications, particularly in the handbooks produced by the National Trust which has owned the estate since 1953 thanks to the will of Sir George Vernon.

The garden as originally designed was of considerable importance being one of those laid to the instructions of George London, the partner of the royal gardener of Hampton Court, namely Henry Wise, but the formal straight lines of yew and box on the south side of the house by direction of Thomas Vernon, did not remain in existence for long; possibly from the 1730s to the 1770s, when Brown became fashionable. The Orangery, more or less as seen today, was built during the 1730s.

The Vernons did not originate in Worcestershire and can be traced throughout many centuries commencing with Richard, Lord Vernon, in Normandy, who was made an English baron during the reign of William the Conqueror; the family now includes the Vernons of Haddon and Sudbury in Derbyshire and the Vernons of Poynton in Cheshire. During the twelfth century one branch of the family settled at Wheatcroft near Northwich in Cheshire, and it was from this branch the Vernons of Hanbury were descended. The Reverend Richard Vernon, one of the issue from Wheatcroft, became Rector of Hanbury in 1580 and remained incumbent for forty-seven years, and it was his eldest son Edward who bought the estate in 1631 from the Leightons. This purchase included the Advowson of Hanbury — that is the right of presenting a clergyman to a benefice in the Church of England — a thought worth remembering when reading further. Edward's grandson, Thomas, a very successful chancery barrister, built the existing house when life had returned to normal after the Civil War, and when the 'Whig' style of administration had returned to power.

Before delving into the stories of a couple who owned Hanbury in the eighteenth century, a few thoughts about the historian clergyman named Nash who produced two massive volumes on the county history of Worcestershire, not only quoting dates incorrectly but also in 1781 referred to the great painted staircase at Hanbury as being created by the German painter Kneller. The Reverend Doctor T. Nash is variously spelt as Nash or Nashe, and his Christian name as either Treadway or Treadaway.

Nash undertook the production of the county history because no other person could be found to undertake the work and he spent his spare time and money collecting details of churches and manors. It should be mentioned that much of his work was based on the writings of the previous Worcestershire historian Thomas Habington – again a spelling question as some authorities use Habbington. This gentleman was, during the early seventeenth century, as a punishment for his involvement with the Gunpowder plotters, confined within the county boundary for the last forty years of his life, and spent the whole period producing copious records of his findings. Nash, who at one time lived in the village of Claines is referred to as an eighteenth-century Worcestershire historian but considerably censured when he acted as art critic in his 'History of Worcestershire' in the mid-eighteenth century. Dr Nash administered as Rector for thirty years, a link in a remarkable chain of Nashs who were vicars in Droitwich from 1688 to 1810. By the end of the eighteenth century old Dr Nash, as he was called, became Vicar at Leigh, where he is known to have preached at least once each year, usually shortly before the tithe audit.

So why did this historian suggest the great staircase was painted by Kneller instead of correctly listing it as one of the works of art of Sir James Thornhill who actually signed the work? The plot becomes even more interesting with the knowledge that Nash was a personal friend of the Vernons of Hanbury who owned the house and visited the family many times. The German painter Sir Godfrey Kneller came to England on the death of his father in 1675 and became portrait painter of royalty; it is therefore very unlikely that he would be involved in baroque painting in a country house owned by a lawyer.

Perhaps a word about the introduction of the baroque style would be appropriate at this juncture. Baroque paintings at so many of the great houses could almost be called enthralling and became particularly important as a status-symbol for the rich after the King had employed Verrio to work at Hampton Court and at Windsor. The great house owners obviously thought their properties deserved equally lavish attention.

The three main painters of the 'baroque' in the eighteenth century, introduced into England between the Restoration and the death of Queen Anne, were Verrio, Laguerre and Thornhill. The style is very distinctive and involved covering walls and ceilings in the great houses and offices, depicted rooms or staircases with open-sided pavilions without roof. Ground level showed scenes between columns on the walls whilst the sky, or ceiling, illustrated mythical figures, gods and goddesses flying about or reclining on clouds.

Of the three, the senior in age and the man thought to have introduced the style into England was Antonio Verrio, who was born about 1639 in Lecce in southern Italy and probably came to England about 1672. Some critics consider his work more gaudy than that of the other two; nevertheless he was in great demand and after some nine years mainly spent working at Windsor and Whitehall, in 1684 became Court Painter following in the steps of Lely who had died in 1680. For about eleven years from 1688 much of his life was spent working at Chatsworth and Burghley, after which he returned to royal favour and worked for the latter part of his life at Hampton Court and Windsor for William III. Verrio died about 1707.

Louis Laguerre was born about twenty-four years after Verrio; he was a French Catholic who arrived in England when he was about twenty years old and worked at Christ's Hospital for Verrio. Between 1689 and 1694 he joined another Frenchman and for much of his time worked at Chatsworth with other time spent at Burghley, Blenheim and Marlborough House in London. At Blenheim he probably produced some of his finest work. Although he continued with some commissions after this period, including that at St Lawrence, Stanmore near London, he was without doubt under the shadow of the third member of the trio, James Thornhill, who had gained much of his skill by copying Laguerre. Laguerre completed more of his artistic work, not unusually in the stairwell, of another Vernon house, Sudbury Hall in Derbyshire nearly twenty years prior to Thornhill's work at Hanbury.

James Thornhill was born about 1675 and, unlike the previous two, was an English Protestant who, it is said, continued the style of Verrio with the refinements of Laguerre; possibly the only English decorator in the grand baroque tradition. He was without doubt favoured because of his nationality and religion when given the commission to paint the cupola of St Paul's Cathedral, for which it is thought he was awarded his knighthood. Thornhill worked at Stoke Edith Park, according to Pevsner's *Herefordshire*, a house newly completed in 1698, the central hall of which had painted decoration by Thornhill. The house, owned by Thomas Foley, a near neighbour of the Vernons, was burned in 1927. He also worked at Chatsworth, Blenheim Palace and Hampton Court. Many years, something like 1708 to 1727, were spent painting at Greenwich Hospital. In addition to travelling in France and the Netherlands, Thornhill was made Sergeant Painter, became Member of Parliament in 1722 for his native town of Melcombe Regis (now incorporated in Weymouth) in Dorset, a Fellow of the Royal Society and Master of the Painter-Stainers' Company. In 1729 his only daughter Jane eloped and married the painter William Hogarth after which they lived in Paddington Village. Sir James was not amused and disowned the couple, until one day Lady Thornhill displayed some of Hogarth's work around the bedroom without declaring the artist's name. Thornhill was, so the story tells, so impressed by the standard of work by his son-in-law that thereafter all appears to have been forgiven.

Reverting to the owners of the Hall, Thomas Vernon the builder died without issue and the estate went to a cousin, Bowater Vernon, who produced a son, another Thomas, one time MP for Worcester, who died in 1771 aged about forty-seven, leaving a widow Emma, formerly a Cornewall of Berrington in Herefordshire, and a daughter in her teens, also called Emma. Both father and grandfather of Emma junior were friends of Nash the historian, in fact Nash was for a time the girl's guardian. On the death of her husband Mrs Vernon at once set about finding a grand husband for the new heiress and a match was made with Henry Cecil, nephew and later heir to the 9th Earl of Exeter.

Hanbury is the focus for some of the most intriguing and fascinating chronicles written — not a single chronicle but many. It has been the subject of facts construed in a form of censure of some of the people involved, the subject for incorrect recording of events and dates, and the basis for the delight of romantic narratives on more than one occasion. The whole premise of these writings are the interpretations of events during a relatively short period in the history of the estate.

The period starts after the death of Thomas Vernon and, as previously written, the widow, Mrs Vernon, was seeking a suitable husband for her only child, the heiress Emma. Actually a suitor for Emma had been considered prior to Thomas's death and the fathers of both parties were in accord, as was the uncle of the proposed groom. The only dissenter to this arrangement was the family friend Nash.

The case now placed before you, the reader, presents to you the facts, the provable facts, and nothing but the facts, starting on 23 May 1776 when a fashionable wedding took place at the moderately new church of St George, Hanover Square, in London, joining together in matrimony Emma Vernon and Henry Cecil.

During the ensuing thirteen years, or a little over, the couple lived at Hanbury. Within the year a son was born, but died within two months; this tragedy was followed, again within two months, by the death of Emma's mother. Hanbury Hall became subject to some internal alterations and the garden on the south side was converted from the elaborate formality of Thomas Vernon to the naturalistic mode of the day; it is therefore evident that the newly married couple were 'making themselves at home'. Henry, in addition to becoming more involved in politics in London and his responsibilities in connection with the fluctuating health and subsequent problems of the King, George III, was appointed Deputy Lieutenant for the County of Worcestershire. In the early days Emma would accompany her husband on the journeys to London, but, as time elapsed, she more frequently remained at home. Almost on the seventh anniversary of the wedding of Henry and Emma, the Curate, William Sneyd arrived at Hanbury from Lichfield. Some three years later Emma and William met at a public house called The Hen & Chickens in Birmingham, and from there the couple eloped. Henry, after surrendering his interests in Worcestershire, commenced his wandering. At this stage the year was 1789 and Henry arrived, by chance, at the village of Great Bolas in Shropshire, and using a pseudonym became engrossed in the village life. The following year, still using his false name of John Jones, he bigamously married the daughter of Farmer Hoggins, Sarah, who it was alleged he compromised. An Ecclesiastical Separation of Henry and Emma was arranged by civil action against Sneyd, albeit this action took place over two months after the bigamous marriage; nine months later this action was promulgated and within three months Royal Assent was given by the King to a Parliamentary Bill of Separation. This deed was followed by a quiet second marriage of Henry, now using his legal name, and Sarah in London. Within ten days of that marriage Emma married William Sneyd.

The activities of the participants of this story during the next six years were considerable. Basically in order of occurrence, starting with perhaps one of the most interesting facts, except a necessary duty to a person of title, Henry's uncle, the 9th Earl of Exeter, about a month before Henry's legal remarriage, made a new Will citing Henry as sole residuary legatee; it was more than two years later before uncle died. Sarah gave birth to a daughter, Sophia, and the following year a son, Henry, who died a few months later; this in the same year as Emma's husband William Sneyd died, that marriage having lasted less than two years. At this stage Sarah had reached the age of twenty years, and the year following she and her husband, now elevated to the peerage as 10th Earl of Exeter − Henry's uncle Lord Exeter whilst attending musical parties and dinners in London having died of a 'chronical disease' − visited his family seat of Burghley House for the first time.

During 1795, the year during which Emma married her third husband, John Phillips, Henry and Sarah revisited Sarah's place of birth, Great Bolas, and Henry spent a great deal of time and money, not only securing the future for his various in-laws, but also by providing gifts and annuities to the younger generations. Apprenticeships were bought, together with various army commissions – one of Sarah's brothers later rising to the rank of colonel. Gifts and legacies abounded and the former property bought by Henry, Bolas Villa, was renamed Burghley Villa. Sarah produced another son, Brownlow, who thrived and ultimately inherited his father's title. Henry maintained contact with the Hoggins family during the remainder of his life, giving support in many ways from financial to agricultural advice.

For Sarah the year 1796 was one of sadness as both her mother and father died with only a few weeks between events; on neither occasion could Sarah attend the funerals having other commitments at the time. Four days after her father's funeral Sarah attended a presentation to the King at St James's Palace; according to Horace Walpole the former farmer's daughter won approval in high circles by her great humility and modesty. In that year Sarah had a son, Thomas, but sadly this proved too much for the young Countess of Exeter and she died at the age of twenty-four years. To complete the life of Henry, in brief, he could not face the return to Shropshire so he sold Burghley Villa to the Reverend Creswell Tayleur from whom he had purchased it, and the sale was completed at the same price of two hundred pounds which John Jones had paid. Politics and government affairs became Henry's main occupation, in addition to the affairs of his estates at Burghley, and for three and a half years he remained a widower. Shortly after being elevated to Marquess he married and his third wife was the divorcee, Elizabeth Anne, Duchess of Hamilton. Less than four years later Henry died at fifty years of age and was interred in the family vaults at Burghley by the side of his beloved Sarah.

Above are the facts as known, all of which can be obtained by reference being made to a variety of works of fact, written by a variety of people; most of the periods mentioned and the dates together with the actual events can be proved from numerous sources including legal documents which still exist. Based on these happenings over the years has evolved three types of writings. At one end of the spectrum there is recorded the historical listings, at the other end there are the writings produced in the fairy-story fashion of the fictitious storyteller, written in a most delightful manner, and in between there are many references to the events presented in many forms, written as a guide for people on the periphery, people of sufficient interest to become knowledgeable of the facts as they affected history, but nowhere are there writings to try to understand why the intrigues took place. Most of the middle guide type of authorship condemns outright the accused of this case; namely Henry.

A short preamble is now required to summarise the salient points in this case as quoted above. Questionable occurrences have taken place: elopement, bigamy and the compromising of a young girl. Individually none of these were unusual during the eighteenth century – perhaps less usual in modern times – but collectively and appertaining to one couple would, even during the period when they were rife, create a scandal. Elopement by the lady of the house with a young curate of the church was rare; more common for the junior member of the household to elope with a servant. Bigamy was a dangerous act if discovered as in the period concerned the penalty was death – using a false name would not exonerate the guilty party. Compromising a youngster was by no means unusual; gentry were no better than others, and juniors, either in age or position, were on many occasions subjected to such behaviour, particularly the masters with innocent country maids.

Why is this case being brought before you? How have previous writers reported the facts of the matter? More importantly, is the impression given by these many writers and recorders presenting for posterity a fair hearing?

The answer to the first question is to enable you, the reader, to consider your verdict and decide which of the parties is responsible, if any, for the sadness experienced by those involved. The answers to the remaining questions are purely a matter for you to decide, but there is, without doubt, a sadness in the reading of the various chronicles in that few extol the virtues of the participants of the story. Without directly quoting, other than in the case of the classical historian Nash, who in life had much to say on a diversity of subjects with great authority, but little of pre-eminent standard, Emma was passionate and headstrong, whilst of her grandfather he had a low opinion but her father he considered virtuous and prudent.

Other published works make a variety of comments on the characters which are interesting. Tennyson's ballad produced in 1833, something like forty years after the event, was considered an abominably bad ballad or an inaccurate poem, or idealized version of events. Perhaps the Poet Laureate could be allowed some artistic licence for a work which reads rather well. On the subject of the marriage of Henry and Emma perhaps there is some truth in the idea that it was almost in the mode of an arranged marriage, the arranging being completed by the senior men of substance.

Of the main character in this saga, Henry, words have been used such

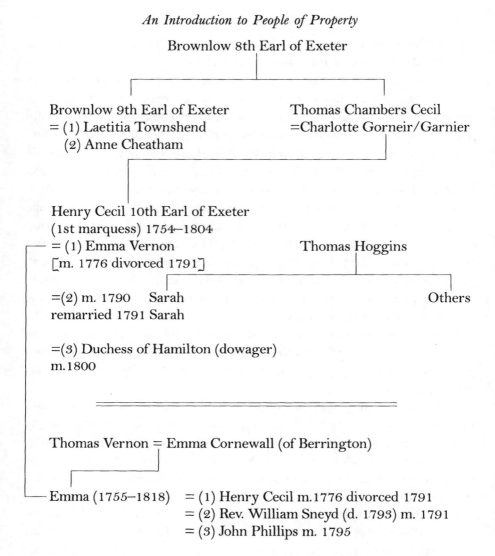

Brownlow 8th Earl of Exeter

Brownlow 9th Earl of Exeter
= (1) Laetitia Townshend
   (2) Anne Cheatham

Thomas Chambers Cecil
=Charlotte Gorneir/Garnier

Henry Cecil 10th Earl of Exeter
(1st marquess) 1754–1804
= (1) Emma Vernon
[m. 1776 divorced 1791]

Thomas Hoggins

=(2) m. 1790   Sarah
remarried 1791 Sarah

Others

=(3) Duchess of Hamilton (dowager)
m.1800

Thomas Vernon = Emma Cornewall (of Berrington)

Emma (1755–1818)   = (1) Henry Cecil m.1776 divorced 1791
                     = (2) Rev. William Sneyd (d. 1793) m. 1791
                     = (3) John Phillips m. 1795

as a bore, extremely devious, a gambler, unscrupulous aristocrat, selfish, extravagant, and as a young man he suffered from insecurity, being thus dependent upon the whims of elders who had confused him from cradle to early manhood. On the last count that could be construed in his defence as, by reading further, this is without doubt a relevant thought. During the period of Henry's visit to Shropshire before he married Sarah, quite understandably many suggestions were made including him being a land-scape artist – he did indeed complete some pictures so that may have been the image he intended – but other ideas followed such as him being a highwayman and leader of a gang of thieves. All very understandable when a man, who spoke like the gentry but wore rough country clothes, arrived amongst the country rustics incognito.

With Henry in the dock as the accused, in order to give a fair hearing of the case it is necessary to go back to the start of Henry's life, and then, having noted the circumstances, try to understand the people of the eighteenth century who represent the basis of the many facets and chronicles relating to the accused. Submission will be made to the effect that if blame is to be apportioned for Henry's shortcomings it must be equally levelled at the adults who controlled his early life.

Whilst it may not be of particular relevance it is worth mentioning that Henry was a direct descendant of the sixteenth-century William Cecil, Lord Burghley, one of the most famous of Elizabeth I's courtiers, the seat from which the families of Exeter and Salisbury emanated. Burghley was, in addition to having one of the most powerful posts in the land, the builder of one of the greatest of country houses, frequently likened to a palace: Burghley House in Lincolnshire. His character and desire to maintain royal favour was such that on more than one occasion he changed religious allegiance purely to conform with that of the monarch of the day. By no means unusual during the period in question, but in this instance with considerably more fervour. Henry of this story was within nine generations of that indomitable founder of the dynasties. William Cecil's son by his first marriage was created 1st Earl of Exeter and it was from this line that Henry originated, but it was not his father, Thomas Chambers Cecil, who inherited the title as 9th Earl but his uncle, Brownlow – a name perpetuated in honour of the 9th Earl's grandmother who introduced a lot of money into the family.

The circumstances of Henry's upbringing were far from ideal as his father, being the younger brother of the Earl, and who has been described as weak and undistinguished, although he was elected to Parliament as one of the members for Stamford at the age of twenty-two, married a dancer named Charlotte Garnier (or Gornier) who was said to be of Basque extraction and may have belonged to one of the company of dancers who came from France each year to perform at Drury Lane and Covent Garden. It is said that she was not conversant with English attitudes and had the conviction that the English were completely devoid of any sentimentality, and regarded the raising of her son as a duty to be performed strictly and in any manner to ensure that the child was not spoilt. Little is known about Thomas' life except that one important piece of evidence shows him to be in Belgium in 1756 when he wrote to one of the neighbours of the 1st Earl making it clear that he had gone abroad at the request of his brother and friends for indiscretions and extravagances in the past; he was asking for support and employment, and in addition he was making it clear that his health was not good.

Henry was born in Brussels in March 1754. There is even less known about the early years of Henry except that he was sent to Eton with a private tutor, Mr Weston, at an age somewhere between eight and ten; he also considered his home as being that of his Uncle Brownlow's at Burghley where he spent his holidays. With the evidence of father being abroad it is fair to assume that mother was also out of the country, and that his uncle arranged for the education and tutor at Eton. When his uncle, the Earl, inherited Burghley it was a property that had been neglected for some sixty years and the restoration was his sole interest in life, and which received all his energies and money. Rarely going even to London until progress of restoration could be seen, Henry as a child without parents was an inconvenience, even if he was his brother's child.

How lonely the young foreign-looking Henry must have been; some days wandering forlornly about the endless rooms and passages, and next amongst a house filled by visitors for the hunting and shooting parties, in addition to the family of the Earl's sister, Lady Elizabeth who had married a Lincolnshire squire, Mr Chaplin. Timidity and agitation had to be concealed whilst trying to please all these new varied adults. A servant woman looked after Henry's welfare and engaged masters who taught him. In time he realized the extent of being heir to his uncle's estate and fortunes and he became accustomed to this new lifestyle.

At this stage his uncle was between marriages and as no issue had been produced by the first union it was conceivable that Henry would be in line for title property and so forth but, alas, his uncle remarried at about the time Henry left Eton. Circumstances changed dramatically.

In 1770 Lord Exeter married his second wife Miss Anna Maria Cheatham, the daughter of Job Cheatham of Sodor Hall in Yorkshire. With the likelihood of him now having a son of his own, Henry was sent to St John's as a fellow commoner at Cambridge. Mr Weston, who it had been planned would accompany him, was dismissed so the change from being one of the 'grandees' at Eton to being one of the lower orders at Cambridge must have had considerable effect on this now sixteen-year-old lad. Universities were at this time described as schools for vice, fallen as low in scholarship as they had in morality, and must have proved difficult indeed. No wonder Henry became even more of an introvert and took shelter behind a mask of indifference and secrecy. For two years only was his stay at university, not normally long enough for a man of good fortune, but what occupied Henry after then is in doubt. Perhaps he travelled to be kept out of the way.

His uncle's second marriage was short lived and childless so Henry was once again back as heir to one of the greatest names and fortunes in the country. At twenty he was elected to represent Stamford in Parliament, perhaps to provide stability for a youth who had now a new position but had inherited his mother's love of frivolous amusement. By the age of twenty-two his fate had been decided and he was engaged to the Worcestershire heiress Emma Vernon. It is not known where the couple met but it is known that Mrs Vernon was strongly in favour of the match to this exceedingly eligible young man, but the historian Nash was more than strongly against the union, referring to Henry's father as a good for nothing and his mother as a mere dancer of the stage. Mrs Vernon was not persuaded that the marriage was not a good one considering the likely future of Henry's inheritance. Lord Exeter was pleased with the engagement and provided an allowance of £3,000 a year for his nephew, and gave over the family jewels for Emma to wear. Even though becoming more and more of a recluse his lordship attended the wedding on 23 May 1776 at St George's, Hanover Square, and was one of the witnesses.

With that concentration on the circumstances in which Henry grew up there is a clear indication that the man could develop with unstable tendencies. Already it can be submitted that if blame is to be apportioned for Henry's short-comings in later life it must be equally levelled at the adults who controlled his early life. A child starved of love is in later years going to be incapable of giving love to others.

The story will continue with a few details of life after the wedding, and the introduction of the villain of the piece – or was he?

As previously mentioned it appeared that the young couple were 'making themselves at home', but there was sadness in that within less than eighteen months of the wedding both the only child died, as did the bride's mother. The child was buried in the family vault at Hanbury Church, where other memorials to the family can be seen. Neither death helped an already questionable marriage, perhaps tenuous, or, as one authority wrote, the bride's father was so desirous of joining his riches with title he over-persuaded his heiress daughter to marry a descendant of the Exeter line. However, the lifestyle of the couple appears to have been one of pleasure throughout the days of the few years that they were to be together.

In addition to this country seat in Worcestershire, the couple owned a house in London, in Albermarle Street, and during the years that followed incessant parties, balls, race meetings and gaming sessions took place, entertaining in a grand manner friends and neighbours at both London and Worcestershire. To impress all and sundry travel was by coach and six with outriders and postilions to front and rear, therefore not surprisingly within a matter of four years the debts of the couple were too great to be discharged, and with economies being made the parties took place less frequently, visitors became fewer and life became dull. Problems started with the relationship of the two and, whilst they may still bed together, the distance between them grew; poorness is relative, as servants were reduced in number, a mere twenty-four to deal with both inside and out. The Vernon fortunes had dwindled and only by the ingenuity of trustees and lawyers was bankruptcy averted.

In the easterly corner of the Hanbury estate stands the church of St Mary the Virgin for which there was no rector at this time, and about seven years after the arrival of the newly-weds a substitute in the form of a curate arrived. This was the handsome, well-bred William Sneyd, whose age was compatible with that of the squire and his wife. Poor lodgings were the only available accommodation for the curate, in fact rented rooms at the smithy. Perhaps circumstances at this time were too convenient. The big house was reduced in staff, the master and wife of cool disposition towards each other, entertaining had been reduced, and this new personable incumbent descended from ancient gentry stock of Keele Hall in Staffordshire was given humble lodgings at the village blacksmith's farmstead. The line of Sneyd from which William was born lived in St John Street, Lichfield in a large house by the cathedral, with father, one-time usher to the King, and this stern, old-fashioned parent lived in state with his two unmarried daughters, Mary and Charlotte. Good looking and presentable the family may have been but of the ten daughters born before William and his brother Edward only three remained; Bessy being the third. Consumption was the problem, a problem which infected almost the whole family. Bessy was disowned by her father when she married the broken-hearted widower of Honora, Richard Edgeworth, who was father of the novelist Maria who was born in Oxfordshire but latterly of the family Greaves of Aston, Derbyshire; that side of the family lived happily in Ireland, a significant point later in the story.

For a few years this gentle, quiet life continued for Henry and Emma at the country property, entertainment being restricted to visits by a few friends and the junior members of the Sneyd family from Lichfield, including Edward, who appears to have had no profession, and indeed the 9th Earl occasionally paid a call, and whenever visits were made for the subdued dinner parties the curate would be present. This state was conducive to the inevitable and little by little the curate and the mistress of the house became more and more friendly when the master was away on business either around the estate or in London. Infatuation was dominating Emma's life, and her personal maid, Bessy, who remained loyal and outlived her mistress, was cajoled into acting as go-between when the squire was inconveniently present. Was Emma the seducer and Sneyd yielding from a false sense of honour? Whichever way the curate would be the beneficiary; comfort in the Hall for the night was much more preferable than sleeping at the blacksmith's homestead at Sanderson's farm.

The clergyman weakly succumbed to deceit in the house in which he had been made welcome; not surprisingly, his father of such staunch upright habits, would never forgive his son who had taken his vows, but the circumstance existed and eventually during one of Sneyd's many illnesses matters came to the fore. There are indications that Sneyd was suffering mentally as well as physically or perhaps simply his conscience overruled his mind, but whatever the reason he sent a message to Henry pleading for a visit to his sick bed at the farm. During the ensuing visit confessions were made that an affair was in progress and Sneyd asked forgiveness; Cecil assumed that the patient was delirious but within days Emma confessed and despite Henry's offer that she could live anywhere she wished, away from him for a year, and if at the end of that time she felt the same he would give her a divorce. She would not be pacified. This was the start of the circumstances for the final stage of the marriage. Emma remained in her own room at the Hall for some days with no contact with other members of the household except her devoted maid Bessy by whom she sent an appeal to her husband for arrangements to be made for one final meeting with her lover, who by now had returned to Lichfield. With Emma giving threats of suicide Henry had little choice in the matter and arrangements were duly made for a meeting at the halfway stage between Hanbury and Lichfield, namely Birmingham, and the public house to be used was the Hen & Chickens.*

It is proven that Emma was not being strictly honest with her husband

---

* The public house referred to in Birmingham with the name of 'Hen and Chickens' is not one of the three which exist today. At the date of the elopement of Emma Cecil and William Sneyd there was a substantial hostelry towards the High Street end of New Street with that name, and this is no doubt the one in question. It was a building of note in that adjoining were brew houses and stabling for seventy horses.

as during the time she spent closeted in her room she was making arrangements herself by amassing clothes, jewellery and any money that she could obtain to take with her to the rendezvous so elopement would be possible. By the time of the journey to the public house she had concealed about her person spare clothes sufficient for a long journey and the jewellery – perhaps some of the family pieces which the 9th Earl had given to her to wear when the engagement was first announced. This was to be her only form of finance when considering that her legal husband was the possessor of all her wealth and estates and she had no access to funds without his permission which would be somewhat difficult; and her lover was penniless. At the meeting point Henry, either acting in a foolish or naive manner allowed his wife with her maid and Sneyd's sister to proceed to the establishment whilst he stayed close by in another hotel – a recipe for the elopement although it is thought that those accompanying Emma, apart from the maid, were not confidants to the act. As previously mentioned the elopement took place, apparently in a post-chaise which was awaiting nearby for the fare.

There are many reports on the further life of these two persons, from the few days in London to obtain more clothing, their stay in the West Country at Thompson's Hotel in Exeter churchyard, rooms for seven weeks at the house of Richard Danning in Dawlish, then to the Blue Ball Inn in Bruton, Somerset for two weeks, always under the name of Mr and Mrs Benson. Towards the end of the year Emma travelled to London where she still had supportive friends in town, some of whom had never been over fond of Henry, and Sneyd visited Ireland to stay with his sister and family and in-laws, the Edgeworths. The following spring Sneyd joined Emma in London and here, in Green Street, the couple had a visit from Henry's solicitor seeking evidence for the divorce; this he obtained by seeing Mr & Mrs Benson living together. Life may have appeared to be improving for the runaway couple with the divorce in sight, but unfortunately the Sheriff's men closely followed the solicitor and this time the bailiffs arrived to try to obtain relief for the debts Sneyd had incurred whilst travelling the country. With no possibility of the money being forthcoming Sneyd was arrested and subsequently placed in Marshalsea Prison, where he suffered a complete mental breakdown. It is far from clear how the debts were paid and Sneyd released, but Emma did have many friends in the capital. The next recorded travel was to Lisbon, in the hope of more congenial weather for the improvement in Sneyd's health, but his consumption deteriorated and in 1793 at Calder's Wells near Lisbon he died and is buried in the English cemetery.

The conclusion can be brief as interspersed with these writers has been mentioned the life, ultimate marriage of Emma and her lover in 1791, and the eventual third marriage she made after her return to England in 1795, with John Phillips of Droitwich. Ironically Phillips was formerly Henry's estate manager at Hanbury and friend and executor who, after his time at Hanbury, became barrister of the Inner Temple. After living at Bewdley, also in Worcestershire, Emma returned to Hanbury with this husband in the year 1804, this being a significant date as it was the year her first husband died and therefore her inheritance was restored. The estate built from money obtained through the legal profession was again in the hands of a lawyer. It is not certain what remained in the house at this date as the contents had previously been sold in 1790 after the marriage break-down. When Emma died in 1818 she was not, at her request, buried in the Vernon vault but by the north boundary of the churchyard; remarkably wrapped by her faithful maid, who had married and settled in England, in the winding sheet that had covered William Sneyd's body twenty-five years previously, while on the coffin earth from Sneyd's Lisbon grave was scattered.

Although Emma died fourteen years after her return, Phillips continued to live at Hanbury for a further eleven years after which he relinquished his life interest in the estate in favour of Emma's distant cousin Thomas Tayler Vernon. Tayler had two sons who inherited Hanbury; the first died after a short life part of that being devoted to alterations to the house during the mid-nineteenth century. As he left no issue his brother, Harry, succeeded him, Harry being created baronet in 1885, and it was his son Sir George, second and last Baronet, who bequeathed Hanbury to the National Trust.

The case rests.

Chapter VI

Dovecotes

The dovecote – or as originally named, the pigeon house – is one of those small buildings which in the plan of any of the old villages or hamlets was an integral part essential to provide service to the community. In hamlets or villages it was there somewhere whether tucked away behind other buildings almost hidden from view, or part of a farmyard, or where there was a manor house then it was probably found within the manor grounds. Dovecotes were essential for providing food before the days of the agricultural revolution in the eighteenth century because, quite simply, the produce obtained from this insignificant little building, frequently the smallest in the vicinity, ensured life for many of the inhabitants.

This situation in itself then created a problem because if the food thus obtained was so essential why not build dovecotes in every backyard? Why not have one in every garden, or at every lane end? Not as easy as that when certain facts are considered. It became so difficult to balance the advantage of the food source obtained, against the costs, that controls had to be introduced to restrict the number of buildings erected – usually the property of the lord of the manor or, in some cases, the cleric, but only one dovecote at each property, although the size was not restricted and could be large enough to house 2,000 nesting boxes; and the use was tenaciously protected.

Why a problem with balance? The cost of producing enough birds to satisfy the population, by way of meat for the table, and eggs, and the fertilizer for the land, was expensive. Not financially expensive, as once the building had been erected it was minimal, merely a question of materials plus labour for a small amount of building and nesting box maintenance, but the cost was in the amount of food these vegetarian birds consumed, and for all the growing crops or vegetation eaten by the birds there was less for the population to eat.

By appreciating these dovecotes many facets of life in the period eleventh to eighteenth century can be learned. There is the diet available at the time and there is the marvel of the architecture and the cleverly contrived use of materials found on site. Possibly the most impressive device is the ingenious thinking behind the means of gaining access to the nesting boxes, as without that access there is little point in building the structure.

In Great Britain there is a very large variety of dovecotes ranging from circular stone free-standing units to timber-framed buildings, which in some cases actually appear to be part of the big house; in these cases the materials used and the overall rendering match that of the estate buildings.

This type of building, of which there is an infinite variety throughout the northern hemisphere, indicates lifestyles and survival from medieval times to the eighteenth century. Survival relied on the food supply and in the days long before preservatives and freezers the maintaining of food throughout the long periods of winter depended so much on the use of natural resources. In 1659 a census indicated that there were in a line from China to Great Britain – Britain being the westernmost point of civilisation – an estimated 200,000 dovecotes and of these 26,000 were in Britain.

The feast of St Michael, or Michaelmas, was a significant date in the calendar to landowners and farmers long before the introduction of silage and imported animal feed were introduced. Hay was the only home produced food for the livestock during the winter months and the number of animals which could be kept depended upon the amount of stored hay; that decision had to be made by Michaelmas. The remainder of the livestock would be slaughtered for early consumption before decomposition set in, or the meat would be salted for future use; that was providing sufficient salt was available. Many farmers and landowners who estimated incorrectly suffered dire consequences, not only in loss of stock but also the standard of stock. It was better to keep too few animals so they at least were in good condition for breeding the following year, rather than keeping too many resulting in inferior beasts, if they survived at all.

The origin of the use of birds to supplement salted meats as part of a diet is lost in the mists of time but it is known that in medieval days the Chinese were constructing dovecotes, and the Romans certainly knew of this important food source. Today dovecotes in one form or another can be traced from China, the whole way across Europe terminating in the British Isles.

It was discovered in prehistoric times that of the pigeon family, that is the bird order of *Columbiformes*, a number of species including those commonly called doves, had certain peculiarities which indicated that they could be controlled to produce not just edible meat, but also eggs, and for the land a fertilizer. Only two or three of the species are suitable for domesticating and these are pigeons rather than doves. This discovery certainly improved the variety of food which would otherwise consist of salted meat or fish; unless you were a member of the landed gentry.

The common wood pigeon, which only breeds twice a year, was not used in dovecotes, although it is well known that country people who did not have access to the luxury of domestic birds took advantage of the prolific birds as part of their diet. The species used for the domestic purpose were those which returned to their 'homes' each day, as long as home comforts existed – hence the sanctuary of dovecotes. The birds are also happy living in large groups. These species had an unusual breeding cycle almost throughout the year. Each pair of birds will, nearly every six weeks, produce two eggs, and the chicks fatten to about one pound in weight before the next two eggs are laid. The parent birds, who pair for a lifetime and continue breeding for about seven years, reject the fattened offspring when the new eggs appear, so there is no loss felt by the parents when the young are removed for the table. Although until about 1880 they were a protected species, it is understandable why antipathy between breeders and farmers, or food growers, exists as pigeons are ferocious eaters, known to consume more than their own weight in one meal.

With this knowledge the pigeon/dove, to which much homage is paid on a spiritual level, being the symbolic representative of the Holy Ghost used from earliest times in Christian art (in accordance with St Luke's iii. 22 at the baptism of Jesus) became sustainer of the body as well as of the spirit.

A fascinating variety of dovecotes, sometimes called 'columbariums' from the family name of the birds, can be found in Great Britain dating from the eleventh to the seventeenth century. Examples include those built into the tower of a castle or keep such as at Tattershall in Lincolnshire; the detached 'stepped' building at Willington in Bedfordshire which is built into a stable block with thirteenth-century attachments housing 1,500 pigeons; circular buildings such as Dunster in Somerset, possibly dating from the eleventh century with over 500 boxes; and at Cotehele in Cornwall. Kinwarton in Warwickshire, which could well have been owned by the Abbey of Evesham in the fourteenth century has 580 nesting boxes, and the building is even more interesting with a fine ogee doorway. The lovely timber-framed seventeenth-century square example at Wichenford with over 550 nesting boxes and complete with a lantern atop a steep roof; or the brick-built type built in the vegetable garden at Felbrigg in Norfolk, built about 1680 with 968 nesting holes each accommodating two birds.

The square or oblong buildings contain various forms of steps or ladders as a means of having access to the nests, whereas circular buildings had, or in many cases still have, the 'potence', in various stages of restoration, replacement or indeed nearly original. A 'potence' is an ingenious movable ladder fixed to the end of two offset horizontal beams which are secured to a central vertical post which pivots on a central block in the floor with a similar inverted block in the roof. Entry to the cote was also to be carefully considered and as can be seen in a number of the buildings they have either a very small door, or double doors, both designs to allow for entry by man but to restrict the exit by the birds. A number of devices were tried over the years to control the louvers at the top of the building, all of which enabled the trapping or releasing of the birds, and different types can still to be seen.

The demise of the dovecotes was a natural progression when two changes took place. One was the weather and the other the introduction of root crops. The climatic conditions changed over a long period of time and there is ample evidence that the mean temperature in Great Britain before the period, sometimes referred to as the mini-Ice Age – basically 1600–1750 – was high enough for vineyards to be grown in northern Britain. Since the eighteenth century the mean temperature has been steadily and slowly rising, although by the end of twentieth century it has not risen to that of the pre-thirteenth century period.

An Act of Parliament was passed in 1761 which, with hindsight, may appear to have been somewhat superfluous. This allowed any landowner or freeholder to build a dovecote on his land, or the tenant to do so with his landlord's permission. The dire need for improvizing ways of catching food had by that date passed and, apart from a few show dovecotes, few new buildings were erected. The sustaining of winter food for human beings was greatly improved by the agricultural revolution in the seventeenth and eighteenth centuries thanks largely to landowners in the eastern counties, particularly Norfolk, by gentry such as Townshend of Raynham (nicknamed 'Turnip Townshend'), the Walpoles of Houghton and the Cokes of Holkham. As a result of their efforts root crops were introduced. The potato introduced from South America into Europe by the Spanish in the sixteenth century, and by Sir Walter Raleigh into Britain in the 1580s, was by no means freely available to the whole population for many years.

Chapter VII

Bess of Hardwick

This chapter of the book was initiated by the unique building in Derbyshire known as Hardwick Hall, that is the 'new' Hardwick Hall – unique in that the design is not in anyway similar to the grandiose palladian style of so many which can be seen throughout the country, although the derivation of the word 'palladin' is expanded upon later. It is frequently suggested that here is the first house of size to be built during this period in England which was not copied or based on the design introduced with a foreign element.

Many of the large houses which exist today emanate from the great landowners of a bygone age and when there were relatively few great estate owners amongst whom could be included the Russells, thus incorporating the Dukes of Bedford; the Dorsets allied with the Sackvilles and the Somersets; the Percys and their great holdings in the north-east of the country – a line also connected with the Somersets; and the Talbots, who dominate the second half of this story.

View the properties of any of these estate builders and there appears to be one single factor in that the men instigated the building, but is this true? Remembering that in many instances the resources for the building of these great edifices was obtained from dowries – marrying-well was one of the objects for many a poorer descendant of a titled family; in fact that was often at the very heart of the marriage. Records show that a number of the greatest manors were not built until after the dowry had been obtained. Little is recorded in most cases as to how much influence the wife was allowed regarding the building, but it is probable that she made some of the decisions.

In almost all respects Hardwick Hall is unique – in one or two particulars it may not be so, this will be debated later – but if the design itself may not be unique the builder certainly is. There cannot have been two Elizabeth Hardwicks! Born of very lowly country landowning stock, herself being employed when a young girl as little more than a 'scivvy' at one of the gentry houses in London belonging to the powerful Zouch family, she reverted to country life in preference to the London lifestyle, except when searching for husband number two; and she married four husbands to gain wealth and power enabling her estates to be consolidated. More than once she misappropriated funds and the rents from part of her husband's family estates, was argumentative with the head of state, and arranged a marriage between one of her offspring to place her almost in line for the crown of England. During her second marriage, and after her fourth husband, this former country girl became a lady of property and had connections with many different dwellings, some of which are detailed later. What better way of displaying wealth and status than in grand buildings?

This story relates to Elizabeth Hardwick, commonly referred to as Bess, born in Tudor times during the reign of Henry VIII, who experienced the rule of five other most famous monarchs, including Henry's offspring Edward VI, Mary and Elizabeth, plus the short period of Lady Jane Grey, and finally dying when King James I of England, or VI of Scotland, was in office. Her life span was probably between the 1520s and 1608, neither date adamantly declared as historians have throughout the years been vague and indeed contradictory as to the actual dates. Latest research has however more or less confirmed these dates, particularly as her death is reasonably certain to have been 1608 and she was supposedly eighty-eight years of age. Bess was not known to admit her date of birth readily, all of which adds to her general mystery. There is no mystery surrounding her climb to a position of wealth which almost rivalled that of that most famous of queens, Queen Elizabeth I, nor is there doubt about her being escalated to the top echelon from humble birth thanks to the very timely deaths of six of the men in her life. She greatly influenced two large estates as they can be seen today, both in the county of Derbyshire, the first Chatsworth, the second Hardwick, and she was the founder of one of the great dynasties of the sixteenth century. There are many other properties which she influenced in the building. She may have started life simply named but on her death she was Elizabeth, Countess of Shrewsbury.

The original Hardwick family home suffered from a Tudor peculiarity when monarch Henry VIII, because of his continual over-lavish expenditure, had a near cash flow problem and his Chancellor of the Exchequer devised many different ways of raising funds throughout the land. One of his most obscure ways was to evoke the old feudal claims of royal wardship over estates inherited by minors; this through the Courts of Wards lead to claiming the right to administer the estate until the heir became twenty-one years of age. Agents were appointed to seek such estates ripe for takeover, circumstances prevailing in the case of the Hardwick lands with the death of Thomas, Bess' father, described as a farmer-squire. The estate was left to nominees but this attempt at securing the lands for his descendants was overruled by the royal lawyers and the lands were ultimately leased to a local businessman named Bugby who could be trusted to ensure the Crown received its due rewards. This decree was called Escheat which was abolished in England in 1870. In Tudor times there was little or no sentiment for children – unless of royal birth – and an unmarried orphaned female was possibly the least significant form of human life.

Thomas and Elizabeth of Hardwick had produced three girls, and one boy named James. Bess was the youngest being born shortly before Thomas's death when he was aged about forty-one years. Sometime after Thomas had died his widow married a widower who was the younger son of a nearby gentry family – unfortunately near penniless – namely Ralph Leche. Ralph already had a number of children by his previous marriage and after his marriage with Elizabeth Hardwick three more girls were born.

The story now continues following the life of Bess, who has been described by historians as of strong features, no beauty and with red hair. Whether the colour of hair is significant remains to be seen. Whatever the personal feelings it must have been a great physical relief when one of the girls left the poor household of her mother, her stepfather, and the accumulated children of three marriages. Bess at the age of about twelve was sent on the perilous five-day journey to London, to the home of the Zouch family; there was a vague family connection between the Hardwicks and the Zouches.

The Zouches were an interesting family founded by Breton Alan-la-Zouch in the early fourteenth century and they obtained great tracts of land in Leicestershire, amongst other areas; the name being perpetuated by the conversion of the Danish settlement of Ashby to Ashby-de-la-Zouch. They became rulers of much of Wales for Edward II but their status was somewhat reduced many years later during the fifteenth century. One of the great Archbishops of York was a Zouch in the fourteenth century.

There were a number of direct or indirect influences between the Zouch family and Bess of Hardwick, the most obvious being the start of Bess' introduction to the upper classes. Ashby Castle was twice the prison for Mary Queen of Scots in her early years of confinement in 1569, and during the penultimate year of her life in 1586, and Edward Zouch, 11th Baron, was one of the judges of this most unfortunate of queens. In the nineteenth century the Zouch title passed through the female line to the Curzon family. Modern-day Ashby is probably best known for its ruin of a castle, largely the result of the Civil War, and for what is possibly a unique ecclesiastical device in the church, a 300-year-old finger pillory. Ashby was a property visited by royalty on a number of occasions, particularly between 1503 and 1634.

Bess was to be in the care of Lady Zouch, whether as ward, infant poor relation, or unpaid 'scivy' is not clear, but what is clear is that the lifestyle of this great and important house introduced Bess to a standard of living at which to aim in her future life. It was by no means unusual in Tudor times and later for the gentry to provide homes for their poor relations whether as a charitable act or to obtain free labour. By 1590, the year of her fourth husband's death, Bess herself employed one of her poorer nephews, George Kniveton, as a page in her household.

It was not many years before Bess, possibly aged fifteen, was returned to Derbyshire, and she fulfilled the position of bride as arranged by her family to an ailing man, Robert Barlow, or Barley in some books. Unfortunately, or fortunately, Robert Barlow died the Christmas Eve of the year of their marriage. It certainly was unfortunate that the Barlows were of moneyless stock but whilst Bess had no claim to any of their worldly tangible possessions, by the marriage settlement she did receive an annuity of £8 15s. per year. This may not have been a fortune even in Tudor times but it was the beginning of Bess' independence for the first time in her life. What is more she now became higher on the status ladder being a young widow, and therefore considerably more attractive in the marriage stakes of the day. Rural Derbyshire was not a draw to Bess and even though her family lived in the district it could not possibly produce any suitable openings for the now ambitious widow. She returned to London and thanks to her now elevated position and no doubt her new connections and those of the Zouches, she became Lady-in-Waiting within the Dorset family.

At 2 o'clock in the morning of 20 August 1547 (the early hour being chosen for astrological reasons as a time when the conjunction of the stars were a good omen) a middle-aged civil servant married his third wife, a childless widow in her early twenties at Bradgate Manor, Leicestershire. The bridegroom, a trained accountant who had recently been knighted for services to the Crown whilst in Ireland, and owned properties in Hertfordshire and Wales with a house in Newgate Street, St Paul's London, was Sir William Cavendish. The bride Elizabeth Barlow.

Bradgate Manor, was the property of Henry Grey, Marquis of Dorset, and father by his wife Frances of Lady Jane Grey who was born here. The Marquis became Duke of Suffolk in 1551, but was executed for treason in 1554. The heath and woodlands which now surround the ruins of Bradgate House is one of Leicestershire's main recreation areas, complete with fallow deer; it was given for public use by a private benefactor in 1928.

The next ten years of Bess' life had considerable effect on her rise to power and wealth. The wealth was partly provided by the state, although not intentionally and only because of the inefficiency of the administration thanks to the continued controversy between inheritors of the Crown and opportune deaths of some of the heads of state; remembering that this marriage took place in the first year of the reign of the weak and sickly Edward VI. Whether Bess was a beauty or not is of no significance, what was proved was she was physically strong and her new husband almost worshipped her, as a result of which a new dynasty was founded. This was William Cavendish's third marriage and he had three children who were living at the time of this latest marriage. William was more than twice Bess' age but perhaps his financial security and rising position in government posts appealed to the girl who had never before experienced stability. Prior to this wedding Cavendish had obtained a number of properties such as Dover Priory, Northaw, Cardigan Priory in Wales, Lilleshall a small former abbey in Shropshire, and Welbeck Abbey long before it was enhanced by the great buildings constructed for the Dukes of Portland as seen today, together with the late-eighteenth-century ground improvements by Repton. That is to name but a few, acquired whilst William committed business for the King and was in league with Thomas Cromwell, before the latter lost his head in 1540, much of this acquisition being during the great orgy of loot which took place during the Dissolution and division of monastic lands. With the power of the gentry lands were commandeered or a nominal payment made, and title transfer legalized by persuasion with the Crown Commissioners.

The first child of this newly married couple was a girl, Frances, being William's ninth child and Bess' first, born in 1548; Bess' half-sister Jane Leche joined Bess in London during the child-bearing period to act as her 'gentlewoman'. This was a useful connection and provided the method for Bess to maintain contacts and be informed of any news relating to her former childhood district. A second daughter, Temperance, was born the year following but was short-lived, but the real excitement came a year later when a son and heir, Henry, was born. The godparents to

Henry indicated the advancing status of the Cavendishs; they included Henry Grey, later elevated to Duke of Suffolk, the Earl of Warwick and, by no means least, the King's youngest child, Princess Elizabeth. By the end of 1551 son number two arrived and was called William, with yet another son being born in 1553 who was called Charles.

Princess Elizabeth and Bess proved to be compatible and, ignoring some stormy relationships over the years, they remained on friendly terms. The Princess was also kinswoman of Frances Grey, wife of Suffolk.

As a result of Bess keeping contact with her half-sister and keeping abreast of the Derbyshire news, she learned that the Agard family who owned Chatsworth near Hardwick were falling onto financially hard times and the manor was put on the market for sale. On 31 December 1549, a little over two years after Bess' marriage to William, Chatsworth was bought in joint names for the sum of £600, not that either the existing house or amount of land was good enough for Bess who was only too well aware of the value of the nearby moorland sheep country and the lead mines in the park. The Crown Commissioners of the day, officially or otherwise, managed to help Bess with her aim by exchanging the lands in William's hands which had little value to him, such as in Cardigan and Shropshire and in Hertfordshire Northaw Manor owned by Cavendish and described by him as uninspiring and too far from London when he was serving the Court. At the same time there was one somewhat run-down estate in Derbyshire called Meadow Place Manor which almost adjoined the Chatsworth estate; rundown the buildings may well have been but the land was of great value as sheep runs, and fairly extensive. The solution was quite simple. The Crown Commissioners were yet again persuaded to exchange ownership one for the other, as they did with great stretches of fertile land by the River Dove. To enlarge the Chatsworth estate even further about 8,000 acres of good sheep-rearing land was bought from the Earl of Westmorland, thus establishing the Cavendishs to the height of one of the great Derbyshire landowning-families.

Being a landowner was an achievement for the woman who as an orphaned girl suffered that difficult life and that long, terrible, lonely journey from Derbyshire to London only ten years previously, but having achieved so much the real status had yet to be considered. The grand house needed to show off wealth which was synonymous with position, and now much of Bess' impressions, particularly from the status of the Zouch household, came to the fore. She appears to have had a natural inclination for building work and the best way to make a great impact on the populace, and particularly on locals who considered themselves as gentry, was by way of impressive buildings. William may have paid for his wife's great ambitions but in truth had little interest in the country estate. He was not a countryman and was far too busy with state affairs in London.

About 1552 Bess, whilst still producing children – she actually had either eight or nine, six surviving infancy – masterminded the start of the building work for the replacement of Chatsworth House, which became a large stone fortress with square turrets at each corner. The turrets may sound familiar with a house Bess built many years later at Hardwick, and others which experienced her influence. To say that William was engrossed in state affairs is an understatement for 1553 was the year the young King Edward died and William's personal involvement was in jeopardy; in fact this was made clear when two of William's patrons who acted as godparents to William's son and heir Henry only three years previously, were summarily decapitated on Tower Hill for their involvement in the plot to supplant Catholic Mary by Protestant Lady Jane Grey. William, politically motivated as ever, declared loyalty to Mary by changing his religious faith from Protestant to Catholicism. This may well have helped when the Lord Treasurer declared that more than £5,000 was missing from state accounts. An interesting comparison of values; it is thought that William received £30 per year as his official salary at the time. The deficit was finally admitted when William, and even Bess, travelled to London for the occasion and appeared in the Court of the Star Chamber before the Queen's judges. Appeals for clemency may not have been completely accepted by the new Queen but by devious postponement no repayment of the debt had taken place by the time of William's death on 25 October 1557, when he was about fifty-two years of age.

This opportune death provided Bess with a breathing space. The legal process for the financial recovery, via Parliament, proved how slow the wheels of law take to turn. Queen Mary was ill and finally died in the autumn of 1558. Bess' astute business mind ensured that Chatsworth was placed in trust for the eldest son Henry, thus removing the possibility of the estate being sequestrated by the Crown to cover the old debt. Bess, now about thirty-two years of age, took advantage of her association with the Princess Elizabeth, and indeed attended the coronation of the new Queen Elizabeth.

It was all very well having a large estate in the Midlands and having funds to maintain a high lifestyle, but with a brood of children to be looked after ranging in age from under ten years to a few months old, male companionship was sought to complete the family. The year after she was crowned the Queen appointed a widower, a descendant of an old knighted family, as Chief Butler of England to deal with etiquette and protocol of court officers, Sir William St Loe, and he and Bess were married in 1559. Although Bess had no further children facts show that this latest William doted on Bess, not only did he finance some of Bess' children's education, but he also provided £1,000 for Bess to pay to the Queen towards the debt of the first William. It is concluded that the remaining £4,000 was written-off. He also made arrangements that the St Loe inheritance, which included the ruined monastery and lands at Glastonbury, should pass to Bess rather than to his brother Edward. It was not long before this faithful act benefited the Cavendishs as Sir William St Loe died in 1564. The St Loe family accused Bess of denying them their inheritance but failed in their attempt to have Sir William's wishes overturned and Bess benefited from the income of the Somerset estates, thus her income from the joint lands was now estimated to be about £1,600 per year.

In Tudor England a woman may indeed have obtained land and wealth by one means or another, but for real status it was essential to own another ingredient and that was position by title. Bess was only too aware of this deficiency, perhaps even more so because of her humble birth. There was one sure way of obtaining this requirement, which would result from marriage number four. Fortunately at about this time one of the Queen's favourites was George Talbot, 6th Earl of Shrewsbury and there were few with greater and more important lineage. His ownership of wealth, land and buildings rivalled that of the monarch, and very conveniently some of his lands were nearby to those of Bess. There was however a matter of an existing Countess of Shrewsbury, a lady called Gertrude, sister of the Earl of Rutland, but she was at this stage ill and had not long to live. Bess became Countess of Shrewsbury by marriage in late 1567, but this in itself produced one great problem. Realizing that there would be costs to pay for this great marriage to title, Bess was prepared for many things but not the sacrifice of wealth and possessions which, on the marriage, would normally be added to the existing Talbot fortunes. The very best lawyers available had to be consulted to devise a suitable marriage contract. Part of the arrangements affected the children of the two parties by intermarriage; Talbot's daughter Grace (aged 8) to marry Bess' Henry (aged 18), and second son Gilbert Talbot (aged 14) to marry Bess' Mary (aged 12). These junior marriages were not unusual in eminent families in Tudor times, and these were sanctified in 1568 at the Sheffield Parish Church a few weeks after their parents' marriage.

After the union the Earl maintained control of his many great houses, his business interests and royal duties thus leaving Bess to control her beloved Chatsworth. This did however keep the couple somewhat apart for much of the time but this may have proved an advantage as the ardour of this newly wedded couple soon cooled. Only the year following, the marriage was placed in jeopardy as Mary Queen of Scots had arrived in London to seek sanctuary from the Queen. George was nominated to maintain restricted travel on Mary at George's castle at Tutbury, and whilst initially even Bess was pleased that such an honour had been bestowed on the Shrewsburys, she soon found the constant attention required by George to act as gaoler somewhat irksome, and this was made worse by Queen Elizabeth complaining about too many favours being given to the prisoner. The Queen also complained frequently about the costs of maintaining Mary's retinue, added to which there were a number of attempts by Mary's supporters to obtain her release. Mary's constrictions were moved to Bess' newly rebuilt Chatsworth and for a while Mary and Bess lived amicably, even producing much needlework together, some of which is now on display at Hardwick Hall.

Many agreements were made between George and Bess both on financial matters and the future security for the children, nearly always on favourable terms for Bess' children. But there was one piece of unfinished business uppermost to Bess, and that was the future of her daughter Elizabeth who justified a suitor of the highest rank possible – according to Bess. Unknown to George, Bess chose one almost as high as one could get, namely the eighteen-year-old Charles Stuart, who became 6th Earl of Lennox, brother of the late husband of Mary Queen of Scots, Earl Darnley, great-grandson of King Henry VII; he was also Queen Elizabeth's first cousin once removed and somewhat near the succession to the English throne. Succession to the English throne was almost an obsession with the Queen and certainly a jealously guarded matter. Rufford House in Nottinghamshire, one of Bess' numerous country seats, was where Elizabeth met Charles Stuart, used by Bess without her husband's knowledge, and where the couple were married.

Bess was only too aware that her choice of new son-in-law would cause considerable displeasure with Her Majesty, but regardless she pursued the matter without any consultation with her husband who would not have approved such an act likely to cause disfavour at this period when relationships were already somewhat strained. Bess must have had great charm as she remained sociable with the Queen even if she and the mother of her new son-in-law, Margaret were sent to the Tower, albeit for only a short time. There was an interesting relationship between Bess and Lady Margaret, Countess of Lennox – Bess of lowly birth with great wealth, and Margaret of high rank by birth but financially poor. Within the year, by November 1575, a daughter was born to this newly married couple and when Bess' son-in-law, who had always been somewhat sickly, died in 1576 Bess being her usual avaricious self, made claim to the Scottish lands owned by the Lennox family. For once Bess lost her case even when the claim was made for the benefit of the new granddaughter called Arbella/Arabella – unfortunately Arabella's mother Elizabeth Cavendish died about six years later whilst in her early twenties thus leaving the upbringing of the young girl in the hands of grandmother Bess.

Alveston in Staffordshire, with its great forests, was another of the Talbot properties as was Sheffield Manor and Lodge where the Earl lived for a time whilst Bess was living at Chatsworth and she was sequestrating the Talbot rents from estates throughout the lands. Here Arabella lived between the ages of six and seven years, and here her mother Elizabeth Stuart died in either 1581 or 1582. Eventually this property passed by marriage to the Arundel family.

The case to obtain the Scottish lands may have been lost but the indefatigable Bess ensured that her existing Chatsworth, both house and land, continued to be enlarged and the legal ownership divorced from the Shrewsburys and securely placed in the hands of sons Charles and William Cavendish. Divisions within the family were now showing themselves in a number of ways, particularly between George and Bess who spent less and less time in each other's company. Clearly George disagreed with the way Bess was acting, even to the point of division between the three sons Henry, William and Charles – Henry, the oldest on the side of his father and the other two supporting mother, hence Henry not being involved in the title of Chatsworth. The financial empire of the Cavendishs was a constant source of disagreement, Bess already having commandeered much of George's former wealth to sustain beloved Chatsworth.

Bess' lack of affection was again shown when her blood brother James, who on attaining the age of twenty-one had inherited their father's estate at Hardwick, was sent to a debtors' prison despite Bess being well able to cover his debts. If only James had had business acumen like his sister to have a mining engineer conduct a survey of the land, they would have discovered the rich seams of coal and there would not have been a financial problem. After James died Bess bought the farm and land at Hardwick from the creditors in 1583 for a greatly reduced price. Bess' avarice continued by diverting income which should have been for the Talbots from the Derbyshire and Somerset estates to the Cavendish empire. Matters came to a head when near all-out war developed between George and his followers and Bess' supporters, but timely intervention by the Queen and her instructions for a Commission of Enquiry to formulate peace between the parties saved complete anarchy and a cool agreement was reached, but yet again the result was in Bess' favour, much to the annoyance of George. George, as Earl Marshal of England, a post awarded after the execution of the Duke of Norfolk, officiated at the execution of Mary Queen of Scots in 1587. Reconciliation was never made between George and Bess and for a while he retreated to the comfort and sympathetic attentions of a lady of his household at one of his manor houses outside Sheffield before he died in late 1590; the funeral took place at Sheffield Parish Church where the couple and some of their children had been married just thirty years previously. Although the funeral of the 6th Earl was reported to be even more lavish than that of the 5th Earl thirty years previously when about 1,200 people were fed, Bess did not attend the funeral and she is not mentioned on the memorial to the great George, 6th Earl of Shrewsbury.

So with the death of husband number four, and the previous death of father which started the incredible career, and then the sad albeit timely death of brother James, Bess' story is almost complete, but not quite. Having risen from poor little orphan girl to one of the wealthiest women in the land, almost competing with the wealth of the Queen, and gaining one of the leading titles in the country; even if her treasure and highly prized Chatsworth was lost to non-favourite son Henry, riches and experience were maintained. The twice rebuilt Chatsworth gave experience in building which appears to have been almost second nature to Bess and after the separation from husband George she accepted the loss of affection and returned to her birthplace Hardwick in about 1584, where even prior to his death, she started to rebuild the old small manor house as a very large family house. It must have been evident that George would not survive much longer and without waiting for the actual event to occur the foundations were laid a few yards distance from the old manor for the new hall which was to be of sufficient grandeur to match the status of Dowager Countess; glass and the size of windows were an undoubted status symbol. This had to show to the world the position of the owner, and this time it is thought, although there is no actual proof, an architect Robert Smythson was employed to deal with some of the technicalities, but basically the outline was from the mind of Bess -- quite remarkable and one of the very few large houses built about this time which was purely English, but then Bess had neither the time nor inclination for the fashionable grand tour of the Continent, and certainly did not have any books to give examples as she is reputed to have only owned six books in her life; she was after all far too busy empire building. Most of the materials for the new house were obtained from one or other of the owner's estates, and the true icing on the cake which can be seen today, is the surmounting on each of the corner towers in six-foot-high letters 'ES', representing Elizabeth Shrewsbury — lest anyone should forget.

Bess died during the cold winter of 1608 at the grand age of eighty years, or was it eighty-eight, but whichever, as one writer suggests she spent her last years with abundant wealth and splendour, feared by many, beloved by none.

In the introduction to this story reference is deliberately made to 'palladian' and whilst it is not intended to become involved with the merits of architecture at this stage Hardwick shows a leaning towards the great sixteenth-century master's influence. Bess may not have owned many books but her involvement with Smythson may be significant in that he certainly would be aware of the works written by Andrea Palladio, his books being used and influencing building work throughout Europe for centuries. Hardwick has two respects which may be in the mode of Palladio; one is the great hall placement, the other the colonnading between the towers. Even if there is no categorical proof that Smythson was involved with Bess for the building of the new Hall there is ample evidence that she was in some way connected with a number of his building projects. Further the three Smythsons were at various times working at one or more of the Talbot sites, whether it be Robert, his son John or in later years, the grandson, Huntingdon, although much of junior's work would be after the death of Bess.

Not all the family properties will be mentioned but a few of the richest possessions should be included such as Wingfield Manor in Derbyshire, built mid-fifteenth century, now no more than a huge ruin unoccupied since the 1770s — another home used by Arabella during much of her childhood, and also where Mary Queen of Scots was held in 1569. The estate is rich with iron and glass works, some of this material being used by Bess for the new Hardwick Hall. It has been thought that most of the materials for the new building were obtained from estates owned by Bess and this is very possible considering such estates as this one. Worksop Manor in Nottingham was possibly one of those influenced by Bess. The building was completed about 1585 — today nothing remains because of a fire in 1761 — but the original structure was with towers, cartouche and screen similar to Hardwick; this was without doubt a Smythson building. Shrewsbury House, Chelsea, London is worth a mention not for the architectural view but an example of its use. After the death of the Earl Bess and her entourage used this London residence as their base whilst the many legal tangles regarding land ownership were resolved. Gilbert Talbot made claim against the now Dowager Countess for the recovery of some of the lands formerly the sole property of the Talbots. Unfortunately for Gilbert he was to learn that he was not dealing with a mere male and Bess having employed some of the finest legal minds available, and bribing the Master of the Rolls, ensured that Gilbert lost most of his claims. About this time records show that whilst Bess was spending less than £340 per year on the building of the new Hardwick Hall, in the eight months of 1591–2 some £1,200 was spent on legal fees.

No story about Bess of Hardwick would be complete without reference being made to her granddaughter. As previously related Arabella – who signed herself and was known by her contemporaries as Arbella – was the only daughter of Bess' daughter, Elizabeth and Charles Stuart, Earl of Lennox; unfortunately Arabella's father died the year after her birth and her mother a few years later, hence her upbringing being left in the hands of grandmother Bess. It should be appreciated that Queen Elizabeth had now been on the throne something like seventeen years and her successor was almost constantly at the forethought of the Court. With the marriage of daughter Elizabeth to Stuart as brother-in-law to Mary Queen of Scots, the family connections were becoming perilously close to descendancy for the throne of England and subsequently being watched with great care. Bess herself naturally considered that her beloved granddaughter had title to the throne and cosseted the girl appropriately. When Arabella was about twelve years old she was invited by the Queen to attend Court, but, so the story goes, the Queen was offended by her childish arrogance to such a degree that the child was sent home in disgrace.

Being a virtual prisoner at Hardwick for many years ended when the succession to the throne had been determined and James was crowned. The year was 1603 and Arabella was now aged about twenty-eight at which point she was again admitted to Court, by no means the end of the story as love then entered Arabella's life. Very unfortunately, the attraction was with Lord Beauchamp's son, William Seymour, who was twelve years junior to Arabella, and he could also claim royal descent. The union could not be tolerated by King James in any circumstances, even to the point when the King instructed the couple must not meet. Love conquering all, they not only met but were married in the early hours of one morning in Greenwich Palace. Less than three weeks later the King was informed with the result William was sent to the Tower and Arabella was imprisoned in the north. On the journey she escaped and almost reached France but was arrested and returned to England, this time incarcerated in the Tower where she died of madness less than five years after the marriage. William independently also escaped at about the same time and did arrive in France living in Paris where he stayed for about five years. On returning to England and marrying daughter of the Earl of Essex he became Duke of Somerset; his descendants became owners of Petworth in Sussex and from this line Her Majesty Queen Elizabeth, The Queen Mother is descended.

Hardwick Hall as seen today is thanks to the fact that the family used Chatsworth as their main seat and Hardwick was for many years little used except as a dower house, particularly during the eighteenth century, but it was maintained by the Dukes of Devonshire who enhanced the antiquarian atmosphere by bringing tapestries, portraits and furniture from Chatsworth and other Cavendish houses. Much of this action was taken by the 6th Duke who inherited in 1811. The contents include many items as listed in the inventory of 1601. The garden is now mainly as designed by Lady Louisa Egerton, daughter of the 7th Duke in the second half of the nineteenth century, with some recent modifications by the National Trust to the herb gardens.

Chapter VIII

Tolpuddle Martyrs

In Dorset there is what may be a unique, certainly one of the most insignificant items in the care of the National Trust. This is in the village or hamlet of Tolpuddle where there is a sycamore tree preserved to remind the modern reader of the conditions which befell the working population in the first half of the nineteenth century. Before relating the story in detail let us have a look at the conditions which prevailed at the time and some of the causes which led to the trial and conviction of six working men.

The memorial referred to later is in effect a reminder of the period after the Napoleonic Wars, the period when agriculture slumped to an all-time low; farmers throughout the land were going bankrupt and the landowners were having a serious change of fortune for the worst. The Government was losing control and the situation was not improved by the developing split between the political parties. Perhaps this period of transition, which included the abolition of slavery within the Empire, the Poor Law amendments, the Workhouse systems, and the great increase in the population was progressing far too fast. It certainly created an atmosphere of distrust, to put it mildly, between master and servant. The suggestion of any type of Trade Union lead to fears in both capitalist system and indeed within the Government.

The labour force was almost on starvation level and in 1834 the almost inevitable took place. Six village labourers met to discuss their grievances of intolerable working conditions and the fact that their wages had been reduced from nine shillings to six shillings a week. This small gathering so worried the farmers and landowners that the 1749 Mutiny Act was invoked and the men were charged with consorting together and administering secret oaths. An example had to be made and, as the judge when sentencing inferred, the object of legal action being taken was as a punishment and also to set an example and a warning to others. One of the important points about this case was that it was held, not in a large industrial area of thousands of working people, but in an almost unknown village in rural Dorset. Communications of the day were difficult and only local newspapers reported the event.

It was not until the men had been sentenced to seven years' transportation and had actually left the country, that the news was heard throughout other parts of England. This created such condemnation and riots in the capital until finally an appeal was launched and eventually a pardon was granted, but with all the many delays the news was not received on the other side of the world until about three years after sentence had been passed. Ultimately the men were brought back to England but only one, named James Hammet, returned to Tolpuddle, the remainder emigrated to Canada. James, when he died, was buried in the local churchyard where on 31 August 1934 George Lansbury unveiled a memorial to James; 1934 being the centenary celebrations of the Trades Union Congress and six cottages in the village were dedicated to the memory of the six country labourers. The 'Martyrs' tree and a commemorative seat are now at the entrance to the old manor which is reputed to be the meeting place of the six. The old sycamore now has a young companion which will eventually replace the original tree.

Chapter IX

Brown and Holland

This section of the book differs from most of the other sections in that, instead of referring to people of specific or allied properties, here reference is made to two people whose lives were devoted to building, modifying or restoring both houses and lands for other people during the eighteenth century. It is not that the two did not own properties themselves, they did own a number, but the interest here is the providing of homes for clients.

The two men referred to are truly synonymous with the property of Berrington Hall in Herefordshire (see Chapter X), and the saying that all people are influenced to a greater or lesser degree by other people or circumstances, or a series of circumstances, prevailing at some point in time, can never be more true than when considering each of these men. Their names were Lancelot, or to use his more popular name, Capability, Brown and Henry Holland junior – one the born landscape artist and the other born into the world of the construction business and architecture. If only the ages had been more contemporary then houses and estates of the gentry built during this period may well have been somewhat different from those seen today.

Other options could have been chosen to illustrate the industry of bygone builders and constructors. Perhaps one of the most famous and well known names being Sir Christopher Wren who was active, although in his seventies, when Brown was born, but Wren predeceased Holland junior by about twenty-two years. Wren was born into a strong royalist, conservative, Anglican family – his father becoming Dean of Windsor and his uncle the Bishop of Ely – he was also fortunate with his sponsors and worked almost solely on ecclesiastical and crown establishments, in addition to having a singularly unique opportunity after the greatest disaster of all times, the fire of London. In addition to being given an opportunity to remodel the centre of London, for which he submitted grandiose plans, part coming to fruition, he was responsible for the rebuilding of over fifty churches as well as the replacement St Paul's. Nearly half have since disappeared during subsequent centuries whether by demolition to allow space for the Bank of England such as St Christopher-le-Stocks, or for Victorian parish modifications, or indeed those destroyed during the Second World War.

A further option could have been the Repton and Nash partnership, both men born in the same year, whereas when Brown was in his thirties and already well established as a landscape artist and by this time adding architecture to his achievements; Holland on the other hand was still a schoolboy. Repton was basically and by nature an artist and was some thirty-five years of age when announcing himself as a landscape gardener for which he had had no training or experience. He did receive many commissions, some say with the reintroduction of flowers into the 'evergreen' Brown methods, but these commissions were on a much smaller scale and virtually slight variations to the existing. His artistic prowess came to the fore with the use of his famous 'Red Book' illustrating before and after as a sales media. Nash, that very different extrovert, started life as an architect and did show considerable versatility by building extremes from Cumberland Terrace in London to the hamlet of Blaize near Bristol, amongst many other projects. The partnership was comparatively short-lived and said to break up when the ever capricious Prince of Wales asked Repton for ideas for his Brighton residence – it was thought that the idea of Hindu style was Repton's – but Nash was appointed to execute the work, so that it became yet another Holland design hidden behind the work of Nash.

Having written thus the writer of this book decided the Brown and Holland partnership executed a greater influence on the English country house and estate than the partnership of others, therefore it is the story of these two which has been pursued.

Before continuing further a brief mention of the political, economic and physical state of the country during the Brown and Holland era may assist the reader, and may well raise more questions than answers covering this somewhat turbulent period of change. Many of the properties mentioned, and much of the financing stemmed from the fact that the gentry were Whigs and thus partly controllers of the country; the period concerned does, however, include that unsettled time when Whigs and Liberals struggled over supremacy in other words mainly a time of Protestant support as religious reform and toleration was to be considered nearly a century later. There were many other unsettling circumstances during this early Georgian period as England home events must include such influencing matters as wars which were still very much in evidence, whether it be the Stuart factions again attempting to invade England, and arriving remarkably near to London in the attempt, or one of the most famous of wars, the Battle of Culloden, which took place during the year following. In addition there were local skirmishes such as the Gordon Riots. Events abroad may also have had some influence, particularly the historically well-known Seven Years War, the capture of Quebec, the American war, further wars with France, and of course, the very unsettling French Revolution, much of which influenced manpower and finances at home. A number of the great landowners' finances may well have been affected by the dramatic outcome of the early eighteenth-century South Sea Company, but much less affected by the great Boston Tea Party. It is even less likely that the establishing of the Board of Agriculture in 1793 would have early effect on the work force but may have influenced the gentry. There were a number of good developments made during this period including James Watt's steam engine, and coal gas being used for lighting, but, to the labourers these would be pure novelties without effect on their lives until the next century. In spite of, or because of, all these events, remembering that a lot of money was made by a few from some of these events, the gentry continued to build, and build on a big scale.

One of the great issues during the period in question was the enclosure of land in England and this had possibly been a bone of contention since the advent of man. It certainly had been the subject of legal rankling since the thirteenth century, and came into more prominence during Tudor times, and even more so during the eighteenth century and the period of this narrative. Not until the nineteenth century was formality of enclosure introduced, prior to which the matter was distinctively contentious as those against had no power to oppose whilst those in favour had complete influence to authorize. A classic anomaly. The powerful landowners became more powerful and the commoner more lowly with the loss of lands. The population by mid-eighteenth century was little more than five million, with no significant increase until after 1760; there was no influence possible by power in numbers even if the landowners were far outnumbered by the lower classes. It has been suggested that the low population was not because they could not produce children, but because they could not keep them out to the very unhealthy state of this somewhat nomadic populace. The poor health was as a result of poor sanitary conditions and little pure water being available, so that the mortality rate was high.

Later in these writings reference is made to the long journeys travelled and it may be of interest to make brief comment on the general state of communications. The civilized Roman roads had fallen almost at the time of the fall of the empire, and within a short lapse to the Saxon period there was little remaining, and so difficulties existed until serious consideration was given to communication as late as the reign of George III. This was the era of Turnpike Acts, the remodelling and maintenance being paid for by the tolls. This indicates that, during the dates of this chapter of the book, transportation was far from easy; certainly facilities were few and the great Scottish engineer McAdam's introduction were not in use for many years to come. Later in this chapter some information is given about George III's son, the Prince of Wales, who, whilst still under age, became besotted by Brighton to which he was introduced by the King's brother, the Duke of Cumberland, much to the annoyance of the King who knew of the duke's notoriety. One historian suggests that it was when the Prince was in partial residence on the south coast that the habit of 'commuting' was introduced, somewhat before the habit became the norm, but perhaps a good thought. It is recorded that His Royal Highness did, in the 1780s, journey from Brighton, departing at about five in the morning, deal with the required business in London, returning to Brighton by late afternoon. A journey of 180 miles, spending ten hours in the saddle. Long and ferocious horse rides were a normal occupation, for both business and pleasure, in the eighteenth century; a practice which in modern times would create a considerable hue and cry of cruelty – for the horse, not the Prince.

Many of these points would have influenced the work of Brown and Holland; the one taking advantage of the less fragmented tracts of land, and the other providing the means for the owners to show to the world their great wealth.

Neither man received during their lifetime any recognition by way of title, in fact both created controversies at some stage of their careers; both were born into the world of commoners and yet, both on very many occasions or when handling commissions dealt directly with aristocrats from princes to dukes, and with a list of clients which reads like a who's who in the world of the gentry. In addition both created such works of art as to be names known to the majority hundreds of years after their deaths.

Why these two should be so important in the line of architecture and design of both buildings and estates will become clear. On the one hand Brown is the name associated so frequently with the larger estates, whereas Holland may not be as familiar but nevertheless is linked with such oddities as Carlton House, demolished in the early nineteenth century, but its life continues by a large number of chimney-pieces and parquet floors being moved to Windsor, the Ionic screen being used by Nash at Buckingham Palace and the portico columns to the side entrances of the National Gallery; and indeed Holland, jointly with his father, was largely responsible for Hans Town which became the forerunner of modern day 'new towns'.

In truth it is no surprise that Brown's name is more famous than that of Holland; the former modified the natural materials of the landscape on a massive scale, while the latter used man-made and adapted materials to construct buildings. The movement of the landscape to conform with Brown's vision, and thereby obliterating the work of previous landscape artists, such as LeNotre, George London, Charles Bridgeman, and Henry Wise, all of whom died within the first third of the eighteenth century, has never been superseded whether because of the curtailing of land enclosure, lack of vision, or lack of financial resources. Never has there been since the life of Brown movement of land on the scale of the Brown era, and that was during the period of small population and no mechanization; there has been a large number of garden modifications and much in the way of destroying the seventeenth and eighteenth century planning but only on a small scale. Little research will show that many small formal areas today purporting to be the parterre built by one of the great gardeners, in fact they may well be to their design, but are copies rebuilt on, in some instances, former vegetable plots created during the troubled times of one of the world wars.

Holland, on the other hand, whilst being involved in many projects, they were basically on a much smaller scale; in addition, the materials – man-made – do not have the durability of natural materials. Holland in his turn modified or covered the work of his predecessors and in due time his work was lost or hidden by that of his successors. It is also of interest that some modern-day experts are in doubt as to the true originator of one or two properties, particularly in London, where Adam has been given the credit for a building which in fact was by Holland. In many instances this confusion is understandable. One name in the group of Holland's successors which is well known is that of Nash, which is to be expected in view of the large number of commissions completed by him. There may be some truth in the words of one architect that Nash was an 'untidy' worker and his buildings required constant repair. There are no longer the resources in this modern lifestyle to replace such as Buckingham Palace or Holland's Carlton House which was replaced by Nash's Carlton Terrace. More information on the subject of these properties is given later in this chapter.

Before continuing in further detail, to attune the reader to the characters referred to it is fair to quote two historical matters. In a letter to Humphrey Repton Holland praised the virtues of Brown, not only as an architect who gave the greatest consideration to every minor detail, from providing comfort for the habitation of all ranks and degrees of society, but he also did this without ever having had one single difference or dispute with any of his employers. Perhaps the best way of assessing Holland is to refer to the personal tribute inscribed on a plinth of a marble bust which was commissioned by Samuel Whitbread, the second, who inherited Southill in Bedfordshire from his father, the founder of the brewery, the work being carried out by George Garrard after Holland's death in 1806. As a point of interest Holland worked at the house in the 1790s and independently Brown had carried out work in the park twenty years previously. The inscription on the plinth reads as follows:

> Business is often friendship's end.
> From business once there rose a Friend.
> Holland! That friend I found in thee,
> Thy loss I feel, whene'er I see
> The labours of thy polished mind;
> Thy loss I feel, whene'er I find
> The comforts of this happy place;
> Thy loss I feel whene'er I trace
> In house, in garden, or in ground,
> The scene of every social round.
> Farewell! in life I honoured thee;
> In death thy name respected be.

For ease of reading, as the ages were so different – Brown 1715 or 16 to 1783 and Holland 1745 to 1806 – this narrative will start with a brief history of Brown's life, continuing into that of Holland then the two jointly for the period when they became business partners, a partnership which only ended because of Brown's death in London in 1783. This period also covers a happy time when the partnership was cemented on a personal note when Holland married Brown's daughter Bridget.

The Holland referred to above is Henry junior as opposed to his father Henry senior, although records show that as early as 1761, at least ten years before Brown and Holland junior became associated, work carried out by senior at Ashridge in Hertfordshire was to some degree connected with Brown, although the work entailed appears to have been slight and included a garden wall.

Brown

Lancelot Brown, the son of a Northumberland farmer, was born in either 1715 or 16, being the fifth of six children, started work at the age of fifteen or sixteen, some say in the kitchen garden, but certainly on the estate of Sir William Loraine who was principal landowner of Kirkharle. This must have provided those grand ideas for which Brown became famous and provided his popularity and great wealth, as the Loraine estate was being remodelled at this time. Work was on such a grand scale as to include the moving of a village, land reclamation and removal of the formality of the French style, and the planting of more than half a million trees. All aspects of Brown's designs in the future and which were to be repeated on over 200 estates, and over thousands of acres of land throughout the country could well have been initiated at this time.

By about the age of twenty Brown observed the completion of this estate transformation and moved south. At about this time William Kent was working at Stowe, Buckinghamshire for Lord Cobham, and Brown was appointed as Head Gardener. Although Kent was actually only in the latter half of his fifties his standard of work was failing and Brown had an easy task of superseding him in importance at the Stowe estate. For about ten years Brown was associated with Stowe and this must have been one of the most important periods in his career, not only for gaining experience of landscaping but also for the introduction to persons of note who became his employers in later life. In addition Brown was, even in his early days at Stowe completing a number of small commissions. The Stowe period came to an end with the death in 1748 of Kent and a year later the death of Lord Cobham.

Hammersmith, in the days when it was a riverside hamlet, was Brown's next address, and perhaps he decided on this area as there were already a number of notable horticultural nurserymen established here. Brown set up what was considered to be an architectural practice; it will be noted that it was architectural and not just landscape work. He had become more and more convinced that the large estates must be considered as a whole, neither house nor grounds looked at individually but the two to be interlinked to give a whole picture. There was, perhaps, another significance in this move to Hammersmith, which, in the eighteenth century was within the Fulham area, and it was also suitable for anyone involved in the construction industry as the main industry of the area was, and had been since the seventeenth century, brick-making.

Humphrey Repton cited Brown as the founder of the English style of landscape-gardening which superseded the geometric style perfected by Andre LeNotre (1613–1700) at Versailles, a French style much copied in many countries of Europe, but it was his own original naturalistic style that Brown pursued for the remainder of his life. Gone too was the period of London and Wise, those great formal garden designers of the latter part of the seventeenth century; gone too, at Stowe and many other estates, was the work of Charles Bridgeman (d. 1738). William Kent, born in 1684, was perhaps the originator of the natural style but Brown took it a stage further. Some commissions involved starting afresh, such as Croome and Longleat, whilst others, and perhaps more frequently, the work was modifying when following Bridgeman's and Kent's type of construction. The visits to properties varied considerably in that one required only one visit and the plan would be grasped and digested by the staff on site and implemented as time, finances and circumstances allowed as at Highclere in Hampshire for the Earl of Caernarvon; other estates would receive many visits over many years before the work was completed. Of his house building it has been said that the exterior was a little clumsy, but the interior gave great success as regards comfort. He realized a great fortune by his amiable manners and high character supported with dignity, and acting as a country gentleman.

The style he used in landscaping was to a large extent repetitious in that his main aim was to bring out the undulating lines of the natural landscape, but furnishing each with a similar set of features. This was sufficiently flexible to allow for variations to incorporate existing features such as at Blenheim where the widened lake incorporated the existing Vanbrugh bridge. This radical change in garden design attracted much criticism, perhaps it was too revolutionary, and even today Brown, according to one school of thought, was an eighteenth-century vandal; certainly there was a great destruction of trees on vast areas of land, but to the gentry of the day it was popular, and to many of the landowners it was more important to have grounds suitable for riding their horses in private rather than formal viewing gardens in a foreign style. In many cases the economics had to be considered. This eighteenth-century period was showing signs of reduced wealth obtained purely by owning land, and 'weed-a-women' were starting to expect more than the paid two pounds ten shillings, or three pounds per year, and when considering that twenty or thirty such staff could be employed to maintain the formal parterres and ancillary topiary work, great savings of wages could result. Of the many reasons given for the growth in the Brown style landscapes throughout the country, the evidence for the popularity is shown by the number of times the style was copied, whether Brown was involved or not. Supporters and critics alike must admit that in view of the short period of the induction of the Brown landscaping, something like fifty years, the ideas have stood the test of time, and there are relatively few who could envisage the impact of a few clumps of trees when they reach maturity 200 years later.

During mature years Brown was severely criticized by Chambers who appears to have accepted a number of occasions to publicly censure Brown's work. Why? Was it some unrecorded past meeting from which this animosity arose or purely professional resentment? There may be a clue for the second reason as on a number of dates Chambers had submitted detailed plains for projects but the commissions had been awarded to Brown. In 1769 Lord Clive chose Brown's plans for Claremont, and during the following year Lord Milton chose Wyatt's design for the house and Brown's plans for the village at Milton Abbas; again Chambers had submitted plans for work he hoped to obtain.

Chambers, that is Sir William Chambers and Brown, both men being born within twelve months of each other, were very different characters and had greatly differing backgrounds. The former born in Stockholm of Scottish descent, was brought to England at the age of two. After his formal education, he spent two years whilst in his twenties in the mercantile marines and a five-year period between 1750 and 1755 in Paris and Rome studying architecture. On his return, apart from writing a book on Chinese building and furniture, he was appointed tutor to the Prince of Wales (later George III). By 1761 he joined the Office of Works, succeeding Flitcroft as Comptroller and by 1782 became head of the department with the title Surveyor-General. His main claim to fame, in addition to designing a number of mansions and the pagoda in Kew Gardens, was the near lifetime's work of building the largest official building in London since Greenwich Hospital, that is Somerset House on the Thames embankment. So named as it was the site on which the great Lord Protector Somerset's Renaissance mansion of 1547 stood – possibly the first true Renaissance building in England. The building could well have occupied much of Chambers' working life as this neo-classical styled, 800-feet-long building was started in 1776 and not completed until 1798. It was Chambers who introduced this style, possibly the first major building of its type in England, from the Continent. Chambers was knighted by the King of Sweden; he became the first Treasurer for the Royal Academy which was housed, with other learned societies, in Somerset House.

Brown, on the other hand, started work as a gardener, obviously had a mental aptitude for landscape design, and had already worked at Stowe for ten years, completed Croome Court in Worcestershire, and remodelled many other estates, before Chambers had finished his education. Very different characters, a great pity one should criticize the other! Later in life Chambers' attitude did mellow to some degree, as will be seen later in these writings when the last few years of the life of Henry Holland are recorded.

It is unnecessary to bore the reader by listing all the multitude of properties and estates with which Brown was involved, but it may be of interest to mention a few indicating the various reasons for the work, and this may illustrate why the expression of 'who's who' is written above. These are more or less in chronological order and prior to the partnership with Holland. Petworth Park in Sussex was an early work for Lord Egremont; Burghley in Lincolnshire, for the 9th Earl of Exeter had innumerable landscape projects and further modifications over something like thirty years; the great George London, a gardener of considerable note, had one of his claims to fame removed by Brown at Longleat in Wiltshire. During about a four-year period remodelling of the views was effected at such widely dispersed estates as Ashridge, Hertfordshire for the Duke of Bridgewater; Alnwick for the Duke of Northumberland; Chatsworth in Derbyshire for the Duke of Devonshire; and Harewood House estate in Yorkshire for the Lascelles family. By 1762 William Kent's landscape at Holkham in Norfolk was being modified and a couple of years later Henry Wise's parterres were grassed over and his avenues of trees were moved to create groups, both these projects for the 4th Duke of Marlborough at Blenheim. In that year Brown was appointed Royal Gardener and managed to resist George III's wish to remove the great formal gardens at Hampton Court.

A year later Brown designed and built a castle, this at Tong in Shropshire. A complete departure from his previous work and one can almost imagine this as being light relief from the many remodellings of the landscape. It was, in truth, a rebuilding of the castle and this medievalizing, according to Pevsner, became an oddly Moorish Gothic fantasy, utterly incorrect – an elaborate piece of Rococo wit rather than a reproduction of the past; nevertheless even Pevsner referred to it as Capability Brown's masterpiece. It was built for George Durant to replace the mansion of the Vernons, unfortunately demolished in 1954. Having said that, it did exist for nearly 200 years.

The above, as the reader will appreciate, is only a short list of the

Brown workload. One's mind can imagine the mileage achieved whether on horseback or in a trap before roads as known today existed. Workload – by now a man in the second half of his fifties, his perpetual ill health caused by asthma not improving, he then accepted the post of High Sheriff of Huntingdonshire to meet popular demand. It is no surprise that help was needed to enable all these commissions to be supervised and in about 1772 Brown made formal partnership with the son of his family friend, Henry Holland.

Holland

The other member of this duo is, in all probability, less well known than Brown, this being Henry Holland, and unless otherwise mentioned, reference is being made to junior rather than his father, also Henry. Holland, similar to Brown, started work at either fifteen or sixteen years of age and learnt his trade by experience, tuition from his seniors in the same trade and, perhaps, more so in the case of Holland than for Brown, reading and studying the writings of the day. No grand tour for either of them. It appears that Brown did not travel abroad but Holland is known to have visited the Continent perhaps more than once. They both experienced the period of great change in their respective businesses, many resulting from the deaths of the leading exponents in their particular field, or changes in attitudes, or changes in the financial status of the clients. One very significant influence does became clear, and that is the great change, perhaps independence may be appropriate, as the Isles of Britain were leaving the centuries of accepting that the Continentals must dominate and lead the fashions when building estates.

The changes were exciting. As an example, the strict rules for the Palladian style of building was at last being questioned for the great mansions for the English gentry. It is a fact that Andrea Palladio, the executant of the vogue, had been born and died in Vicenza, 41 miles from Venice in Italy in the sixteen century, but one good reason for his having so many followers was the book which he produced in 1570. It is thought that Palladio was himself inspired by the writings of the only written exposition to survive from antiquity, that being the ten books written by Vitruvius in Rome before or about the first century. But the Palladian style was devised to meet the requirements of the Venetian patrons with specific instructions that the building must serve all utilitarian purposes, but at the same time present a well-balanced and dignified exterior. The published work of 1570 was avidly used as the bible for many of the greater construction projects, and Inigo Jones, who introduced the revival of the Palladian style into England at so many estates had died mid-seventeenth century, so by the eighteenth, even early eighteenth century, change was due, and this was the time Holland became involved. In addition there were a number of deaths of those long-standing supporters of the Paladian style, all within a relatively short space of time: Campbell (1729), Leoni (1746), Kent (1748), Burlington (1753) and Gibbs (1754).

Henry Holland junior was born in 1745, his parents being Henry (b. 1712) and Mary, née Byrom (b. 1716), and it would appear that at this time the family were living in Fulham, London. Father Holland already had a thriving construction firm, although he is recorded as being the builder of properties, rather than as the architect. Certainly it is recorded that Henry senior worked at such places as Bowood in Wiltshire and at Ashridge in Hertfordshire. The Holland family history can be traced back a long way and there are many stories about the fortunes and debts over a number of generations, the fortunes apparently being made by the holding of offices to Crown and Country. but the debts resulting in supporting the wrong side! It has even been suggested that one Cornelius Holland had a rank within the government of the day to justify the thought that he was involved with the decapitating of Charles I. All very intriguing but, perhaps, not to be dwelled upon at this stage, as the subject of this story was not born until 20 July 1745.

Holland joined the family business about 1760 which is in itself an interesting year as it is about the time Robert Adam returned from Italy, Adam probably being a more familiar name than that of Holland. Age-wise the two differ in that Adam was seventeen when Holland was born, but that is not sufficient difference for them not to have crossed paths a number of times. In fact Holland was very aware of Adam and could well be accused of having some Adam type work in mind when dealing with interior decor later in his life. He was more reserved, if the word flamboyant can be used for Adam. More than one twentieth-century history book illustrates the similarity between the two as the writers have created some debate as to who was actually responsible for some of the works. The difference between these two designers can be seen clearly at Berrington Hall in Herefordshire, but that is going too quickly as Berrington was not until Holland had been working something like eighteen years and much was to take place before then.

To concentrate on Holland's main period of working life is to refer to a relatively short period, namely when he started to appear in the family firm's books, about 1767, to the end of the eighteenth century. It could be said that Holland followed the era of Wyatt but without the Wyatt pursuit of novelty and extravagance in that Holland reverted to more strict neo-classicism. If Henry Holland followed Wyatt it could also be said that he was the forerunner of Soane, who started as an apprentice for the newly formed partnership of Brown and Holland. Soane became an important architect by rebuilding the Bank of England and colleges of both Oxford and Cambridge, amongst others; he obtained his knighthood in 1831, some time after this story ends. As already stated Holland died in 1806, but for a number of years preceding his death there were only a small number of commissions fulfilled; he died in the house which he built off Sloane Street at the age of almost sixty-one.

But the thirty-odd years reviewed here were extremely productive and long lasting; and the amount and type of involvement with some clients was sufficient to enable Holland to be recorded in history. Almost twenty years of his life were implicated with that most extraordinary of royals, George Augustus Frederick, Prince of Wales, sometimes Prince Regent, and eventually King George IV, the monarch who was kindly called the first royal patron of architecture since the Stuarts. Henry Holland, in conjunction with his father, was devising what may, many years later illustrate the technique for satellite towns juxtaposition to large cities.

Before the 'satellite' stage Holland was involved in the building work of many London houses, sometimes just minor alteration sometimes additional wings; there are today a considerable number of the larger London residences which contain the Holland influence. Many have, of course, by the twentieth century, been modified a number of times and it is not always easy to distinguish the Holland work. During the first year in which Holland appeared in the firm's books an important event took place, not that Holland would have appreciated it at the time. Clive of India, Lord Clive, returned to England for the last time and, the important point being, he obtained Claremont in Surrey. The importance to Holland was, although it took a couple of years to progress, the rebuilding of Claremont was designed by Brown and built in collaboration with Holland; the work continuing for at least three years. Three years of working together is quite a long time, but it obviously was satisfactory to both parties as about the time of the culmination of that commission a partnership was formed between the two. It was a pity that Clive did not gain happiness from the rebuilding of Claremont, but instead he died by his own hand, after being censured for his conduct in the sub-continent, at his Berkely Square address within two years of the estate being completed.

The 'satellite' town previously referred to gives another opportunity which reflects on the relationship of the two families of Brown and Holland. During the eighteenth century, and indeed a practice which still continues today with any far-sighted construction firm, is that investment is made whenever suitable land for possible future development becomes available. The firm of Holland was very much aware of this and became involved with the area, now modern Brompton, being bordered by the existing Sloane Street, King's Road and Brompton Road; this approximately 89 acres. It appears that Brown was the original contact as he had worked at Caversham in Berkshire for Lord Cadogan during the 1760s; Cadogan married into the Sloane family and hence the valuable estates of Chelsea were brought into the family. Sir Hans Sloane, who was of sufficient importance in the medical world to become president of the Royal College of Physicians, owned the manor of Chelsea. It was he who presented the freehold of the Chelsea Physic Garden to the Society of Apothecaries in 1721, and part of the British Museum; the Natural History Museum was founded on his lifelong collection, estimated to have cost more than £50,000 but was bequeathed to the nation on payment of £20,000 to his family. At one stage there was a thought that the collection should be housed in Buckingham House but finally this was considered to be too expensive so Montague House, in Bloomsbury, was used instead. Sloane Square and Street, and other properties with the name, were named after Sir Hans. The whole new town project was large and somewhat protracted, the aim being to provide dwellings for the upper, middle or professional classes, and some of the early occupants included Mary Russell Mitford, Lady Caroline Lamb, Jane Austen, Gainsborough's widow, and even the son of the famous architect Flitcroft. The concept appears to have been sufficiently well received as to be cited as the model for a number of future, later referred to as 'new towns', such as Camden, Kentish, Somers and Canning towns. Inevitably replacements and modifications started to take place a hundred years later with the expiration of the leases. The name 'Hans Town' appears to have become lost in the mists of time, rarely can it be found in the history books.

The actual construction of Hans Town extended during almost the whole of the 1770s and this proved to be one of Holland's very active periods both in his business and personal life.

During 1772 the partnership of Holland and Brown was formalized and this whilst the work was being continued at Claremont. The actual house, described as a rambling building, with a brick, castellated facade by Vanbrugh was owned by the widowed Duchess of Newcastle and the commission brought to light a number of interesting facets, but there is more than one story attached to it. Some say Brown designed and Holland built, others say the other way round. It would appear as a joint venture, one modified even further years later by John Soane. There are also many stories about the actual cost ranging from £100,000 to about one third of that figure, the latter being considered to be nearer the truth. In the world of building it is not always easy to categorically state that a material was used by one constructor before any other, and this very much applies to the material used to create Scagliola. This is the term given to the artificial decorative marble to be found in so many properties; it is a most effective pseudo-marble based on the use of plaster of Paris. The use can actually be traced back to the early Florentine builders, and revived in the sixteenth century with an introduction into England about 1750. James Wyatt is usually given credit for its first use in England, this for the Pantheon in Oxford Street which was begun in about 1769, but eventually demolished although not until 1937. The hall columns of Claremont must have been as early when the plasterer William Pearce used the material, and at Stowe Holland employed the Italian Domenico Bartoli who was responsible for the jasper columns. Giving the due credit is perhaps not important, the importance lies in the use of this material which gives such pleasing effect without the very high cost of transporting, importing and installing either columns or sheets of marble which are indeed heavy and difficult to handle.

At the same time as the partners were involved in a number of commissions the marriage took place between Henry Holland and Brown's daughter Bridget. Four children were born to the happy couple during the following five years, the names used carrying on both family traditions being Bridget, Henry, Mary and Harriet. The fifth child was born three years later, called Lancelot after his grandfather. It was four years before Charlotte was born, and the last child Caroline was the year after.

For about seven years, from 1775, Holland acted as Clerk of Works at the Royal Mews, Charing Cross, and he became Justice of the Peace in 1778.

In addition to bringing up the family, acting as Clerk of Works at the Royal Mews and as Justice of the Peace, a number of other commissions were being carried out in various parts of the country. From Cadland, Southampton (a property sadly lost in the 1950s to make way for part of the Fawley Refinery), to Stone in Staffordshire (modifying the Crown Inn); from Benham, working for William, 6th Baron Cravon, to a church in Kent, namely St Michael's at Chart Sutton, where on at least two occasions plans had been prepared for the restoration and modifications.

It was about this time, 1778, that an eminent Tory landowner, Thomas Harley, required a house to be built on a newly acquired estate in Herefordshire, and as Brown had already worked for the family at nearby Eywood it was logical that he should be invited to receive the commission for this new property. On this occasion Brown worked in conjunction with Holland, in fact Brown working exclusively on the estate grounds and son-in-law, Holland, dealing with the buildings. Much more detail can be read about this property and the owners, including the relationship with the gentleman after whom that most famous of London Streets, Harley Street, was named and their successors in Chapter x.

In the 1770s the partners worked on other Staffordshire properties, one of which gives a good illustration as to the fate of many a great house. A Tudor gabled house called Fisherwick, owned by Lord Donegal, had received modifications to bring it up-to-date by both Brown on the estate in the 1760s, and by Holland on the house in the 1770s. His Lordship died late in the century and his successor sold it to a private individual who, within a matter of a few years, sold it lock, stock and barrel for the value of the materials.

The year 1783 was, however, an even busier year but also a year of sadness. Early in February of that year Brown died and this left a void in Holland's life as the affable Northumbrian had been connected with the Holland projects during the whole thirty-eight years of Henry's life. Three months later Mary Holland, Henry's mother died at the age of sixty-seven. Life carried on and so did business and during this year a sequel to a project performed six years earlier took shape. During the 1770s Holland, as part of his London commissions, became involved with the work on a number of clubs, one of which was Brooks's, which the Prince of Wales joined during the year of his coming of age, and the time when his father, the King, agreed that the heir should have his own property. Perhaps the introduction of the alliance of Prince and Holland was the Brooks's Club connection and at that time there were few architects with the same experience as Holland. Fortuitously Carlton House, not far away, had been empty since its abandonment on the death of George III's mother in 1772 and this was to be the new royal palace. Within three years Holland had converted this address to what was described by some as one of the finest royal palaces in Europe, not in size but in facilities and artistic design, and it was partly in use within two years even though work was still progressing. Rather unfortunately for the Treasury the affections of the Prince had changed to Brighton to which he had been introduced by the King's brother in 1780; he became almost besotted with the thought of living on the south coast and the purchase of property there resulted in Holland continuing to work for royalty, which in total was the case for the best part of twenty years. The initial building work was to convert, modify and extend some existing buildings to the standard of that required by the Prince, work which was carried out over many years, in fact the constant modifications continued long after Holland withdrew from service to the Prince largely because His Highness employed other little-known architects to interfere. What is now known as the Pavilion at Brighton is far from the original plans of Holland although the various attachments were built on or over Holland's work.

Whilst the Carlton House, and later the Brighton House, projects were in operation Holland was responsible for a variety of jobs including the development of the port on the Forth and Clyde Canal, the sea loch later becoming Grangemouth, and a number of commissions for Earl Spencer at some of his London properties. Frederick, Duke of York employed Holland for work at Oatlands, Weybridge, Second Earl Spencer had modifications completed at Althorp, and for many years the fifth Duke of Bedford, who was greatly involved with a number of theatres and inns in London, employed Holland to redesign and rebuild a number of them. One of the common problems with theatres, and indeed with many of the houses of the day, was the scourge of fire, a subject which Holland had been interested in and taken precautions against in much of his building work. The Duke also employed Holland for the remodelling of his home Woburn Abbey. That is not all that was occupying Holland during the years of trying to satisfy the Prince at Brighton, for he was commissioned for the second phase of work at Broadlands, modifying Debden Hall near Newport in Essex and Park Place, Henley, with yet more work for Whitbread at Southill, Bedfordshire, and the designs for Wimbledon House in Surrey.

Holland may have started work at an early age but the thirty years practical work gave him the opportunity to write articles on one of his favourite subjects, agricultural dwellings, for publication in the trade journals. He also became involved in the founding of the Architects' Club, and it says much for the man when considering that membership was exclusively for those in the profession who were Gold Medallists or members of the Royal Academy, or one of the European Academies. Members of the club incorporated such as Dance, Wyatt, Adam, Soane and Sir William Chambers, a name previously mentioned in connection with Brown, but the relationship between Chambers and Holland was very different despite Holland's lack of background – obviously his achievements had qualified him to become one of the elite.

There are still many, many properties at which Henry Holland worked, some during the Brown partnership, some working independently, but many are not obviously Holland's, some need to be looked for, but they are there. He continued working and designing architecturally for a few more years and unfortunately was, a few years before his death, aware that Porden was working for the Prince of Wales at Brighton, and as history shows after Holland's death, Nash took over.

Chapter X

Berrington Hall

Berrington Hall in Herefordshire may not be the most visited of the great English houses, but it is one deserving scrutiny rather than just a quick look round the rooms which are open to the public. It justifies further and further investigation, and by pursuing enquiries the real worth of this house and estate is appreciated. Below are observations giving some of the background to a few of the people, and their circumstances, associated with the property.

The early days of the estate reveal owners who, in their time, were important history makers, and the present house was built during a turning point in the designs of architecture. During the building period the two hundredth anniversary of the death of that great Italian building designer who influenced so many of the large houses in the British Isles was being celebrated. Andrea Palladio, who was born and died at Vicenza, 1518–1580, was the chief exponent of the new Roman as opposed to the Renaissance architecture, and his influence on foreign styles was enormous. By the date of the building of Berrington much of his severe symmetrical lines had benefited by being softened by the introduction of more artistic work.

Berrington Hall can best be described as of medium size, although it has comparatively few rooms, and it certainly is not one of the great palaces with which the architect became involved some years later, but it can also be described as handsome. Certainly the present site, which is some thousand yards south-west of the original manor of the estate, commands a position, deliberately, to provide the best possible view using the natural landscape of the Black Mountains, Brecon Beacons and Radnor Forest as a 'back-cloth'. Medium size it may be but it has all the required service areas from larders to laundry, from dairy to depository for coal (in the semi-basement), from stables to staff quarters; in other words it has all that is required to be a self-contained estate.

A visit by those interested will whet the appetite for such questions as to why the estate was positioned in its present form, who the owners were, and how the finances were raised in an area not part of the hub of business or commerce. Below is a brief insight which may answer some of the questions.

The original estate owners were of the Cornewall dynasty, a name mentioned in association with the Battle of Agincourt, and their story unfolds later with the tales of Kinlet Hall, Moccas Court and Burford, whereas the instigator of the new house was Thomas Harley, the son of an earl who made progress in the political field by being outspoken against a revolutionary politician of the day. It was he who provided the capital for the building work by being an eighteenth-century entrepreneur and partly financing the Government in the American exploits. Perhaps the financial downfall of the Cornewalls in the 1720s allowed the estate to be sold. The last private owners were the Cawleys, all these families being of moderately local stock. The building and landscaping of the present estate from 1775 into the 1780s was fulfilled by two of the greatest architects and landscape designers of the period, and it was during this period, when these two were business partners, that the work was executed. In addition the architect married the daughter of the landscapist, the two men being known as Henry Holland junior, and Lancelot (Capability) Brown. Another marriage, perhaps an even more important one, took place during the final stages of the interior decor of the house, and this was the owner's heiress daughter marrying the son and heir of Admiral Rodney.

It was this Rodney, George Brydes, who was born into poverty, went to sea at the age of fourteen, became a captain whilst in his twenties, had a long and distinguished career being considered a very important naval man between the 1740s and 1780s, and one of the most effective admirals of the day. Amongst his many exploits he distinguished himself in many battles, relieved Gibraltar by utterly defeating the Spanish fleet off Cape St Vincent in 1780, and defeated the French in the West Indies, thus saving George III the considerable embarrassment of losing the much-prized jewel of Jamaica – good news for the cricketers – Jamaica having been captured from the Spanish by Admiral Pen and General Venables whilst Cromwell was Protector in 1655. Rodney was made a baron and the baronetcy was passed to his son George on his death in 1792; it was this son who married the daughter of the owner of Berrington. It remained a Rodney home until sold by the 7th Lord Rodney to the Cawleys in 1901. The third Lord Cawley surrendered the house, park and pool to the Treasury to pay estate duty resulting from his father's death.

The new and present owners, the National Trust, new owners being from 1957 when the estate was transferred to the Trust through the Land

Fund procedures, have, during the last two decades of the twentieth century, carried out extensive restoration both to the building and the grounds. The unusual step of removing trees and shrubs has restored the original view from the house. In fact the columns of the portico were deliberately placed to enhance that view so the visitor can now see what can best be described as a very beautiful 'Constable'-like scene, complete with pool (a 14-acre lake) and background of mountains.

Like most construction firms the team of Brown and Holland were involved in more than one scheme at the same time. About 1778 they were providing plans for the new house on the Berrington estate whilst remodelling Cardiff Castle for Lord Mount Stuart. Brown had previously worked for the 3rd Earl of Oxford at nearby Eywood (now demolished) and it was therefore logical that Brown and Holland should be chosen to construct the house and estate for the Rt. Hon. Thomas Harley, third son of the 3rd Earl of Oxford and Mortimer. Berrington may have benefited from the timing of the marriage of Harley's heiress daughter, Anne to George Rodney son of Admiral, later Lord Rodney, in April 1781. The house was not finished but expediency ensured decor suitable for the reception was ready in time. Dolphins and sea horses can be found within the building as respect to the new naval connections. For more details of the Brown and Holland careers and their partnership see Chapter IX.

The Harleys and Others

The Harleys were long-time owners of Brampton Bryan Castle, in addition to Eywood and they became Earls of Oxford (second issue) from 1711, being strong Whig parliamentarians. It was the 2nd Earl, Edward, after whom the London Street 'Harley' was named; the street which housed such notables as William Beckford, W. E. Gladstone and J. M. W. Turner, before being dominated by members of the medical profession. Young Thomas Harley, in modern parlance, would no doubt be classified as an entrepreneur, in effect his fortune from banking financed the cost of pay and clothing for the British Army in America. Money loaned to the Government was of great benefit which resulted in his MP status for the City of London, he was at one time one of the youngest Lord Mayors of London. Perhaps he really made his name by publicly denouncing the declarations of the MP John Wilkes.

The vagaries of being in or out of favour, whether connected to royalty, gentry, politician or commoner, was never more apparent than during the seventeenth and eighteenth centuries. A prime example of this is perhaps the little-known eighteenth-century MP John Wilkes who during his seventy year life, born in 1727, experienced the extremes from fines and imprisonment to being MP more than once, and Lord Mayor and Sheriff of London. At one time an obelisk stood in Ludgate Circus to commemorate his mayoralty. His controversial stance and subsequent penalties were, however, self-inflicted because of his habit of being too outspoken and opposing opponents without discretion, so ably confirmed by his founding of the papers *The North Briton* in 1762. Wilkes even declared a passage in the King's speech as being a falsehood, not being satisfied with attacks on Bute and his successors in the premiership. He was involved in the 'Essay on Women' resulting in expulsion from the House of Commons, twenty-two months in prison and at one time a £1,000 fine; his involvement in so much litigation subsequently had disastrous effects on his financial status. Even the great William Pitt the elder, somewhat of a turncoat, found Wilkes' attitude too outspoken for him to continue with their association. The public denouncement against Wilkes by young Harley would certainly not have been to his detriment.

With the above preliminary it may now be of interest to go back in time to the earlier days of the Harley family, starting with the earliest known home of Brampton Bryan which they held since the thirteenth century.

Accounts of the seventeenth century English Civil War relate stories of gallantry by the ladies and their female staff whilst their menfolk were away on government or crown business, or fighting at some skirmish in distant counties. These heroines of the period organized defences of their properties and many were defeated only by treachery. The story of Mary, Lady Bankes of Corfe Castle in Dorset, has been told many times, but there were others such as steadfast Lady Brilliana, Lady Harley who, whilst her husband was at Westminster, held the family seat at Brampton Bryan mansion for a number of weeks before it was finally destroyed by fire in 1643. Brampton Bryan Castle was one of the many defences against the Welsh and known to have been in the care of Lord Kinlet of Salop in the twelfth century, as Bernard Fitz Unspec (or Unspac or Ospac), probably a courtier, became Bernard de Brampton. The following century the property passed to Robert Harley and by the fourteenth century Bryan de Harley was rebuilding the defences. It was Sir Robert Harley who departed from his now fortified mansion and handed over the care to his wife Brilliana. The destroyed mansion was replaced by a new building for Sir Edward Harley in the 1660s and today the remaining parts of the old castle are used as a feature in a privately owned garden; it was used in the TV film *Howard's End* with Anthony Hopkins.

Kinlet, Moccas and Burford

Trying to trace the Cornewall family history before and after their ownership of Berrington is not easy as various writers contradict other writers. A certain amount of conjecture has been used by some authors, whilst others categorically contradict their predecessors. With this in mind, the following brief résumé gives one or two known facts purely as a guide. Almost all accounts show that the name is derived from Richard, Earl of Cornwall; the name becomes variously spelled Cornwall, Cornewall, Cornwalle etc., so one or more of the spellings may be shown below.

The Cornwalls were in possession of the ancient deer park of Kinlet in Shropshire from the end of the thirteenth to early fifteenth century, and it is recorded that Edward I gave custody of Bryan (can be Brian) to Edmund Cornwall. In the paragraph referring to Brampton Bryan Castle the Lord of Kinlet is mentioned. Let it suffice to accept those facts and then accept that branches of the family held Burford and Berrington by the fourteenth century. The owners of Kinlet have changed by the marriages of successive heiresses from the days of being owned by the Bramptons (or Brompton), thence to the Cornwalls, who gained ownership by Edmund marrying Elizabeth Brompton, the Cornewall residence lasting somewhat over one hundred years, the whole of the fourteenth century. There then followed the Blounts, who were knights of the realm, courtiers and soldiers; (were these related to the Blounts of Mapledurham House in Oxfordshire?), then the Lacons, as Rowland's second wife was Dorothy Blount and their only child Anne, married William Childe. Some of the Childes were Doctors of Law and MPs; and so to the Baldwyns who had been fortunate in marriages and were great landowners. The Baldwyns – or Bawdewyns and later Baldwin – to inherit the Kinlet property changed their name to that of Childe, and it was at this time, in the 1720s that the last and present Kinlet Hall was built to replace a number of previous manor houses. This eighteenth-century building constructed for William Childe MP, was based on designs by the well-known Midlands architect Francis Smith, frequently referred to as Smith of Warwick; in that county a number of houses to his design can be seen. Whilst the former Kinlet village has disappeared, a visit to the estate church of St John Baptist will reveal a number of very fine monuments and tombs in memory of various Blounts and Childes, and a fifteenth-century alabaster effigy to the daughter of Sir John Cornwall. The Childe family left Kinlet about 1930 and since immediately after the Second World War it has been used as a preparatory school.

It is now clear that the Cornewalls possessed Kinlet for a relatively short time into the fifteenth century, and it is also known that the principal family seat became Berrington, but only until their financial status deteriorated about the 1720s. However, during the middle of the seventeenth century Edward, the younger son of the family at Berrington had made an interesting marriage and the Moccas estate now appears on the scene.

Moccas Court, Herefordshire

What tales could be told if the old vernacular buildings of the venerable estates could communicate. What history could be learned, what intriguing gossip could be heard. Never more so than from the ancient Norman church on the Moccas estate. A building which has itself experienced changes has born witness to the comings and goings of the inhabitants of castles, more than one manor house, and some interesting owners throughout the past hundreds of years whilst the present manor house or Court is new, a mere eighteenth-century structure. Four-square to the wind has the village and parish church stood these past centuries. The additional work within the building took place with decorated windows in the thirteenth and fourteenth centuries, and, much later, repairs by Westmacott in 1803 and restoration, including the new ceiling, by G. G. Scott junior in 1870. The church has associations with the famous diarist R. F. Kilvert who was curate at nearby Clyro before being vicar at Bredwardine until his early death in 1879.

In the days when the original church was built there were three local castles each of which, by marriages and changes in ownership, has a bearing on the story of the owners of the Moccas estate.

The de Freyne family lived at Moccas Castle in the thirteenth century and records show that Sir Hugh de Freyne received licence to crenelate, albeit that ownership was temporarily suspended by the Crown when the building conditions were not met but after title was restored the family continued to live here until the 1370s. The Merediths had ownership briefly from the mid-fifteenth century but by the mid-sixteenth century the Vaughans were in possession and it is this family and their descendants who enter into the story of the owners of Berrington Hall. The Vaughan family seat in the seventeenth century had become Bredwardine Castle and Moccas was allowed to fall into ruins. Bredwardine is known to have existed as a wooden stronghold in the eleventh century when held by John de Bredwardine, and the Baskerville family had possession by about 1277. In the 1370s, through marriage, it became a Fouleshurst property, and a Cheshire family, but on the death of William in 1439 ownership reverted to the Baskervilles, who lived at Eardisley Castle. William Baskerville received licence to hold services in the chapel at Eardisley which was the seat of the Earls of Hereford, the long-established Bohun family and that line did not die out until about 1372.

Bredwardine, now in the hands of the Vaughans, is thought to be the site on which they built their mansion in about 1640, and it is known that some of the stone from Bredwardine was used for the building of Moccas Court from about 1775. The 1650 marriage of Edward Cornewall was to Francis, widow of Henry Vaughan and their son, another Henry married a Dutch heiress which provided sufficient funds for purchase and consolidation of all the Vaughan lands. With this increased wealth the Cornewalls held their place in society as politicians and served in the Navy and Militia, and as magistrates. Henry and his Dutch wife produced a son called Velters, a name with Dutch influence, and he became an eminent MP serving in the House of Commons representing Herefordshire for over forty-six years in seven successive Parliaments. He was also famous for his stables of horses for which he had a passion. Although Velters married three times only his third wife produced any children; one son, Frederick Henry, who died in infancy and one daughter, Catherine, who was born in 1752. Catherine therefore became sole heiress and at the age of about nineteen she married a wealthy man from a house called Carshalton in London. Under the Will of her father, Velters, who unfortunately died about three years before the wedding, a condition of the marriage was that her husband must change his name and accept the Arms of the Cornewall family, this he did and therefore Sir George Amyand became Sir George (Amyand) Cornewall, Bt.

This young groom, aged twenty-three at the time of his marriage, and Catherine could now bring new life to the old Moccas estate, and this they did by building a new modern house on a site overlooking the River Wye and employing 'Capability' Brown and others to layout the park. At various times he also employed Repton and Nash; Nash for the building of the distinctive cottage-style lodges, likened to those built to Nash's design at the hamlet of Blaize near Bristol. This was about 1801 to 1804 when G. S. Repton was working in the office of John Nash. This eighteenth-century house can be seen today, the architect was the little known Gloucestershire man, Anthony Keck, and it is known that Adam prepared some drawings for the house. It is of red brick built above steep slopes to the valley of the River Wye overlooking the old deer park with many ancient trees and the interior containing some fascinating Adam-style decor.

Sir George Cornewall, unlike his parents and brother whose life spans were short, lived to be over seventy years of age, and the Cornewalls remained at Moccas until 1916. The father of the present owner inherited by way of a cousin.

Carshalton and the Amyands

So far in this narrative the Cornewall family have been traced to Kinlet in Shropshire during the fourteenth century, to Berrington and Burford in Herefordshire from the fourteenth century to the 1720s. As previously mentioned at Moccas the introduction of the Cornewalls was by Edward from Berrington marrying Francis Vaughan in 1650, but by 1768 the last of that line was Catherine and, as mentioned, her new husband George Amyand who changed his name and the Cornewalls thereafter remained holders of Moccas. Perhaps now is a good time to enquire into the background of the Amyands a new dynasty introduced into England during one of the many turbulent periods in Europe in the sixteenth and seventeenth centuries.

Going back in history there is nothing new in people emigrating from one country to another whether for political or religious reasons. Early in the eighteenth century some of the Scottish Jacobite supporters of the Stuart claim to the British crown lived in exile in France or Italy; years prior to that the French industrialist population was greatly reduced by many emigrating to either the Low Countries or to England because of changes to the Edict of Nantes. The Amyands were Huguenots, in other words French Protestants who, during the period of the Edict from 1598, were moderately safe from persecution but on the Revocation of the Edict in 1685 they were no longer protected and during this exodus the Amyands fled from their native Mornac. Amyand is a name rarely found in general history books but found in the annuals of parliamentary history. Grandfather Amyand was astute enough to anticipate a problem and emigrated and by the year of the Revocation had became a naturalized English subject. Claudius became sergeant surgeon to George II, but Claudius's son George chose to be a financier and banker rather than follow into the medical profession. His business attainments were good and with money from the financial and merchant business he bought Carshalton in Surrey, and the same year stood for Parliamentary election for Barnstaple. Part of his financial interests involved him in the East India Company, and by 1764 he was given a baronetcy. Regrettably he had little time to enjoy this new position as he died within two years; his wife the former daughter of a Hamburg merchant died the following year. He had been 46 and she 42 years of age. The four orphaned children were George, the one who became Cornewall, a younger son John who died at an even earlier age than his parents, about nineteen, and two daughters both of whom married well, one to the Earl of Malmesbury, the other to the Earl of Minto. Financially the children could certainly be considered 'comfortably-off' inheriting substantially from their father and from their German grandmother.

Today the most interesting landmark on the Carshalton estate is the water tower, but more of that later. Much of the park is now used as a public recreation area, while the house a mere eighteenth-century structure built around the core of an older house, has been a school since the nineteenth century. The estate predates the Domesday survey but let the story commence later than that covering a few people of note. Sometime in the seventeenth century part of the lands were owned by the Arundells, may have been as Dower lands. An Edward Carleton appeared on the scene shortly after and he had the house built that is seen today; the architect remains unknown. The grounds were originally laid out by that great historic gardener Charles Bridgeman. Carleton was a merchant sometimes involved in the tobacco trade amongst other profitable ventures but the risk of all merchants was such that by 1713 Edward had become bankrupt.

Carshalton House became the residence of Dr John Radcliffe of Wakefield who became a Member of Parliament and was medical adviser to royalty including William III and Queens Mary and Anne, but was far too outspoken for his own good. His tenancy at Carshalton was short-lived as he died in 1714. From his great wealth his name is well perpetuated by the library, observatory and infirmary at Oxford bearing his name.

Another merchant then became resident at Carshalton, but this one had far greater diversity of interest in the world of trade than Edward Carleton; this was John Fellows, later Sir John. Fellows is frequently given credit for the building of Carshalton House but there is documentary evidence which cites his predecessor, Carleton, as being the instigator. Fellows became involved in the morally questionable South Sea Company as a result of which he spent a short time of imprisonment in the Tower and lost his fortune. Sir John's younger brother Edward bought Carshalton; Sir John died two days later at the early age of fifty-four. Edward died six years later aged fifty-nine. Another of the Fellows family inherited. It was Sir John who rearranged the water system at Carshalton, and this has left an inheritance of a unique eighteenth-century Waterhouse, or

Water Tower (possibly constructed 1719–20) now in the care of the Carshalton Water Tower Trust. The water system on the estate has been referred to as the best surviving example of domestic water architecture of the period, the water courses being diverted to fill the tank within the tower and thus supply water to the house and to the bathroom at the base of the tower. Although the actual bath is now covered over the Dutch tile lining remains in situ.

Lord Anson, of circumnavigation of the globe fame, leased the property from 1749, but when he purchased Moor Park in Staffordshire in 1751 the actual owners of Carshalton, the Mitchells of the Manor of Hemingford in Huntingdonshire, now Cambridgeshire, held it until the great sale of 1754 to George Amyand. And as is known, George flourished and in 1771 on his marriage to Catherine moved to Moccas Court Estate.

Burford Parish Church and Burford House

No epistle on the subject of the Cornewall family can be considered complete without a mention of Burford House and Church. The manor of Burford belonged to the Mortimer family throughout the thirteenth century, passing to the Cornewalls by marriage in the fourteenth century; the Cornewalls were Barons of Burford from that period until the eighteenth century. Burford Castle, when the official seat, stood approximately on the site of the present house.

Possibly the most important of the Cornewalls was Sir John, and it was he who commanded a division at the Battle of Agincourt, after which he was given command of the army of occupation of France. He became the second husband of Princess Elizabeth, daughter of John of Gaunt, sister of Henry IV. There is a very fine painted alabaster effigy above where the Princess was buried.

Burford Church was well documented in the eleventh century Domesday survey and obviously has received many restorations and modifications over the years, resulting in a somewhat irregular shape, as seen today, because of successive additions of aisles and chapels. One of the last major works was by that nineteenth century architect, famous for construction at Buckingham Palace and Admiralty Arch, Sir Aston Webb. There are a number of other extraordinarily fine tombs and monuments to the Cornewalls including a 'heart tomb' to one killed in Cologne, and a life-size effigy in wood to another.

The most outstanding of all the memorials must be the triptych. To refer to this as being one of the most remarkable in England, is to be conservative. It is unique, and that is no overstatement, although it should be mentioned that it is unique in size and importance; there are two other triptychs in the North of England which also combine religious with secular images, but not of the same magnitude. It needs to be seen to be appreciated. This sixteenth-century work of art, painted by an Italian Melchoir Salaboss, better known as Gheradino Milanese, has, within the central doors three life-sized portraits of the ninth Baron, his wife and their eldest son the tenth Baron. In addition to a number of pictures of the Nativity, Crucifixion and Resurrection and representation of the Last Judgement, there are figures of saints, evangelists, apostles and coats of arms. A painting beneath the two central doors depicts the figure of Edmund Cornewall in his death shroud; he was known as the 'Burford Giant', and was actually seven foot three inches tall. Interestingly the church houses a number of other monuments to the Cornewalls and to the Rushout family.

By the 1720s as the Cornewalls were heavily in debt the last Baron, Francis, emigrated to Jamaica, and the dilapidated castle and estate was sold to William Bowles, owner of the Vauxhall Glassworks; some years later the castle was demolished and the new house built. The great-grand-son of William Bowles, George Rushout, the 3rd and last Lord Northwich built additions to the house, although these were later demolished, and on the death of Sir Charles Rushout in 1931 the title died out and Burford passed to the Hon. Mrs Francis Whitbread, daughter of the 4th Lord Sudeley. During the Second World War the house was used by a girls school from St Albans, thence briefly as a school for the deaf and dumb, before being bought by the three Treasure brothers. It is now run as part of the famous nursery of Treasures of Tenbury.

Chapter XI

Tithe Barns

Tithe barns may initially appear not to be commensurate with a book entitled *People of Property*, and yet as a property in their own right they certainly were an integral part of the life of people. Few who are interested in buildings and who visit estates of yesteryear cannot have seen, and possibly enquired of, the use of these, the largest and most spectacular of the estate buildings wherever they have survived. They are old, old by the very nature of their purpose, providing a function common in the medieval period and before, but even in the twentieth century that function has left a legacy modified by Acts of Parliament during the nineteenth century.

This heritage of a completely different type of building provides cause for further investigation and thought; an inquiry which can produce facts on a subject which created contention during more centuries than possibly any other single subject. A situation which had necessitated a national survey throughout England and Wales, the size of which could be almost likened to a mini-Doomsday report of the eleventh century, but this in the nineteenth century.

Reference to tithes, originally one tenth, can be traced to the Bible Old Testament when Moses commanded the payment as mentioned in the Book of Deuteronomy, although it is known that tithes which were a set proportion of products from both agriculture and habitual employment were paid by civilized people before the coming of Christianity. Later Egbert, Archbishop of York around AD 750 is known to have instructed the clergy to teach people to pay the tithes.

The one tenth could be from the produce of the soil, profit from handicraft or merchandise, and products from animals such as butter and eggs. The system was simple as these tithes were paid to the church to maintain the parish clergy, and any surplus would be allocated to cathedrals and monasteries. It was a system which worked and was justified as taxes are justified in modern times. The inception of tithes payable to the church authorities was during the period when organized civilisation began; the time when the church provided most of the country's legal system, dealing with the formality of marriage, wills, sexual offences, and adultery. The monasteries were, between the fifth and twelfth centuries, the only seats of learning for higher education of the sciences, history, languages, arts and medicine. In other words the Church was all powerful and although the taxes created disputes and a constant source of friction, particularly in the seventeenth century, it was not until the eighteenth century that formality was confirmed and payment of tithes commuted to real charges. At this stage the changes and modifications to the basis for payments was dealt with at a local level only and the national law was not formulated until later. Even in the eighteenth century some imprisonments were enforced for non-payment in some kind, but by this period the church authorities introduced reforms, this at the time when the Tithe Commissioners were considering the introduction of the Commutation Act. The church authorities themselves, who had a basic objection to any control by government, considered changes and money raised by voluntary subscription came to the fore, much as the free church had instituted since their formation. The arrival in the eighteenth century of non-conformity in religion had a detrimental effect on the system, and many changes since medieval times enforced more radical revision to the procedure.

As tithes originally were due to the church incumbent this could include the vicar or rector or a lay 'impropriator' – a good example being a purchaser of former monastic lands – all of whom possessed the right whether descended from or acquired by purchase, the wealth frequently being given to those already wealthy. Especially true during the time when the younger sons of gentry were filling the niche vacant as curate or church dignitaries. The poor lay brothers remained poor even considering the greater value of tithes resulting from advances in agriculture, but tithes were crucial to their existence. The ecclesiastical authorities took action to economize and reduced their number of offices, in addition the due tithes were claimed from landowners rather than the tenants.

The early nineteenth century was appropriate for efforts to be made to clarify, even justify, this type of tax to be collected as civilization had advanced sufficiently for the matter to be reviewed as one entity. Income tax was on the statute books, piecemeal perhaps, by the early years of the century, but tithes, or payment in kind, were still required. The Tithe Commutation Act, finally passed in 1836, was based on what was probably the most detailed statistical inquiry held and the volumes of information collated enabled hundreds of parliamentary acts to be passed. The Tithe Commissioners were supplied with details amounting to something like

15,000 maps and plans involving over thirty million acres of land, plus masses of detailed facts on disputed areas, at a cost of over three million pounds, so fair consideration could be given to the formulating of law. A large amount of money was spent to establish facts but the actual value of tithes in monetary terms, although difficult to actually quantify because of lack of comprehensive records, at the time of the survey would be in excess of four million a year.

The above may appear a far cry from the original purpose of the tithe barns, but nevertheless the more modern action was as a direct result of the concept of taxes by tithes.

Below is a short list of the buildings which can be seen and thought over today. It is not by any means a complete representation for various reasons. A number of barns were demolished where development or redevelopment was required, particularly during the first half of the twentieth century. One or two have been resited either in total or in part – which rather defeats the object of preservation – and at least one has been parcelled stone by stone and moved to America to act as a 'folly' in the garden of a wealthy American magnet.

The barns, usually associated with wealthy monastic foundations, are not necessarily to be found near a monastic house as the building could serve a wide area and be a type of collecting point, conversely in some more concentrated prosperous district there could be more than one barn for a single abbey, such as Shaftesbury reaping the benefit from both Tisbury and Bradford-on-Avon. Whilst the three towns were some distance apart the Benedictine Shaftesbury Abbey, founded by King Alfred in AD 880, and where King Canute died in 1035, held power over a large tract of land. Ignoring some of the peculiarities those which remain in situ as originally intended provide examples of some extraordinary wooden superstructures of such size that they require examination to be appreciated. The actual building in most cases follows a pattern with variations as to the porch position as some entrances and exits are on opposite sides and some at opposite ends, thus enabling the carts to drive through rather than the need for difficult manoeuvre of turning within the building. The weight of the roof, frequently consisting of flat stones, although some were of thatch, over an area of roof up to 300 feet long and possibly covering a pitched roof over a building thirty feet wide, indicates that the stresses and strains of the building industry, this purely in timber, have been appreciated before the thirteenth century.

Cholsey in Berkshire – now Oxfordshire – reputed to be the largest of the recorded barns being over 300 feet long has now been demolished. It was possibly connected with the large eleventh-century church of St Mary which was extended during the thirteenth century.

Middle Littleton in Worcestershire near Evesham, buttressed like a church, at over 300 feet in length it is one of the largest and finest in the country still in existence, but the projecting wagon porches have not all survived. It was built for the Benedictine monks of Evesham and may be earlier than the thirteenth century. It is part of a group of buildings which included the Elizabethan manor house. Once it would have been used for the produce from the nearby fertile Vale of Evesham. The interior woodwork is a particularly fine example.

Abbotsbury in Dorset is perhaps the largest of its kind to exist, over 270 feet long and 31 feet high and was formerly, in the fifteenth century, roofed with flat smooth stones but is now thatched and houses a museum of times past. The size indicates the area it served and provided storage for the produce due from the tenants who farmed the monastic settlement estate. The Abbey, which gave the village its name, is down to foundation level in part but the only nesting colony of mute swans founded in the eleventh century by the Benedictine monks to provide meat is maintained nearby.

Frindsbury in Kent is classified as one of the longest, actually about 220 feet, of the surviving barns in Kent which was built about the year 1300 to store the grain and other foodstuffs paid in kind to the monks of Rochester.

Tisbury in Wiltshire – included amongst the collection of medieval buildings at Place Farm, once the grange of Shaftesbury Abbey, stands the reputed largest original thatched barn in England at about 200 feet long.

Bradford-on-Avon in Wiltshire, one of the best preserved in the country, was once a granary for the Abbess of Shaftesbury Abbey and dates from the fourteenth century. Prosperity of the town was based on the wool trade founded about the same period and the increased wealth and production necessitated the building of a barn measuring about 167 feet long and 30 feet wide.

Buckland Abbey in Devon at nearly 160 feet long is another considered to be one of the large barns in Britain, and similar to one or two others, is heavily buttressed. Buckland was the last Cistercian foundation in England established about 1273, and a good illustration that tithe barns were not built as part of a great estate as it appears today, but when constructed it was an abbey on this site and not until after the Dissolution was it converted to a private home. The position of barn in relation to the house appears at a number of large estates, but in each case it is where the barn originally served the church and it did not serve the landowning gentry.

Great Coxwell in Oxfordshire, west of Faringdon, was built mid-thirteenth century and belonged to the Cistercians of Beaulieu Abbey, Hampshire from grounds granted by King John about 1204. The building is some 152 feet long and the end doors are of a later period, eighteenth century; perhaps larger wagons were then introduced?

Bredon in Worcestershire. Traffic on the M5 motorway passing the area above the village of Bredon can easily identify the great tithe barn which originally belonged to the see of Worcester until the inevitable sixteenth-century passing to the Crown. Although there is no trace of the eighth-century monastery which was served by the barn, which is about 132 feet long and dated within the fourteenth century, it can be seen as having somewhat differing proportions in that the ridge rests on gabled end walls 42 feet high. The side walls are only about 12½ feet high thus producing an extreme pitch to the roof which is of stone shingle. Unusually one of the porches is raised in height to allow for the inclusion of a small room complete with fireplace, possibly to accommodate the monk or bailiff in charge of the receiving and dispatching of the tithes.

Ashleworth in Gloucestershire, near the tidal River Severn and about six miles north of Gloucester city, is with a group of buildings which includes a mid-fifteenth century Court house; the great barn was possibly built about 1500. In length about 125 feet the timber posts support a great expanse of slate stone roof.

Coggeshall Grange Barn in Essex is important and one of the earliest surviving timber-framed buildings in Europe. It was built in the twelfth century for the monks at Coggeshall Abbey.

Lacock in Wiltshire. The tithe barn of the fourteenth century now houses an exhibition to the pioneer of photography Fox Talbot of the nineteenth century and it would have been part of the abbey estate founded by Ela, Countess of Salisbury, to accommodate corn and, being in sheep country, possibly fleeces as payment in kind to the Abbey. Ela Devereux held various unique claims to fame, one being that she inherited her title at the age of eight; she married the illegitimate son of Henry II, was the only woman to hold the post of High Sheriff of Wiltshire, and on the day of the founding of Lacock Abbey she travelled sixteen miles on horseback to lay the foundation stone of an abbey for men. Her husband was the first man to be buried in Salisbury Cathedral of which he and Ela laid the fourth and fifth foundation stones. Lacock was said to be the last religious foundation to be dissolved at the Reformation.

That short list partly indicates the variations between these great old buildings found throughout the country. There are many more which can be easily located from tourist guides. Apart from providing a source for the study of ancient construction methods they act as a reminder of one of the oldest taxes on record. In summary, tithes were in Saxon times reasonable for providing the church with funds, they had become common practice during the Norman period, were then included in Canon Law – therefore compulsory – and not rescinded until well into the nineteenth century by which time this wealth tax had become too fragmented and national legislation intervened. It is many years since payment by goods has been accepted, but thanks to the preservation by many it is possible to see a number of these tithe barns, one of the majestic buildings of medieval times.

Chapter XII

Claydon House

Claydon House in Buckinghamshire may have been given into the care of the National Trust for preservation on behalf of the nation in 1956, but it is not as familiar to most people as many of the other great stately homes. And yet Claydon has an equally fascinating history, and associations with as large a number of people of character as almost any other property. The existing structure built mid-eighteenth century is in size a mere third of that of the original – which lasted little more than thirty years – but the portion remaining must be considered one of the gems of the Trust's holdings. Many of the great family members of note may have lived before the massive rebuilding work of the 1760's, but they and their employees at the time of the reconstruction were decidedly worthy of comment.

The very reason for the construction of the short-lived building justifies further investigation, particularly when realizing that in truth the reason for the ever-increasing building work was for the sake of competing with a neighbour and political opponent, but did this warrant being beggared by the act? The actual constructors of the edifice were themselves of such character as to be recorded in history; on the one hand an overseer whose greatest love appears to have been spending money – provided it belonged to someone else – and an artist who could achieve decoration which had no equal. Whatever the reason and subsequent effect of this reconstruction today there is on view art of the very best standard in the form of carvings, plasterwork and the most superb staircase.

In addition to the number of personalities within the family who owned the property from the seventeenth century there is a strong association with a nineteenth-century nurse who could claim to be one of the most famous members of her profession of all times, her name becoming a household word, and she spent the latter years of her life in the present existing house as her sister married one of the owners. Apart from the obvious benefits of this property being preserved there materialized a subsidiary benefit in that thousands of documents were discovered including letters, legal papers, invoices, shopping lists, instructions to staff and so forth from which a vast amount has been learned about the seventeenth- and eighteenth-century life.

To start at the beginning, the family – the Verneys – can be traced back to owning estates at Claydon about 1463, but they did not live on the present site as the property was leased to a family called Gifford who held a one-hundred-year lease from the 1460s. This was duly renewed at the end of the term but a little over halfway through the second term – that would be about 1620 – the owner, Sir Edmund Verney, being dissatisfied with the standard of maintenance of the estate, took repossession. Prior to this move the Verney family lived at a property some three miles distant called Hillesden House, which was the home of Sir Thomas Denton whose daughter Margaret married Sir Edmund Verney in 1612. This must have been rather a large household as both families produced many children: the Verneys twelve children (it is recorded that eight were born at Hillesden), and at least ten grandchildren, and the Dentons eleven children and twelve known grandchildren.

Inevitably during this period of history the Civil War influenced lifestyles, and loyalties became somewhat confused between the Royalist and Roundhead supporters; the Dentons were confirmed Royalist but the Verneys, apart from Sir Edmund who gave his life as standard bearer to the King at the Battle of Edgehill in 1642, remained undecided. In fairness it was obvious that even Sir Edmund was not completely against the Parliamentarians but by this date he was over fifty years of age and had been associated with royalty all his life. Reference should also be made to the Denton family and an unexpected outcome of the war was that Sir Thomas's fourth child, Susan, married the Parliamentarian Captain Jecamaih Abercrombie who was one of the plunderers of the Hillesden estate. Perhaps, fortunately, Sir Thomas had died ten years before the war as he would not have been happy at his daughter's choice for marriage. The estate was in the hands of his son, Sir Alexander, who died about the middle period of the uprisings, not of a bullet but of a fever. When Abercrombie was killed near the Royalist-held Boarstall House in Buckinghamshire in 1644, Susan insisted he was buried by the Dentons at Hillesden. Another famous name associated with the many troubles at Hillesden from the inevitable skirmishes to the poaching of deer, was John Bunyan who was one of the Roundhead soldiers – perhaps he was there when Hillesden was pillaged and the house destroyed by fire the year of the death of Susan's husband. It was fortunate that the two families, Dentons and Verneys, remained closely associated and after the disastrous fire refuge was taken at Claydon.

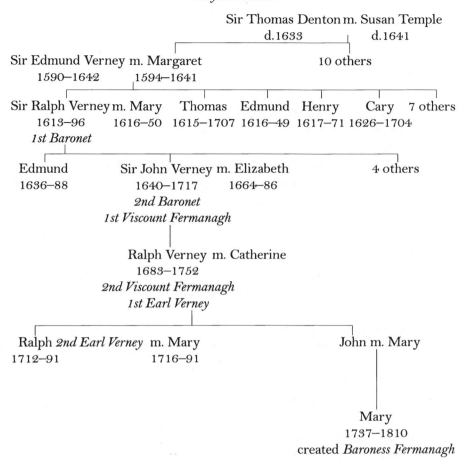

Sir Thomas Denton m. Susan Temple
d.1633 · d.1641

Sir Edmund Verney m. Margaret · 10 others
1590–1642 · 1594–1641

Sir Ralph Verney m. Mary · Thomas · Edmund · Henry · Cary · 7 others
1613–96 · 1616–50 · 1615–1707 · 1616–49 · 1617–71 · 1626–1704
1st Baronet

Edmund · Sir John Verney m. Elizabeth · 4 others
1636–88 · 1640–1717 · 1664–86
2nd Baronet
1st Viscount Fermanagh

Ralph Verney m. Catherine
1683–1752
2nd Viscount Fermanagh
1st Earl Verney

Ralph *2nd Earl Verney* m. Mary · John m. Mary
1712–91 · 1716–91

Mary
1737–1810
created *Baroness Fermanagh*

During the period when the Civil War was becoming more and more certain, the thoughts of Sir Edmund Verney must have been mixed, on the one hand he understood the Parliamentarians' point of view but on the other hand he had served the royal household from an early age when he joined the retinue of Henry, Prince of Wales. On the early death of the Prince, Edmund's services were transferred to the Prince's brother thus his allegiance was to Charles I, and on Charles's succession Sir Edmund was made Knight-Marshal of the Palace. To Sir Edmund the King's Majesty was sacrosanct and without doubt the King was defender of the true Church, but nevertheless the rights and wrongs of the looming war were viewed with no conviction. The day for decision arrived when that early non-decisive battle took place at Edgehill. There were no second thoughts for Sir Edmund and he carried out his duty acting as Standard Bearer, perhaps some of his thought being devoted to his wife who had died, apparently suddenly, the year before. During the three-hour battle Sir Edmund, like so many others, lost his life although his body was never actually identified except by a ring on his hand which was confirmed as that which the King had given to his servant the year previously.

The new head of the Verney family, after the death of Sir Edmund, was Sir Ralph, head of a large divided family, albeit that it appears to have been Sir Ralph who was of differing thought to his three brothers. Perhaps the manner of his father's death influenced Sir Ralph's attitude and certainly his brothers, Thomas, Edmund and Henry, were critical that Sir Ralph should favour Parliamentary views rather than for the King. At one time Sir Ralph was MP for Aylesbury but he lost his seat in the House of Commons because he would not take the Covenant and commit England to a Presbyterian form of church government. Being unhappy with the state of affairs throughout the country, similar to so many families during this period in history, Sir Ralph and his wife Mary decided to go into exile and to leave the country and Claydon in the care of his many uncles and aunts at nearby Hillesden House. There were also his sisters Penelope and Margaret, whose main worries appear to have been their objections to sharing the same maid. Although protection of the Claydon estate had been offered by King and Parliament, Cromwell sequestered everything which forced Mary such grief that she returned to England on a number of occasions to appeal before Parliament for the return of the lands. Eventually she was successful but the hardships took their toll and she died on a return visit to France in 1650. Sir Ralph considered selling the estates at Claydon but the reduced price of land, thanks to the Civil War, made that idea not viable, added to which he did not wish his wife to be buried in France but in England, so when he died he could be buried nearby so their spirits may ascend to heaven together. Not until 1653 did Sir Ralph return to Claydon but the family never returned to the united group of past years, in fact the family diminished as brother Edmund was murdered in 1649, sister Susanna died two years later, and his brother-in-law John Denton, who had married sister Penelope, had died in 1644. The year following another brother-in-law, Tom Gardiner, who had married sister Cary, was also murdered; that same year Cary with her new daughter in sadness returned to Claydon; mention is briefly made about Cary later in this story.

By the year of his return to the family seat at least four of Sir Ralph and Lady Mary's children had died, but during the next two years the reinstated head of the household worked avidly to restore the estate and replenished the gardens growing fruits and vegetables, reintroducing livestock and attempting to make the estate self-sufficient again. Employment was given to local people and the existing rambling Jacobean building was repaired. Unfortunately, two years after his reinstatement Sir Ralph was arrested and sent to prison in London; the reason, as was not unusual during this period, was not made clear. Even after his release there was the continual threat of confiscation of property and control of his movements. The Restoration of the Monarchy in 1660 brought the return of ownership of Claydon to the Verneys; Ralph was made a baronet and took his seat in the House of Commons once again. Life gradually returned to the normal seventeenth-century style and quietly, for the next thirty years, Sir Ralph remained, did not remarry and died after a long illness by which time he was eighty-three years of age.

Before relating a few idiosyncrasies of some of Sir Ralph's brothers and sisters a few notes on his nature may be of interest, much information having been learned from papers discovered at the property. Sir Ralph, later to be elevated as the first Baronet, was purported to be a kind and worthy man and just, as well as a liberal landlord but with very distinct boundaries. Before the Civil War dominated lives throughout the land females took little part in anything other than social activities and although education was encouraged it was restricted as to subjects. Sir Ralph's children had been to one of the increasing number of boarding schools – at a cost of £25 per year – and benefited from such, particularly an orphan ward. The girls however were rebuked if they had a wish to learn such as Greek, Hebrew or Latin and must be content to learn French by way of poetry and plays, at the same time learning the rudiments of housekeeping; the Bible must also be studied. Sir Ralph had definite ideas as to the female positions and frowned on those taking posts as preachers; fortunately this tendency was restricted to the unimportant non-conformists, an attitude to be changed for all times partly as a result of the Civil War during which so many women, especially members of the gentry, had literally held the forts on a number of occasions. Throughout his life Sir Ralph, that magnanimous landlord, maintained the view, and instilled it into his children, that class distinction was to be maintained.

A number of Sir Ralph's brothers and sisters are worth mentioning at this point, starting with his brother who was younger by just two years, Thomas, although nearly always referred to as Tom. A brother who was so very different from other members of the family and one cited by many contemporary writers as being the 'black sheep' of the family. The term could intimate a plausible even endearing character whereas Tom's true nature, as gleaned from many documents contemporary with his era, indicate a self-centred, spoilt child who certainly accepted no responsibility for family matters. He could actually be described as a beggar by nature who avoided serious situations only by the help of his father or elder brother. During his father's lifetime Tom was financed to emigrate to Virginia and establish a plantation in Barbados; but these, as indeed all his exploits, did not last long, a state of affairs which could also be said of his volunteering on a warship and as a soldier in France and in Sweden. Each return home left a trail of debts and quarrels; he may have publicly criticized his elder brother for not fighting for the King, but Tom still relied completely on that brother to obtain his release from a debtors' prison and to obtain his freedom from the Fleet where he was taken after the surrender of Chichester. Embroiled in both financial problems and quarrelling he would use veiled threats of suicide if he thought he was not receiving the immediate and urgent attention to improve his welfare, which he considered he should receive from his family. On one occasion he faced the possibility of a duel, requesting his younger brother, Edmund, to act as his second, and Tom's only worry was his standard of dress for the event. Eventually he became weary of all his activities and returned home to offer his service to the King's army. During his life Tom married three times but each wife produced neither wealth, status nor issue. When he died he was over ninety years old and his estate amounted to twenty-two shillings and one penny.

Previously it has been mentioned that Sir Ralph's brother Edmund was murdered before Sir Ralph returned from France and a brief word is justified on the short life of this member of the family who was born about three years after Ralph. In character he was more like his father than Tom and he could not understand why brother Ralph did not fully support the King. Whether Edmund fully understood that his father had misgivings about the Civil War could be questioned. Although a great family man with much affection for his sisters during his younger days, with his father's blessing he served in the Scots war and also with the English regiment in the Dutch service. On his return to England from the Continent Edmund joined forces for the first Battle of Newbury; he was knighted in 1644 and appointed Lieutenant-Governor of Chester. After the surrender of Chester he returned to Paris but returned to take part in the last struggle against Cromwell at Drogheda on the east coast of Ireland, and it was here that he was murdered in cold blood by a common soldier.

The last male member of the family of this generation to be mentioned in these notes is Henry, born about four years after Sir Ralph. Henry had a passion for horses and later soldiering, both being satisfied when he received a commission as a Major of Horse in Sir Ralph Dutton's regiment; a post he obtained thanks to the influence of Sir Edward Sydenham who had succeeded to the position of Knight-Marshal on the death of Henry's father whilst acting as Standard Bearer at the Battle of Edgehill. Henry was a member of the escort party when Queen Henrietta Maria returned to England with stores and money to help the Royalist cause. Interestingly Henry met the King whilst on this duty, and records show that the King gave him a cold reception – remembering that this event took place in February 1643, a mere four months after Henry's father had given his life at Edgehill – a circumstance which do not make the King any more lovable. Promoted to Colonel, Henry had a questionable affair with a lady in Dorset, a quarrel with his major whom he shot dead in an inn, and was imprisoned in Portsmouth. It was oldest brother Ralph who interceded, yet again, before he left for the Continent, and managed to obtain Henry's release. With no other claim to fame Henry spent the remainder of his life in London borrowing money from friends and relations, frequently alienating himself from his brothers over the subject of money. He died at the age of fifty-four unmarried.

The tenth child of Sir Edmund was Cary, who unfortunately does not appear to have had a happy later life. Before his death Sir Edmund had arranged a marriage for his daughter into the Royalist Gardiner family, her husband being Captain Thomas, son of Sir Thomas Gardiner the Solicitor-General of Cuddesden near Oxford. As Cary's new husband was in the King's army at the Scottish Wars he was away from home for lengthy periods; later he was taken prisoner at Windsor during one of his travels. Perhaps as a result of his new brother-in-law Sir Ralph Verney having no commitment for either side in the war, the Captain was released when Ralph appealed to Parliament. Regrettably the Captain died in a skirmish near Aylesbury in 1645. A daughter was born to Cary in the October who was far from healthy and with sight problems resulting in near blindness in later life. The problems of daughter Margaret were not made easier by the attitude of Cary's parents-in-law who, because their son's heir was a girl instead of a boy, grudged even accommodation and withdrew their hospitality, and reduced any settlement. Cary, at eighteen years of age, left Cuddesden and sadly returned to her family at Claydon where she received greater family attention. Margaret may have had a sight problem but was about fifty-seven before she died without having married. Cary did remarry later and left several children when she died aged about seventy-eight years.

The above gives an insight into the personalities of some of the children of the Standard Bearer to the King, and shows that Sir Ralph returned to his hereditary position on his return from exile in France, and it was he who produced the heirs for the family seat. Whilst his father had twelve offspring Ralph and his wife Mary had half that number with only two reaching maturity. The first was Edmund, named after his grandfather, and young Edmund became what many would describe to be a typical country squire being large and gently boisterous but at the age of thirty-five was over twenty stone in weight. Most regrettably his wife, yet another Mary in the family, became insane and so violent that at one stage she broke most of the windows in the house. She was not only a serious threat to herself but also to others or anyone nearby by using scissors and knives to inflict injury. Many 'quack' remedies of the day were tried and failed and she died completely insane. With Edmund's kindness and patience tested to the full he predeceased his father by about eight years; no doubt his great bulk contributed to his early death at the age of fifty-two.

Sir Ralph's second son was John who inherited the title and the estate on his father's death in 1696. A very different character and unlike his father he was referred to as being antisocial and described as unemotional; nevertheless he married three times and became very prosperous being a leading figure in trade with the Middle and Far East. Only about two years after inheriting Claydon this 2nd Baronet was created Viscount Fermanagh in the Irish Peerage.

Sir John's son, another Ralph, was to continue the hereditary line and in 1743 he was created 1st Earl Verney, a title which did not last long.

The second and last Earl Verney was the son of the last mentioned Ralph, the first Earl, and it was thanks to his father and grandfather ensuring the prosperity of the estate after the family had been ruined during the Civil War that this incumbent inherited in 1752 great wealth. The house however, apart from containing more up-to-date furniture, replacement windows and modern lamps, remained the old out-of-date Jacobean building. The 2nd Earl could indulge in his favourite pastime of supporting the arts and spending money, which he did; very different interests to those of the last two generations. In addition to his inheritance Ralph married a very tolerant Mary, the daughter of a City merchant who brought a considerable fortune into the Verney family. Leaving no one in doubt as to his wealth Ralph's mode of transport was a coach and six escorted by 'a brace of tall Negroes, with silver French horns and perpetually making a noise'. His real ambition was to rebuild Claydon House and searching for ideas he visited all the country houses in the district. The property which was to become his undoing was that built not many miles distant at Stowe for the Grenvilles, the Tory Earl Temple, a man of greater means and a political rival for leadership of the County of Buckinghamshire.

The Earl continued to act in the manner of the newly rich when dealing with his rebuilding programme; instead of employing an expert architect for the technical specifications and to oversee the project he became involved with a dubious personage by the name of Sir Thomas Robinson. Robinson had many claims to fame as a Yorkshire squire who owned and rebuilt Rokeby Hall – a property renowned by Scott's poem years later – he, Sir Thomas, at one time son-in-law of Lord Carlisle (to obtain prestige), married secondly the widow of a rich Jewish ironmonger to gain finances – she he abandoned – and was also a friend of the architect Burlington. Other notable aspects were him being appointed as Governor of Barbados, an appointment which ended with a dispute over other people's money which had been spent without authority, plus his connections with many multifarious financial investments one of which he persuaded the Earl to become embroiled in and become a member of the Directorate. There was no doubt that the Earl was easily parted from his money but over the next thirty years an extraordinary building was nearly completed. To the disgust of Robinson Verney employed yet another character with a strange history by the name of Luke Lightfoot who was at best described as an eccentric, but also as a carver and master builder; he was already employed by Verney to carry out work at the Curzon Street address where the Earl possessed a London home. Work at Claydon became almost unending, so did the costs, and eventually Lightfoot was accused by his employer of dishonesty having spent in the region of £23,000. A case was heard in Chancery, Lightfoot was declared bankrupt and ceased trading in the building world.

At this point it must be said that in spite of, or because of, the above today can be seen some of the most remarkable, if not some of the finest work of carving and plaster work to be found anywhere in the country. It is perhaps sad that much of the construction work of the period was destroyed within a few years as reported below. Some of the wood carvings produced as samples or as experiments can be seen, a few were made into the library steps; these samples were originally designed for the staircase balustrade but not actually used as the stair balustrade is of wrought ironwork in the form of garlands of ears of corn which enhance the treads of many types of wood in parquetry fashion. Art of the very best and without doubt a masterpiece, produced by questionable characters.

Thirty-two years after inheriting a vast fortune the Earl went bankrupt and fled to France. His fortune had been spent on the rebuilding of Claydon in an over-glorious manner, and spending large amounts trying to improve his political status with that controversial statesman Edmund Burke, funds which produced no return. The main contents of the house were sold before he left the country.

For the second time then, the head of the Verney family had left Claydon to live in France. The first was Sir Ralph, the 1st Baronet, who departed the shore of England because of lack of political conviction during the Cromwellian upheavals, his return being considerably marred by the sad loss of a number of family members. The secret return for the second absentee, another Ralph but three generations later, was also sad but in a different way. His return to Claydon provided a legend which relates the story of a stable lad discovering an aged man roaming within the empty, rambling, unfinished building, and the youth covertly providing basic comforts for some weeks, shortly after which the Earl died. His death at the age of seventy-eight did however take place in London, a matter of weeks after the death of his wife Mary.

In all honesty the Earl could be referred to as a very unwise man when dealing with his financial affairs but he was not only over-generous to satisfy his own comforts and whims but was also an over-liberal patron to the less fortunate. More than one received his patronage, such as the poet Robert Bloomfield, the former labourer who became a self-made author, ultimately ending life questionably of insanity.

Leaving no heir the property passed from the 2nd Earl to a niece who was the only child of the Earl's brother John. The year after she inherited Mary did concede to accepting the title Baroness Fermanagh and proved to be of very different character from her uncle. Economy became paramount to the extent that two thirds of the Earl's buildings were demolished; one authority does suggest that this action was partly because of lack of secure foundations for the Robinson construction. The fact remains that at present a greatly reduced building represents the family seat − thankfully containing much varied art − but the house stands without a suitable front door.

Baroness Mary had a half sister, that is the daughter of John's second marriage and she married the Rector of Middle Claydon. Mary and her half sister were very close, the two, Mary and Catherine, being raised together during childhood and by Mary's Will Claydon became Catherine's property.

Two generations later the owner became Sir Harry Calvert who adopted the name Verney when he inherited Claydon, and his second wife was Francis Parthenope Nightingale, hence the connection with the nineteenth-century nurse whose name became a household word. In the nineteenth century nursing was far from being a profession, those purporting to be a nurse were either the charitable moral conscious younger members of the upper classes, or the lower classes hoping to provide service for the price of a gin. Florence Nightingale, who without doubt emanated from the former group – her Christian name reflecting the city in which she was born, as indeed her sister's name of Parthenope was the old name for Naples – at an early age determined to pursue her ambition to aid the less fortunate and alleviate suffering which was rife. The rudiments for health care were quickly learned, together with the understanding that training, which at the time did not exist, was essential if improvements were to be made to nursing services. Having spent some time in hospitals in Germany and France Florence's connection with the philanthropist Sidney Herbert proved invaluable and, although she was about thirty years of age before breaking away from parental objections, the post as Superintendent of the Institute for the Care of Sick Gentlewomen in Harley Street was obtained. Organizational ability and tireless energy in pursuit of her aim qualified her, when a little more than a year later, she accepted the post abroad at the request of Herbert who was by this time Secretary of State for War. The battlefields of the Crimean War, or more precisely the hospital near Constantinople, needed her services and here her name became legend. Within a few years Florence Nightingale became internationally famous – 'the lady with the lamp' – a number of these years struggling with poor and deteriorating health as a result of her workload, but she not only survived a fight against her own death but to her, more importantly, she won the fight against the authority's complete lack of concern on medical matters. Ten years after her first appointment in Harley Street she founded the first nurses' training school at St Thomas's Hospital.

With failing health Florence retreated to a private life, much of the time being bedridden, but continued to write nursing manuals copiously, and much time was spent at Claydon where her sister lived. She outlived her sister by twenty years and was buried at East Wellow in Hampshire near Embley Park, the place where she spent her youth.

Today The National Trust maintains the estate of Claydon and the results of the various Earls Verney can be seen including the artistry of Robinson, the former Governor of Barbados, and Luke Lightfoot the superb designer of chinoiserie; and there is on show the Florence Nightingale room housing some of her mementoes; not forgetting the staircase which has no equal.

Chapter XIII

Stourhead

K ent may be known as the Garden of England, and perhaps justifiably, but equally justified in the eyes of many parts of the world, Britain is known as the land of the gardens. With a brief glance at the variety of sizes and styles and the number of these revered plots throughout the islands this opinion can be understood. Having said that British gardens are not unique, although developed over centuries to suit the terrain and climate, but for centuries ideas have been copied from other countries and continents whether it be the Dutch or Far Eastern pattern, as indeed the Japanese in modern times have gladly introduced into their native lands the English image.

Influences on the British garden have been many and must include the intrepid travellers who, many times risking life and limb, have imported plants from around the globe and changed the type of plants grown in this country today. Names which are perpetuated in the names of the plants illustrate the travels of people such as David Douglas who returned with trees from America; Robert Fortune and his exploits in China; E. H. Wilson, one of the most prolific plant hunters of all times, returning home with new varieties of rhododendrons amongst other species; George Forrest and Reginald Farrer who introduced the alpine garden. The father and son team of the Johns called Tradescants who left fame by being both importers of plants and layout of gardens. John the Younger should also be given credit for passing to his friend Elias Ashmole the noteworthy collection of artefacts inherited from his father and thus providing the material for founding the Ashmolean Museum. There were a number of great nurserymen who changed the imagine of the garden such as George London and Henry Wise who benefited by receiving royal support.

The great parks as known today may have been very different if a number of landscape designers had been of dissimilar personalities, and to mention just two who readily spring to mind, one being Brown – Capability – who placed his mark on nearly 200 large estates, and his near successor, Humphry Repton, known for his famous Red Book, prepared to illustrate his ideas for the benefit of his clients. In the nineteenth and into the twentieth centuries the name Gertrude Jekyll should be included; unfortunately of the 300 or so gardens which she designed, albeit on a much smaller scale, few remain in the original form.

None of these great parks and gardens would have been possible but for the families with the real money whether they were bankers such as the Rothschilds and Hoares or perhaps some members of society not over-burdened with riches but who could be described with near obsessions with impressive estates either because of their love of gardens or merely to make an impression. For pure pleasure and delight there are such sites as Exbury in Hampshire, where the Rothschilds banking funds have been used to maintain and enlarge the varieties of rhododendrons and azaleas producing one of the largest collections of these spectacular plants to be seen anywhere in the country. The relatively modern Inverewe in Ross-shire and on the other side of Scotland in Grampian the much older Pitmedden made possible by the revenue of a lawyer and supporter of the Royalist faction. Occasionally garden history books provide information of a particularly choice relationship between master and servant and this is never more true than at one of the finest of gardens in Wales at Bodnant where generations of owners and gardeners have worked in liaison.

This chapter of the book is not, however to be devoted to gardens or gardening but to illustrate the life of people responsible for one particular garden, or should it be called a park? South-west of Salisbury Plain, at the conjunction of the counties of Wiltshire, Somerset and Dorset lies the hamlet of Stourton and here, since pre-Conquest times, there has been an estate owned by the Stourtons, the lordships being the premier barons of England. Today the estate embraces the landscaped garden which can best be described as a unique contributor to the world of art. It is Stourhead gardens, known and admired by so many, although they were not introduced until the eighteenth century.

The property in ancient times was certainly well documented by such eminent historians as John Leland recording his meandering during Tudor times, and continued in the voluminous notes of the Wiltshire antiquary John Aubrey more than a century later.

The Stourtons, whose history can be traced to the eleventh century, were somewhat of an anomaly but one thread from those far-off days to the more modern construction of the gardens during the second decade of the eighteenth century, is the inclusion in the family coat of arms of six springs which created the source of the river and provided the water for the lakes in the park.

One member of the old family is known to have married a daughter of Godwin, the first Earl of the West Saxons, known as the Earl of Wessex, one of the most powerful men in the kingdom and one of the sons of Harold II, his name being perpetuated by the Goodwin Sands. A son of that union, Robert, was granted licence to build Stourton House which, according to a number of historians, was of great size and in some form remained in existence until Henry Hoare demolished the building about 1718.

During the fourteenth and fifteenth centuries the heads of this worthy family held many positions of note from members of Parliament, Privy Councillor for Henry VI, and Treasurer to the royal household, being elevated to Baron Stourton in 1448. Although staunch Catholics the 6th Lord supported Henry VIII and his ending of Papal control in England, the result being that his son obtained Kilmington Manor which was previously owned by Shaftesbury Abbey until the Dissolution of the Monasteries. The circumstances that followed were perhaps unfortunate in that the 8th Lord, whilst acting as Deputy-General for the King at Newhaven, left the estate management in the hands of a man called Hartgill who, according to his lordship, greatly mismanaged the affairs. Charles, his lordship, was known to be impetuous and violence ensued but the justices found in Hartgill's favour and Charles was imprisoned in the fleet. During a temporary release for the purpose of a reconciliation and to allow for payment as compensation to be made to Hartgill, both Hartgill and his son were murdered by the baron and his men; subsequently the murderers were hanged in Salisbury Market Place.

Another member of the Stourton family to spend time in the Fleet prison was Edward, 10th Baron, who although somewhat older than others of the conspiracy, was involved in the Gunpowder Plot of 1605. Edward was one of the brothers-in-law of Tresham and, maintaining the old Catholic faith, faced trial with others before the Star Chamber and was finally fined £6,000 for his part in the act but actually appears to have paid only £1,000 in total.

With the above occurrences and the fines imposed by the Parliamentarians, and the damage sustained to the estate in the mid-seventeenth century during the Civil War, the fortunes of this ancient family were in decline. By the early eighteenth century creditors enforced the only course of action possible and the 13th Lord Stourton sold the estate to Henry Hoare, the banker for nearly £20,000. The great open-roofed hall described by previously mentioned historians was replaced by the revolutionary Palladian-style house christened Stourhead. The Stourtons are today represented by Lord Mowbray, Selgrave and Stourton. The Mowbray line became extinct on the death in 1475 of John, the 4th Duke with the estate being divided between the families of Howard and Berkeley, and the barony falling into abeyance, but it was revised for Alfred Joseph in 1877 as 20th Baron Stourton, and his son in 1893 became the 24th Baron Mowbray. The ruined Bramber Castle in Sussex was the Mowbray family seat many years ago.

As the starting date of the Stourhead masterpiece was during the second decade of the eighteenth century none of the famous landscape artists previously mentioned can have been involved. It was before the days of Kent, Repton and Brown – Brown would have been the most likely designer to be involved but he was not born until a year or so before the commencement date and he did not relinquish his Stowe responsibility until over thirty years later. It is fair to assume that the concept was that of Henry Hoare who started the garden layout when the house was built round about 1717, although his son, also Henry, completed the gardens when he inherited the estate after his mother's death in 1741.

Tracing the ancestors of the Hoare family before the momentous occasion of the purchase of Stourton, as it was then known, is difficult but perhaps not of importance. The relevant starting point is with a horse trader who envisaged an improved lifestyle for his son and subsequently managed to arrange for Richard junior, who was born in 1648 to be apprenticed in one of the highest and most influential trades of the period, namely the world of the goldsmiths.

Goldsmiths for many years had ruled the finances of the country, both of the monarch and Parliament; it was from the goldsmiths that money was raised to finance the endless wars. The seventeenth century was possibly when they were at their most powerful and it is easy to quote names known to this day. Francis Childs, the son of a Wiltshire clothier, was apprenticed to a goldsmith and married into the fortune of another of the trade; Child's Bank being founded about 1670. Thomas Coutts the son of an Edinburgh provost, moved to London to work for a goldsmith firm founded by John Campbell and under the direction of this entrepreneur Coutts Bank was founded about 1690. Richard Hoare made advances in meteoric fashion whilst in his twenties acting for the Royal Exchequer and founding Hoare's Bank.

Banks during this period were not the substantial businesses as known today but were moneylenders, but moneylenders in a big way both nationally and internationally. There were however problems created by so much financial control being enjoyed by a relatively few people, added

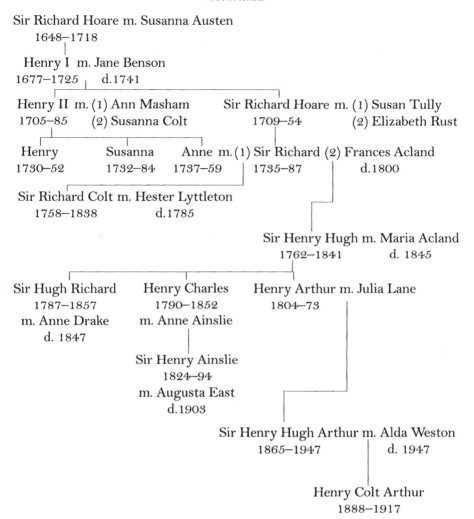

Sir Richard Hoare m. Susanna Austen
1648–1718

Henry I m. Jane Benson
1677–1725   d.1741

Henry II m. (1) Ann Masham   Sir Richard Hoare m. (1) Susan Tully
1705–85   (2) Susanna Colt   1709–54   (2) Elizabeth Rust

Henry   Susanna   Anne m. (1) Sir Richard (2) Frances Acland
1730–52   1732–84   1737–59   1735–87   d.1800

Sir Richard Colt m. Hester Lyttleton
1758–1838   d.1785

Sir Henry Hugh m. Maria Acland
1762–1841   d. 1845

Sir Hugh Richard   Henry Charles   Henry Arthur m. Julia Lane
1787–1857   1790–1852   1804–73
m. Anne Drake   m. Anne Ainslie
d. 1847

Sir Henry Ainslie
1824–94
m. Augusta East
d.1903

Sir Henry Hugh Arthur m. Alda Weston
1865–1947   d. 1947

Henry Colt Arthur
1888–1917

to which the currency in use was open to abuse. The golden crown originally introduced during the reign of Henry VIII became subject to serious defacement as the gold content of the coin had a far greater value than that of its face value which lead to the illegal exporting of gold filings removed from the outer rim of the coin. This was a common practice and it will never be known how many fortunes were based on this enterprise. Controls were necessary and the Act for the introduction of the Bank of England was passed in 1694. Richard Hoare joined the others who objected to this forming of control but he and the others continued to prosper.

Richard had come a long way from the circumstance when he was seventeen and was first introduced to the world of the goldsmiths. In less than ten years he became virtual leader of the business and had business associations with the previously mentioned Francis Child, also with Charles Duncombe of the park of that name in Yorkshire. On the succession of Queen Anne Richard received a knighthood, later representing London in Parliament and became Lord Mayor of the City in 1712. One of Sir Richard's prime interests was increasing his wealth and he was involved in the ill-advised speculation named the South Sea Company; fortunately, for one reason or another the money invested was withdrawn during the period the shares were at their peak and subsequently Hoares avoided the crash of 1720, their fortunes were safe and could, on the death of Sir Richard, be passed to son Henry. Three of Richard's older sons had predeceased their father and of the remaining sons – Richard had eleven boys in total – only one other became involved with the bank.

Much took place during the next few years with part of Henry's inherited wealth being spent on the purchase of Stourton, the demolishing of the old hall and starting of the replacement house near the same site. Henry had married Jane Benson the sister of the Palladian revivalist and amateur architect William Benson who had, in 1718, replaced Christopher Wren as Surveyor General, the result being that Stourhead was one of the first to be built in the new idiom as the design was detailed by Colen Campbell acting as Benson's deputy. Henry outlived his father by a mere seven years during which time he established the family title in this area of Wiltshire, and although his father would have seen the original purchase being completed he died the year after, whereas Henry would experience the near completion of the main 'square' of the house. The Benson-designed portico was not built until mid-nineteenth century and the two wings housing the library and picture gallery not until the end of the eighteenth century in the days of Sir Richard Colt Hoare who is mentioned later. Henry died whilst young and by many historians he is recorded as Henry I, 'Good Henry' – because of the amount of charity work he supported.

Henry II inherited but did not move into Stourhead until his mother, Jane Benson died in 1741 and he returned from abroad. This Henry, apart from being known as Henry II, has been given the name of Henry II 'The Magnificent' because of the creation of the gardens. In the text above referring to Sir Richard is mention that three of his sons predeceased their father, and throughout the Hoare family history there has been the sadness of deaths at an early age. This state of affairs continued during Henry II's life in that his first wife died, perhaps not unusual during the period in childbirth, and within a year he married again, this time to

Susanna Colt, who died within five years. Henry did not marry again although he lived to the age of about eighty, and he outlived all his three children. His son Richard died at the age of twenty-one. The wealth of Henry did not entirely satisfy his desires in that he always considered that the deserved social status had not been reached. For his daughter Susanna he arranged her first marriage to the son of the Earl of Cork but the Corks considered it an inferior match. They appear to have overlooked the deficiency when Henry settled on his daughter – money, jewellery and a house in Lincoln's Inn Fields in London with an estimated value in the region of £40,000, more than twice the value his father had paid for the whole estate three decades previously. Henry was still concerned about the lack of a male heir so Anne, the last born, the year before her death at the age of twenty-seven, became the first wife of her cousin, Henry's nephew, Richard Hoare who was elevated as 1st Baronet. Anne and Richard had a child named Richard Colt Hoare who ultimately became 2nd Baronet. The 1st Baronet's second wife was Maria Acland of Holnicote in Somerset.

The work during the life of Henry II certainly justified his title 'The Magnificent' for the concept of the garden. The original idea of the gardens was possibly Henry II's and it has been suggested that the money and concentration on this project was as a result of the loss of his family. When his second wife died he was only about thirty-eight years of age and he had the finances and the interest to construct the masterpiece. One modern historian has suggested that the overall design of the park has a likeness to the stylized landscape in the paintings in the school of the Italian Salvator Rosa, but these works of art appear far too gloomy and dramatic to have any bearing on the design. It is more likely that the final layout was as a result of the natural topography of the site and the available resources including water. Henry may have been aware of other landscape projects of about this period including that constructed to the idea of William Kent for the Earl of Burlington at Chiswick, immortalized by the painting of Hogarth's friend, the eighteenth-century English landscape artist George Lambert. Interestingly Burlington borrowed heavily from Hoare's Bank to finance that work. Perhaps the Stourhead show ground gave incentive to other landed gentry to similarly beautify their parks and thus borrowed from the newly formed banking institution belonging to the Hoares – a satisfactory arrangement to improve Henry's income and status.

Even with the restricted communications of the day, Henry would no doubt be aware of other estate reconstructions of the period, of which there were many. At Stowe in Buckinghamshire the Temple family were developing an even larger pleasure ground, with over thirty different buildings by the year 1760, and rather than merely constructing paths round lakes as at Stourhead, these gardens were designed for walking around for owners and visitors, much as the house was. There were a variety of paths provided to allow for a choice of short walks or longer routes ideal for the new lightweight chaises or for riding on horseback. The buildings provided points of interest or may be used as banqueting rooms where later courses of a meal could be enjoyed, or perhaps just for an afternoon picnic.

Nearer home in Wiltshire the Lansdownes were employing 'Capability' Brown at Bowood, and there were a number of parallels with the newcomers, the Methuens, at Corsham Court, where Brown acted as architect for additional building to the house as well as the landscape work. Repton also worked on these gardens forty years later including installing the lake in accordance with Brown's design. Stourhead House may have been one of the first Palladian style but by mid-eighteenth century the north facade of Corsham was replaced using a similar style. Today at Corsham can be seen a great variety of pictures including a Salvator Rosa landscape – an artist previously mentioned – and a watercolour of the south front by John Butler which was reputedly commissioned by Sir Richard Colt Hoare.

During the early days banking was not considered an honourable trade, hence Henry 'The Magnificent' buying favour with the Cork family for his daughter. Money could acceptably be accumulated by a variety of means during the period of Henry, whether by paying homage to the nobility, from the spoils of war, or by formulating laws and charging exorbitant fees to rule on their interpretation; as indeed today the borrowing of money for a mortgage against property purchase is acceptable, but borrowing money under a hire purchase agreement or through the even older trade of pawnbroking is definitely *infra dignitatem.* Henry was obviously aware of this and not until many years after the founding of his bank did banking become a respectable trade. Henry's other great fear was recession and he took appropriate action to ensure that should the banking business suffer his beloved Stourhead would not become subject to creditors. Before his death the banking business was passed to his son-in-law and his West Country estates into the hands of his grandson; Henry then retired to Clapham. Perhaps Henry had knowledge of the change of ownership of Corsham into the hands of the Methuens because Sir Benjamin Hoskins Styles, Bt., of Bowden Park, also in Wiltshire, who had bought the property only in 1716, forfeited everything when the estate got into Chancery in 1745 as Sir Benjamin was one of the many unlucky directors of the South Sea Company from which the Hoares were so fortunate.

Many years before his retirement however, Henry II arranged for the building of a number of 'eye-catchers' or points of interest around the lake. Whilst the famous landscape architects may not have been involved in the building of the park, the famous building architect Henry Flitcroft, who received the patronage of Lord Burlington and who had been involved with James Gibbs with the interior of Ditchley Park in Oxfordshire in the 1720s, designed and built the first garden building at Stourhead, 'The Temple of Flora' in 1744, and twenty years later built 'The Temple of Apollo' which formerly accommodated the statues in niches; they can now be seen on the roof of Stourhead House. During the time between those two constructions 'The Pantheon' was built to house Rysbrack's statues of Hercules. John Michael Rysbrack was a Flemish sculptor who was born in Antwerp, came to England whilst in his twenties and was fortunate to have as his patrons the architects Gibbs and Kent, in addition to that of Henry Hoare. The early fourteenth century Bristol High Cross was removed from Bristol and erected at Stourhead in 1765. The Grotto is an interesting concept and possibly following the vogue of the day. By the early eighteenth century cold baths became the fashion, many houses having them within the building of the main house but at Stourhead, similar to many others, they were in the grounds and a separate building was constructed to include changing rooms. A statue of Neptune – or in the case of Stourhead a River God – was the norm. A further parallel with Corsham, perhaps, as Brown constructed a separate bathhouse within the grounds about 1760. The vogue may have been derived from the thoughts of the eminent doctor William Oliver who considered a cold plunge beneficial but they were not new even at that date as a public cold bath was built in Clerkenwell in 1697 and many other towns followed suite – not advised, apparently, for daily use but good on a weekly or monthly basis, and even more so as a social occasion!

As previously mentioned Henry 'The Magnificent' departed from Stourhead to retire to Clapham in the hope that there would be no connection between the banking business and Stourhead should the economic uncertainties of the day prove too great and the Hoares' financial state place at risk ownership of the Wiltshire lands. Henry's early retirement was not by today's standard early as he was in his late seventies when the banking work became the responsibility of nephew Richard, the 1st Baronet, and the Wiltshire properties came into the hands of his son, and Henry's grandson, Richard Colt who subsequently inherited the baronetcy on the death of his father – another early death which took place only four years after Henry's retirement.

It appears that Henry agreed with the marriage between his daughter Anne and nephew Richard almost on condition that Richard remained in the bank, a profession which at this stage had more or less been accepted and had almost become an honourable profession. Richard Colt, in accordance with his grandfather's wish, relinquished any connection with the banking firm, but with estates covering thousands of acres in the counties of Wiltshire, Somerset and Dorset which produced a very healthy income, the personality of Richard was satisfied. He was very much an academic being classified as one of the foremost antiquarians of the period and his love of fine articles was assisted by his patronage of artists and furniture makers including the younger Chippendale. Yet another early death was that of Richard Colt's wife, Hester, who died giving birth to a son. During the following years Richard became an inveterate traveller, first to Italy, followed by a number of other countries; at about this time it is recorded that he travelled more than 6,500 miles during a twenty-two month period and the journey involved some 580 different stages. A number of travels were subject to journals including those to Ireland, Elba, Malta, Sicily and Italy. His archaeological and literary interests covered the ancient and modern history of Wiltshire together with the translation of the twelfth-century Welsh historian Giraldus Cambrensis whose works embraced the English conquest of Ireland. As a bibliophile, together with the collection amassed during his travels, resulted in his home, Stourhead House, being modified and extended with two wings being built either side of the Palladian square building; one to house the library, the other the picture gallery. The gardens were by no means neglected during Richard Colt's ownership and he arranged for something in the region of 90,000 trees to be planted and some of the first rhododendron Ponticums; the grounds were extended northwards and the paths improved by laying gravel for the benefit of visitors.

With the death of Sir Richard Colt in 1838 – his effigy can be seen in Salisbury Cathedral – the property passed to Henry Hugh, Colt's half brother who became 3rd Baronet and had the portico built to the original eighteenth-century design for the house by Colen Campbell. Within about three years the 3rd Baronet was succeeded by the 4th, Sir Hugh Richard. Interestingly this was the first direct inheritance from father to son for well over one hundred years. During Hugh Richard's residence many more trees were planted including conifers with Douglas Firs. The old Kilmington Manor, mentioned in the text in relation to the Hartgills and the hanging of Lord Stourton, was demolished. The 5th Baronet took possession somewhere near sixteen years after the demise of the 4th. He was nephew to Hugh Richard and may have been a politician but unfortunately was also a serious gambler as a result Sir Richard Colt's books and other valuables were sold to cover his debts. His lack of control over his expensive habits saw his dismissal from the bank and he survived on an allowance and increasing debts. Fortunately, although the house was for sometime unused, the estate was in the hands of a trustworthy steward.

The 6th and last Baronet to live at Stourhead was Sir Henry Hugh Arthur, yet another nephew, who was also the end of this most interesting and notable line. Sir Henry's son, Henry Colt Arthur, was killed during the First World War, an act which continued the sadness of the family line since the seventeenth century. Henry Colt had, during his short life, acted as land agent for all the various properties on his father's behalf; most of these properties in Dorset, Somerset and Wiltshire being sold before and during the Great War. The 6th Baronet during his fifty-three years at Stourhead planted many varieties of azaleas and rhododendrons. He and his wife, Alda Weston, coped with a number of problems, not least of which was a very serious fire to the central part of the house during 1902 and the reconstruction was to the design of Sir Aston Webb.

The house, collections and estate of 3,000 acres were bequeathed to the National Trust by Sir Henry and Lady Hoare who reigned for so many years and died on the same day in March of 1947. For 230 years the estates of Stourton/Stourhead were under the control of the Hoare family and the legacy of the village, built expressly to accommodate the visitors, and one of the finest gardens in Europe is permanently preserved for the years to come. How happy Henry I and Henry II must be that their pride and joy did not fall into the hands of creditors.

Chapter XIV

Oxburgh Hall

The Oxburgh estates in Norfolk can be traced back to the eleventh century when in the possession of relations of the Conqueror, this at a time when the area consisted of waterways and fens and properties were in effect islands surrounded by low flat countryside as it was not until the eighteenth century that land drainage became a serious project. The very name is perhaps derived from 'burg' or fort – hence higher ground – coupled with where oxen were kept. That is one of a number of conjectures. It is recorded that by the 1220s the old manor of Oxburgh came into the hands of the de Weyland family and about 160 years later by inheritance to the Suffolk family called Tuddenhams. Sir Thomas, the inheriting cousin, became embroiled in legally questionable activities and thirty years after gaining the property was executed on Tower Hill. It was the exploits of Sir Thomas which lead to the ownership of Oxburgh coming into the hands of a family called Bedingfeld and they remained owners by direct line of descent for nearly 500 years.

About twenty years after Sir Thomas inherited Oxburgh England became dominated by a civil war, not the more famous Cromwellian affair – that took place 200 years later – but nevertheless a very real war covering something like a thirty-year period and a war largely as a result of nobles raising arms as supporters of either the white rose or the red rose antagonists. Hence the War of the Roses – the one being the Yorkists (Richard of York) with the support of Warwick, the other the Lancastrians (Henry VI). It was indeed a real war which may have been started by Richard claiming the throne when Henry became insane and, like the seventeenth-century conflict, many royals and lesser personages were murdered throughout the lands. The resulting effect was the introduction of the Tudors to the throne of England, a dynasty which proved to last a mere third of the years of their predecessors, the Plantagenets. With this lengthy strife the nobility and gentry lost stability and provided many stories showing conflicts between families and advantages being taken of the unsettled period.

Comprehensive records were made of events and the feelings of important people by one particular family who wrote copious letters and documents extending through the years 1422 and 1509. These papers, which provide many records of actions during the upheavals, have survived to this day and late in the nineteenth and early in the twentieth centuries they were collected, edited and saved in volume form. The documents, commonly called the 'Paston Letters', were those written by, or to, various members of the Norfolk family called Paston, William Paston being justice of the common pleas under Henry VI. Apart from the general facts relating to history, the Paston Letters also prove that one member of their own family was a lawyer of questionable methods, gaining possession of Caister Castle near Yarmouth by a Will of doubtful authenticity, a matter which ultimately became the subject of a legal wrangle between the lawyer and the Duke of Norfolk, and later required the intervention of the King.

This illustrates the use of documents as the foundation for stories of history and the name Paston is a good choice to use as an example as that family, and the family of Bedingfeld, were inter-linked by marriage a number of times. It is known that with the execution of Sir Thomas, who had divorced his wife and had no issue, his sister Margaret inherited the many estates of her brother and married Edmund Bedingfeld of Bedingfeld in Suffolk. Bedingfeld, or Bedingfield as it is now known, lies between Eye and Debenham. Further connections with the fens and wetlands are shown as although Bedingfield is roughly forty miles from Oxburgh the name Eye is Saxon for island and at Debenham wetland rush is still used for weaving in the cottage industry.

Even after the joining together of Edmund Bedingfeld and Margaret Tuddenham the Bedingfelds continued to live at their estate near Eye and this remained the case until after Margaret's enhancement of wealth – therefore after Sir Thomas's execution and the deaths of Margaret's husband, Edmund, their son Thomas and his wife Anne, née de Waldegrave. It was Edmund and Margaret's grandson, another Edmund, who with this new considerable increase in financial resources moved to Oxburgh and built a new moated fortified manor sanctioned by a Charter signed by Edward IV. Built in 1482, or a few years prior, it is a most impressive brick structure with the original very large gatehouse, possibly one of the largest fifteenth-century gatehouses in England. The Bedingfelds have always been Catholics and Royalists and as a true Yorkist Edmund was, at the time of the Coronation of Richard III, created Knight of the Bath.

To remain a Royalist and Catholic must have required a considerable amount of diplomacy. The Royalist leanings were well rewarded, albeit to prove a disadvantage at times, but Catholicism was about to demonstrate a serious disadvantage. With the Tudors superseding the Plantagenets within a few years moves were being made for the religious divorce from the Church of Rome. Surprisingly Sir Edmund, according to reports, even with his strength of Royalist feelings, did not attend the King at his downfall on the field of Bosworth; that decisive battle which changed the course of the English monarchy. However, less than two years later he did show his true colours by supporting Henry VII at Stoke for which he received further honours and lands in Yorkshire.

The Battle of Stoke of 1487 shows yet again how the unsettled period continued as this meeting of forces was as a result of the crowning in Dublin Cathedral in Ireland of the impostor Lambert Simnel as King Edward VI. One of the leaders of the Irish and German mercenaries involved in the 'Simnel Plot' was the 9th Baron Lovell who had received Richard III's favours and had been created Viscount Lovell in 1483; he also held positions such as Chamberlain of the Household and Chief Butler of England thereby becoming a man of extreme power. Lovell had supported Richard at Bosworth and after the defeat he fled to Flanders but returned two years later for this new uprising. Lovell's disappearance after the Battle of Stoke has been the subject of conjecture ever since. Was he actually killed on the battlefield, if so his body was never identified, or did he drown whilst trying to escape by swimming the River Trent as some thought, or did he really escape to his home at Minister Lovell in the Cotswolds, and was it his skeleton which was found during the first decade of the eighteenth century in a cellar-type room of the Minster? An unfortunate end to the man who had befriended the ten-year-old who later became King Richard, because it is well recorded that Lovell was one of many who taught the youth in the arts of knighthood at Neville Castle near Middleham in Yorkshire. Whatever the true story it was some of his estates which passed to Sir Edmund Bedingfeld.

With the death of the builder of Oxburgh inheritance passed first to the eldest son, Sir Thomas, followed by the second son, Robert, both of whom died without issue, then resting with the third son who, like his father, was called Edmund. Edmund was about sixty years old when taking over the responsibility of the estate, but before the actual inheritance he had the unenviable task of maintaining control of the King's former wife, Catherine of Aragon, that is after Henry had changed his affections for Anne Boleyn. Catherine's confinement was at the medieval castle of Kimbolton, at that time in Huntingdonshire, and before Vanbrugh's rebuilding which is now used as a school. The period during which Sir Edmund acted as gaoler was, according to the records, difficult diplomatically and financially; both subjects were frequently a test of diplomacy, as with many matters dealing with the King, however Catherine's life expired less than three years later. It was four years before Sir Edmund took control of Oxburgh and during that time he was still involved with the King, particularly when being in attendance at the arrival of wife number four, Anne of Cleves.

On the death of Sir Edmund in 1554 his son, Sir Henry, became owner; a son who had already taken part in historical events from the Norfolk rebellions lead by another Catholic, Robert Kett, a quarrel based on the enclosure of common land, also to providing a protective force for Queen Mary when she moved from Kenninghall in Norfolk to Framlingham Castle. He continued his support when Mary made the move to London and for this Bedingfeld was made Privy Councillor amongst other important offices. During these troubled times the Princess Elizabeth was in real danger and for her own safety held in the Tower of London, actually in the care of the Lieutenant of the Tower, namely Sir Henry Bedingfeld and he continued to act as one of the gaolers when Elizabeth moved to Woodstock Palace. Not surprisingly after Mary's death and Elizabeth's succession Sir Henry was deprived of his various offices, but at this stage he had acquired the family estates and withdrew to the country. It is reputed that the new Queen forgave her former gaoler for the period she was held almost a prisoner. Because of the change of religious faith by the monarchy which was spreading throughout the country, instigated by King Henry, the continued staunch Catholic beliefs of the Bedingfeld's faith was proving somewhat expensive – even more so during the seventeenth century civil wars at which time the continual Royalist allegiance, in addition to Catholicism, had considerable effect on both family and estates. Extra taxes and fines were frequently levied against the supporters of the Church of Rome, and against those who did not attend the Church of England.

It was Sir Henry's great-grandson, although knighted during the early days of the wars, who suffered imprisonment in the Tower during his mature years and his lands were questionably sold by the new regime after the surrender of Oxburgh to the Roundheads, and the buildings damaged. Support for the King had proved expensive both in money and estate damage but with hostilities over the son of Sir Henry's second wife, another Henry, succeeded and was created Baronet by Charles II after the Restoration. This Henry (1613–1685) married one of the Paston daughters. Successively generations of the Bedingfeld family suffered more because of their religious beliefs than damage from picks and shot, and as Catholic children were forbidden education in England their training took place on the Continent.

Thanks to a number of well-chosen marriages funds were available to maintain the house and estate. A nineteenth-century joining of families was that of Sir Henry Richard, the 6th Baronet, to Margaret another and the last of the Paston family who formerly owned estates which today constitute part of the Queen's Sandringham lands. To avoid the loss of the Paston name and arms Sir Henry obtained licence for the name to be added to that of the Bedingfeld thus Sir Henry being named Sir Henry Richard Paston Bedingfeld, Bt., a name perpetuated to this day.

The trials and tribulations of maintaining the Catholic faith by the Bedingfelds, like many important families, a restriction introduced in the sixteenth century, did not end until the nineteenth century with the passing of the Catholic Emancipation Act of 1829. At last the many facets of the constraints were lifted whether it be the effect on education, the control of travel, the hindrance of promotion within the forces, the limitations of inheritance or appointments to some high offices or even marriages. Gone was the need for Catholics to use false names when enjoying privileges offered to Protestants, or to provide secret chapels or hiding places for supporting priests such as those found in many large houses throughout the country.

Oxburgh Hall, like so many of the British country houses, became threatened with annihilation by the middle of the twentieth century, perhaps the greatest threat since being built during the latter part of the fifteenth century. This state of affairs existed because of taxation and changes in social life, but the sale which may have resulted in the demolition was reversed by the great efforts of the Dowager Lady Bedingfeld who influenced help from relations and friends, and a number of Trusts, and was able to present this house to the National Trust for permanent preservation. This philanthropic act by the Dowager, who was buried behind the estate chapel on the day she would have reached the age of 102 years provides sight of a beautiful building visited by monarchs and their retinues on so many occasions over the centuries, with many contents including tapestries by Mary Queen of Scots and Bess of Hardwick, and the famous French garden constructed in the nineteenth century.

Chapter XV

Peto

Harold Ainsworth Peto may not appear to be a candidate for inclusion in a book entitled *People of Property*: he was not one of the 'landed gentry' and he did not influence history as did so many of those who are the subject of other chapters of this book, in fact many people who know the name will associate him with gardens rather than with estates. Quite true and as previously mentioned this book is not intended to be on the subject of gardens nor gardening but in the case of Peto he certainly justifies being included in *People of Property* purely on the grounds of his influence on so many gardens which enhance estates. Of the properties Peto owned, only one will be mentioned at any length, that being his final abode but a few others which received his attention will be subject to comment. Of his life only a brief resume will be made covering many salient stages; readers wishing for further details will discover much has been written about this garden architect designer.

The son of a constructional engineer Peto was born in 1854 and joined in partnership with the architect Sir Ernest George whilst in his early twenties. He was very involved in the designs for buildings within the inner London residential area continuing the trend possibly set by the nineteenth-century prolific architect Norman Shaw: those high gabled houses of which so many can be seen today. For a brief period of the George/Peto partnership they were joined by Edwin Lutyens – prior to his knighthood in 1890 – but Lutyens left the firm to join his old friend and mentor Gertrude Jekyll who gave him the commission to build that most famous address of Munstead Wood. Lutyens had therefore little tutored training and was possibly trained by experience and the help of his connections. Peto's partnership with Sir Ernest was dissolved in 1892 after which Peto spent a considerable time on the Riviera making frequent visits to Italy. Here he continued to study architecture together with interior designs and gardening. Sir Ernest continued to be a prominent architect into the Edwardian era with his alterations to whole areas of residential London by the use of red terracotta facades introduced in the 1880s; in 1910 he designed the Royal Academy of Music.

Peto continued to take an interest in architecture designing a number of charming houses in both the British Isles and on the Riviera but as a garden designer he became outstanding. People like Robinson had more or less successfully revolted against the over-fussy Victorian ideas with imitation Italian styles incorporating elaborate patterns with the use of bedding plants. Architects of the Victorian era in reality knew little about the art of garden design and had neither the time nor the inclination to be involved in this requirement, considering it not part of their brief, and it was, as many thought, below their status. Peto was different and about the time of his leaving the partnership with George he was one of the most successful garden designers in the British Isles although he was not alone in thinking of the garden as part of building work, and allied to it, not treating the building and the plot as two entirely separate parts, but as a whole. Peto had a leaning to the formal but tempered by the use of trees, shrubs and plants which constituted a major part of any layout. With his Italian experience more than one aspect of land design emerged and the Renaissance and Italian bric-a-brac acquired during his travels could now be assembled at a property he bought in 1899, being Iford Manor in Wiltshire.

Peto as an ardent lover of formal and classical within the garden amply illustrated this, not only in the construction at Iford but also during a number of commissions which he received in the first decade of the new twentieth century. A year or so after acquiring his Wiltshire property his thoughts must have been occupied by a project required for the 1st Lord Faringdon at his Buscot Park address in what was then Berkshire, now Oxfordshire. The scheme required a visual connection between the house and the great lake at the opposite side of a wood. Peto was without doubt the man for the job and, as can be seen today at this property in the care of the National Trust, there is a link from one to the other within a cutting through the wood enhanced by a water feature of considerable length consisting of a variety of fountain, waterfalls, rills and pools with the occasional bridge over, the whole being bordered by box and yew. Perhaps this could be called an elongated water garden which provides both the connection of house and lake but also furnished a view of the 'eye-catcher' temple built on the far bank of the extensive sheet of water.

Of the many other Peto projects only a few will be mentioned here but one or two of the more interesting must include Wayford Manor in Somerset where basic design took place about 1902, and a few years later at an important house in Wiltshire called Heale. The manor is of Carolean period being well associated with Charles II; it has a commercial plant centre and the garden is frequently open to the public. About 1901 the owner of Heale House employed Japanese gardeners to create an area with appropriate plants, also some buildings such as a tea house, a lacquered bridge, and suitable stone lanterns were lodged at particular points. West Dean in Sussex received Peto's attention in about 1910 when a 300-foot-long pergola was built. There were in addition many other sites visited or at which Peto was employed – one of the largest perhaps was in County Cork on what is known as either Ilnacullin or Garinish Island in Bantry Bay; here was a project to build a villa with garden, mixing the formal classical with nature. The villa never materialized but the garden was to a certain degree completed. Many of the above are open to the public within the period accorded by the owners, some on a commercial basis, others occasionally under the National Gardens Scheme or the normal opening hours of the National Trust.

To obtain full appreciation of Harold Peto, his last home of lford Manor in Wiltshire is the place to visit. Records appertaining to this area of Wiltshire go back a long way including the time when a Roman settlement was nearby, then the William the Conqueror period to the fourteenth century, when within a short distance the owning monks lived at Hinton Charterhouse. This was the Abbey founded by the great Ela Devereux as mentioned within Chapter XI of this book. The old bridge complete with Britannia which now stands opposite the main entrance to the house is said to be a relic of the monk's building work. The property changed hands a number of times and for some period was owned by mill owners and clothiers allied to nearby Bradford-on-Avon and the local industry associated with wool. Now the lengthy plot is roughly divided into three terraces but these are ingeniously inter-linked. At every corner and with every view there is a classical or natural point of interest whether it shows to best advantage a column or series of columns, an urn, a vase, a statue, a bust, a section or whole doorway, a capital, or indeed the cloisters. They are all there to be found, placed just at the correct point to merge the art of architecture and garden design which was exactly the aim of that outstanding designer Harold Peto.

Chapter XVI

Ickworth

Throughout history there have been characters worthy of note: there have been eccentrics, nonconformists, or call them what you will, they have been different and added jest to the norm and one of the greatest of such characters in the eighteenth century was not only a member of the aristocracy but also a member of the Church. A man who was subject to favouritism on the one hand, and ridicule on the other. He was also the subject for many writers over the years and provided an insight into the lifestyles of himself and others during the period in question. Raised to the rank of Bishop, Frederick Hervey can be cited as one of the characters of note by anyone's standard.

Discover any estate in the geographical region of a former abbey and not surprisingly records will show that centuries ago the lands were owned and controlled by the Church when in its heyday. Ickworth estate in Suffolk, being in the region of one the most powerful abbeys in the land, based at Bury St Edmunds, falls into this category. The abbey records can be traced to the first century and later; in the fifteenth century it is noted that a tenant married a man from Bedfordshire by the name of Thomas Hervey, and whilst little may be known of that union the lives of many of their descendants are well annotated.

By the seventeenth century the head of the family became John Hervey who, like many of the family, was involved in politics; he was created Baron in 1703. In 1710 John demolished the original sixteenth-century manor house on the Ickworth estate and cogitated over building a new house, but during the intervening period the family lived in a modified farmhouse now referred to as Ickworth Lodge. Intended as a temporary residence it remained the family seat at Ickworth for about a hundred years, accommodation being supplemented by the use of their town house in Bury St Edmunds. A number of eminent architects were invited to submit plans for a grand new house but all came to nought. In 1714 John was created Earl of Bristol for his support of the Hanoverian succession; he was the 1st Earl, second issue as previously the title had been held by

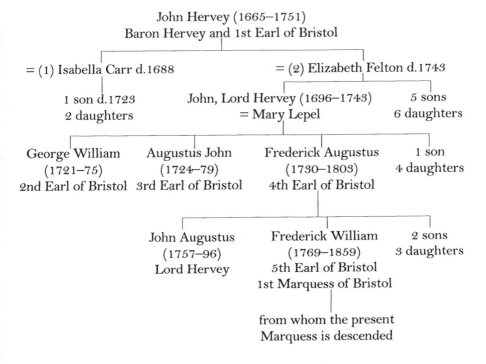

John Hervey (1665–1751)
Baron Hervey and 1st Earl of Bristol

= (1) Isabella Carr d.1688　　　　= (2) Elizabeth Felton d.1743

1 son d.1723　　　John, Lord Hervey (1696–1743)　　5 sons
2 daughters　　　　　= Mary Lepel　　　　　　　　6 daughters

George William　　Augustus John　　Frederick Augustus　　1 son
(1721–75)　　　　(1724–79)　　　　(1730–1803)　　　4 daughters
2nd Earl of Bristol　3rd Earl of Bristol　4th Earl of Bristol

John Augustus　　Frederick William　　2 sons
(1757–96)　　　(1769–1859)　　　3 daughters
Lord Hervey　　5th Earl of Bristol
　　　　　　1st Marquess of Bristol

from whom the present
Marquess is descended

the Digby family but became extinct on the death of the 3rd Earl Digby in 1698. The new 1st Earl, in addition to politics, followed another family trait of producing many offspring – his father being the third child of a family of seven – whereas John, who died at the age of eighty-five, during his two marriages begot twenty children. Of these children the one to continue the line was another John.

John, Lord Hervey married a maid of honour to Queen Caroline, Mary Lepel, and his short life – he predeceased his father by eight years dying at the age of forty-seven – can best be described as a full one. He was a writer and prominent in the social life of the day, both he and his wife being members of the Court of the Prince of Wales (afterwards George III), a Vice-Chamberlain and intimately involved with King George II and his Queen, he wrote amusing memoirs of that reign but ceased his writings on the death of the Queen. His amorous tendencies certainly appear to have been mixed in that between the ages of twenty-five and forty he sired eight children by his wife, and these celebrations of births seem to have been interspersed with affairs of a different kind involving such personages as Stephen Fox – a mere eight years his junior – and Horace Walpole nearer twenty-one years junior; there was also a foreign Count and others. Whilst Hervey supporters, amongst whom must be included the Queen, qualified him as charming, witty, and shrewd but amoral, others less favourably impressed called him spiteful, malicious and effeminate.

It was perhaps unfortunate that the Walpoles were so prominent at this time as it is known that Hervey paid visits to the family seat at Houghton Hall, attending the twice yearly parties given by Sir Robert for his government colleagues and the local gentry. Hervey was twenty years junior to Robert Walpole who had many critics such as Fielding, Pope and Swift sometimes referring to him as ruthless and corrupt. Sir Robert inherited his father's estate of Houghton, entering Parliament whilst in his twenties supporting the Whig administration; he held a number of offices before being condemned for corruption after about eleven years, but re-entered the Whig cause on the Accession of George I. The abortive South Sea Bubble did not help Walpole's reputation and future years proved a greater disaster establishing that he may have been a good administrator but dealing with foreign problems was alien to him, and the problems with Spain brought his career to an end. Nevertheless in 1742 he did receive the honour of becoming the 1st Earl of Orford, 2nd issue as the first issue was to Edward Russell, nephew of the 1st Duke of Bedford, but this became extinct on his death in 1727. The title continued after Sir Robert's death, first to his son and then to his grandson before eventually passing to Sir Robert's youngest and fourth son, Horace.

Horace, the author and writer of letters, may well have existed within the shadow of his father but he was gullible to advances by older men, particularly one whom he considered worldly-wise and sophisticated such as Hervey. Reputedly Hervey advised his young friend on career matters persuading him to take more interest in the classical Gothic of the day rather than the whim of the moment which was chinoiserie. There was a compromise in that the younger man followed the Rococo-Gothic style. Writing was also a common interest between them as Horace continued writing the memoirs of the reign of George II after Hervey abandoned his similar work on Queen Caroline's death; *Memoirs of the Reign of George II* became one of Horace's classics. Perhaps Horace had been in the shadow of his father but he left for posterity perhaps the first Gothic mansion, Strawberry Hill, adding a name to a type of architecture, which is where Horace settled in 1747; he also left in excess of 3,000 letters providing an insight into eighteenth-century life and times. The title of 4th Earl of Orford was not received until he was in his seventies but on his death the title became temporarily extinct and Houghton passed eventually into the hands of the Cholmondeley family. Strawberry Hill, after a period with the Waldegraves, was dispersed at a famous auction in 1842. The title was recreated for Horace's cousin, Horatio, Baron Walpole in 1806 and continues today with the family seat being at Wolterton Park, Norfolk.

With the early demise of John Hervey he never reached earldom status but by his productivity of children ensured the future family line and his first three sons were in turn created Earl of Bristol. George William, one-time ambassador in Ireland, held the title 2nd Earl from 1751 until his death in 1775; Augustus John was 3rd Earl from 1775 to 1779; and Frederick, who was the next member of the family to produce future descendants, held the title of 4th Earl from 1779 until his death in 1803. On Frederick's death the title was conferred on his youngest child and second son, Frederick William who also received the elevation to Marquess.

Frederick Augustus who was born in 1730, thanks to his brother George, became Bishop of Cloyne in Ireland and before he was forty years of age improved his position to that of Bishop of Derry, one of the wealthiest sees in Ireland. Acting as a church dignitary he was one of the few Herveys not to be involved in Parliamentary politics, but by all accounts he would have been a diplomat of some considerable standing if his influence in Ireland was an example of his persuasive prowess. From this see, which was more than just lucrative but also one providing influence and power in the country, his income was substantial and further improved by careful manoeuvring of land receipts from the diocesan funds to the pocket of the incumbent. It would appear that the Bishop's priorities were not as expected as the first was travel, the second architecture, and the third the Church. He may have proved popular with his affable manner but not with everyone, and certainly not with George III who made clear his feelings by reproaches – the King was already embroiled with ecclesiastical problems in Ireland.

A brief insight into his love of buildings shows that the Ulster coast was to be the site for the first of the Bishop's building work where the over-large mansion named Downhill House was started in 1775. Built on land previously owned by the diocese, but which one way or another became the personal property of the Bishop, the house, ten years after its commencement, was being given its final dressings. Less than eighty years later a disastrous fire virtually destroyed the house although twenty years later it was rebuilt. On the Earl Bishop's death Downhill was left to a cousin whose descendants lived there until 1950. The house, now a ruin, and the estate is in the hands of the National Trust and this includes a small complete building known as the Mussenden Temple, named after one of the Bishop's relations. This little building, based in design after a temple at Tivoli, shows the great love Hervey had for circular structures – an interest much pursued with his next two building projects. On the edge of the estate above the cliffs the temple built between 1783 and 1785 was originally fully equipped as a library; it remains now as a complete building.

The second larger-than-life house to be built was Ballyscullion and this a foretaste of Ickworth. Complete with multi-storeyed central rotunda and two side wings some distance from the centre being connected by curved corridors. The building which commenced a little more than twelve years after the start of Downhill (about 1787) was based on the principle of an island residence in the Lake District, Belle Isle, which nearly divides Lake Windermere in two was the site for the owner Mr English to build a round house started in 1774 and based on Villa Vicenza in Rome. The architect was John Plaw who was also fascinated by circular structures, although his thoughts were more on the scale of rustic cottages made of tree trunks – a subject he, like others, wrote books about at the end of the eighteenth century. Cottage, rustic or otherwise, Belle Isle was not. It was of sufficient size to be the subject of derogatory remarks from many – including William Wordsworth who in his writings *The Prelude* referred to it as a 'pepper-pot'. Mr English became so upset at the constant disparaging comments that he sold it at a financial loss to Isabella Curwen, the heiress of Workington Hall; a hall built for one of the oldest Cumbrian families who can be traced to the eleventh century. The ruined eighteenth-century structure is part of the town's recreation grounds of Curwen Park, and the Curwen family still maintain Belle Isle. The eighteenth-century remains are all that exist of the replacement for the original fourteenth-century family seat at which Mary Queens of Scots was entertained during her flight to Carlisle after the Battle of Langside in the sixteenth century.

The formulation of a central rotunda was therefore not a revolutionary idea but the construction of Ballyscullion, which although roofed and furnished, was never completed, but it satisfied the Bishop's wish to pursue the circular form. By this time the Bishop was Earl Bishop having inherited the title as 4th Earl on the death of his brother Augustus John. To complete the history of Ballyscullion, about ten years after the death of the Earl Bishop the house was dismantled and the portico used as the entrance of a Belfast church.

Before mentioning a few points on the subject of big house number three at Ickworth, it would be appropriate at this stage to relate one or two of the facts known about the greatest character of them all, Frederick Augustus Hervey, Deacon, Bishop, and later Earl. Frederick was born in 1730 and his father died whilst he was in his forties at the time when Frederick was fourteen years of age and studying at Westminster School. His mother continued to live in her father-in-law's house, which would be Ickworth Lodge as now known, and Frederick when in his teens went to Cambridge University although left at the age of twenty-one without the formality of sitting for a degree – the degrees came later as the right of a nobleman's son. It would have been normal for the younger son of an Earl to seek a suitable financially secured young lady, but Frederick at twenty-two married a girl of nineteen called Elizabeth Davers. This marriage was not the best for unity within the families as the Herveys were staunch Whig supporters and very involved with party matters, and the Davers on the other hand were Tories.

The newly married couple lived with their first child near Peterborough and within a short time Frederick's career took a change of direction. At Cambridge there had been an idea of pursuing the law, but this admittedly without conviction; now younger brother William who had originally intended entering the Church changed tack and joined the army. Frederick reconsidered his position and wholeheartedly took interest in an ecclesiastical following. The actual qualifications obtained to be an official of the Church appear vague but reference is made in records and letters to the effect that Frederick completed a 'do-it-yourself' education period reading any books, old or new, that he could obtain on religious matters. However achieved, by his mid-twenties he had been made Deacon by the Bishop of Ely, and the following year was ordained as a priest. Ten years later the clergyman and his wife set off on their first continental tour through Brussels and Switzerland and nearly the length of Italy. During a stay in Naples a message was received saying that Frederick's brother George had been appointed Lord Lieutenant of Ireland and he wished to appoint Frederick as First Chaplain. The return journey was faster than the outward one. Frederick now had his sights set on high office in the Irish Church and had not long to wait as the following year the Bishop of Cloyne died and his position was soon filled, but it was hoped that this would be a mere transit post as there were higher offices to achieve. Transitional it may have been but not for long as shortly after accepting that appointment the Bishop of Derry died and in May 1767 Frederick was duly consecrated as the new Bishop in Dublin Cathedral. At this stage there can have been no doubt as to the Bishop's justification in being in office as degrees had already been received from Oxford and Cambridge and to add to those a doctorate of Divinity was given by Trinity College, Dublin.

Less than three years later the Bishop was off on his travels again, this time wife and children staying at home apart from thirteen-year-old son, John Augustus who was already a midshipman and this trip was to be the lad's 'grand-tour'. This continental visit lasted almost two and a half years and not surprisingly the Bishop received on his return the royal rebuke. Frederick may well have become interested in topography during his visit overseas some four years previously as much time was spent studying land formations and an ascent of Vesuvius was made. People were also visited including such notables as Voltaire at Ferncy and the Pope in Rome – a contradictory pair!

Within three years of their return home the Bishop's brother, who had made the Bishopric possible, died. This had a number of effects on his Lordship's position: one was his yet greater financial means, but the other a family matter relating to inheritance of title. Frederick's brother Augustus John, who became 3rd Earl with the death of George, had married Elizabeth Chudleigh which was a union performed in secret when the groom was twenty years old. Some years later she became mistress of the Duke of Kingston and later bigamously married him; this created one of the great eighteenth-century scandals – many years later she died abroad where she had been living since the death of the Duke.

Still as Bishop – the Bristol title was to remain with Augustus for a few more years – his Reverence returned to the Continent, one excuse for his absence from office being given that a health cure was needed. On these travels more and more time was spent seeking and buying works of art and Italy was the country most favoured by the wandering cleric who did indeed from time to time suffer health problems, although usually contracted from location epidemics. Spring 1779 saw the travellers return home by devious routes which lasted for six months, all this during the period when wars of various kinds were smouldering, most importantly as far as the Bishop was concerned, between Ireland and France. Within months of this return Frederick's brother Augustus died at the family home in St James' Square, London, namely Bristol House, therefore the Bishop now became Earl Bishop with an even greater income. For a while the Earl Bishop spent time in Ireland living at Downhill whilst his wife lived at Ickworth Lodge; later he joined her and in 1782 Lancelot Brown was at Ickworth possibly selecting the best site for the proposed new house the Bishop had had in mind during all his years of travelling. Later that year a rift developed between his Lordship and his wife and by

November the Bishop returned to his office in Ireland. After an alleged mild affair with a cousin, Mrs Mussenden, Frederick's main focus of interest was politics and religious reform in Ireland, travelling back and forth between Ireland and the Continent which now occurred so frequently that the Bishop did not even make excuses whether on health grounds or not for being absent from office. It is reputed that his patronage at hostelries abroad was starting to be noted and years later the establishments became known as Bristol Hotels – whether he had stayed there or not; some accommodations maintain the name even to this day. During one of these visits Bristol commissioned John Flaxman the sculptor who was living in Rome at the time, to produce a work based on the Fury of Athamas and this work of art can now be seen in the staircase well at Ickworth. In 1791 Frederick left Ireland for the last time, again making excuses for his departure as having bad health. It is known that he was in Rome in 1794, and in 1798 during the invasion of Italy by the French the collection of works of art obtained by the Bishop were confiscated and his Lordship imprisoned for nine months. On release he did not return home but stayed in Italy, leasing a house in Florence at one stage, and during his wanderings in 1803 he died. The British Minister at Naples arranged for the mortal remains to be returned on board the man-of-war *Monmouth*, suitably disguised to satisfy the superstitious sailors by the coffin being contained in a packing case labelled antique statue, not to Derry which he had neglected over the last eleven years, but to the vault in the church in Ickworth Park. Of the fate of the many properties purchased by the Bishop in Italy there is considerable doubt and mystery but many of the works of art did arrive in England after his death.

Of the building works, with the success of first Downhill and then Ballyscullion, during the travels of his lordship the new house for Ickworth was uppermost in his mind. During the visit in 1792, which proved to be his last, it had been decided as to the form it should take, that is another Ballyscullion. The construction started in 1795 but on his death work stopped and did not recommence for twenty years and it was not until 1829 that the family moved in. Little will be related on the subject of Ickworth as it stands today – many learned writers and historians have put pen to paper on the subject, but it should be mentioned that the house as envisaged by the Earl Bishop is largely to his design – or that of builders and architects whom he was frequently employing, dismissing, and replacing. Details however have changed to some degree, particularly when realising that the inside such as the stairwell was a void at the time of his death and the rotunda had nothing but a temporary roof cover. The present staircase well has been completed to a superb design and contains the Flaxman sculpture commissioned during one of the many peregrinations by his Lordship.

Finally, the title passed to Frederick Hervey's youngest child, a son called Frederick William, who became 5th Earl of Bristol and who was elevated to Marquess in 1826, from whom the present Marquess is descended. It was this thirty-odd year old who had the decision to make as to whether the partly built-over elaborate house should be demolished, or whether it should be completed. Thanks to the correct choice being made today there is available for all to see a unique, nay extraordinary, house which must warrant the title of one of the gems within the portfolio of the National Trust, and most importantly there stands in the park an obelisk erected in 1817 by the people of Derry proving that, despite his many absences, this larger-than-life character was immensely popular.

Chapter XVII

Packwood House

A ny estate or property which existed during the seventeenth-century English Civil War can harbour interesting stories of the people of the day. Packwood House in Warwickshire may not be a grand manor nor claim an extensive period garden, but as the small house of a yeoman the estate predates that frequently referred to questionable period of history, and has indeed stories to tell about people of both that period and of other times.

People at opposite ends of the spectrum, such as one of Oliver Cromwell's generals, Henry Ireton, and Charles II were both entertained here, albeit at different times and the latter's visit was somewhat shorter than that of the former. A story of dubious authenticity refers to this period of which more is written later. In the very early history 'central-heating' was introduced not in the house but in the garden; some years later a layout of trees in a unique fashion allegedly depicting a biblical scene was planted. During the twentieth century Queen Mary visited whilst a local industrialist, Alfred Ash, was devoting a financial fortune to refurbishment in the grandest of fashion. Today there is on permanent display a superb collection of tapestries, including an example of the products from one local tapestry factory, the owners of which actually owned the estate even if not residing there; but do not be fooled by the painted canvas!

There certainly is no doubt that Packwood estate in the Forest of Arden predates the seventeenth century as records show inclusion in the eleventh-century Domesday Book. Before the Dissolution the owners were the Coventry-based Benedictine Monks, and after their curtailment of the various possessors, the most notable were the Sheldons of Warwickshire tapestry factory fame. By the end of the sixteenth century a local yeoman by the name of Fetherston bought the property with the timber-framed building of about 1560, the Fetherston name being traceable in the district from the mid-fifteenth century. In one connection or another the Fetherstons remained associated with Packwood for the following 270 years during which time the L-shaped wing was added and other modifications made. By the eighteenth century there was a joining by marriage with another local family, the Dilkes of nearby Maxstoke Castle, a splendid fourteenth-century, moated, square-plan castle originally built for the Earl of Huntingdon. The name of the family became Fetherston-Dilke which is perpetuated to this day. The thirty-six years after the Fetherstons was a period of mixed blessings with a number of different residents; this state of affairs terminated, again after a thirty-six year interval, with the purchase in 1905 by Alfred Ash whose son after massive restoration, donated the whole to the National Trust.

The John Fetherston of the Civil Wars period, who trained as a barrister, appears to have had political dexterity, or perhaps no intense feelings for either side because he provided accommodation for Henry Ireton, one of Cromwell's generals, before the Battle of Edgehill; a room has been named in his honour. It is said that nearly nine years later Charles II received hospitality in the same house after his defeat at the Battle of Worcester. No room has been named after him! Perhaps Fetherston's lack of conviction saved Packwood from destruction during these turbulent times.

General Ireton was a man of great power indicated by his inclusion in the signatories on the warrant of execution of the King. He had been formerly trained as a lawyer, and to Cromwell he was of considerable support, a relationship bonded further by the marriage of Ireton and Cromwell's daughter, Bridget. There is an intriguing story about an occurrence whilst he was at Packwood during October 1642; a story which has many variations in the telling but basically the story goes as follows. Ireton's son saw from the window of the room at Packwood one of his enemies hiding in the bushes, this hiding individual being in love with the lad's sister. With the alarm being raised the offender was caught and subsequently imprisoned in Kenilworth and there to await death as curfew tolled the following morning. The General's daughter, being the other half of the pair of lovers, in due time climbed into the belfry and steadfastly clung to the clapper of the bell thus preventing the ringing of curfew and so saved her lover from death. Romantic as the story may be the facts are that Ireton and Bridget Cromwell were not married until 1646 so who was the son, and who was the daughter old enough to reach the bell? In 1642 Ireton would have been about thirty-one years of age but there is no record of a previous marriage and even if there should have been a son and daughter they would have been somewhat young to be lovers and climbing bell towers!

A more easily substantiated report refers to Cromwell – no connection with lovers and bells – but with his financial affairs. Financial benefits from his official offices were required before he could provide dowries for the marriages of his daughters, and this he received during the 1645/6 Parliamentary year. Awards were made to him by Parliament, much of the money from the Duke of Buckingham's estates, thus Cromwell was able to afford to move to a larger house as well as providing financial security for his family. Henry Ireton and Bridget produced one son and four daughters, but the marriage did not last longer than five years as he, whilst representing Cromwell in Ireland, contracted a fever and died – surprisingly he did not perish by the sword. Packwood appears to have taken no further part in the Civil Wars and no damage was sustained.

The remainder of this short tale of one of the most charming Tudor houses in the Midlands can be as calm as the lifestyle of the estate after the seventeenth century. During the following centuries, particularly during the eighteenth, much in the way of maintaining and updating was completed and today can be seen the moulded brickwork, pilasters, cornices and roundels preserving a most important example of this type of building in the Midlands. There was in the garden the introduction of the innovation of heated walls by a fire being built at the base of a wall with flues thus protecting tender fruit tree buds from frost. The walled garden layout can now be seen with a gazebo at each corner, although these were not constructed as one project but some added later as a drawing of 1756 shows only one such building. The replacing of an old orchard by a special arrangement of trees is one of Packwood's great attractions. The inference is that the story of the Sermon on the Mount is depicted by the use of yew trees of differing sizes starting with The Multitude, then The Apostles, The Evangelists, with The Master at the head. Whilst no documentary evidence confirms this as being the original aim it is certainly evocative of the theme. At one side of the house, in the open air, a pool or cold plunge has been built this was at the time the fashion, as mentioned in chapter XIII of this book whilst referring to Stourhead; as the King was maintaining the mode at most of his royal palaces why not the country gentry following suit?

The greatest upheaval to affect Packwood after the eighteenth century was to arrive after the purchase by the previously mentioned Alfred Ash in 1905. The word upheaval is not the correct word, as that indicates the place was possibly pulled down and rebuilt – exactly the opposite took place thanks to the very great love and money which was showered on both house and garden. The estate was placed on the open market in 1904 to be sold by auction, and many fates could have befallen the property had it not been for the foresight of Alfred Ash, a descendant of Doctor John Ash who founded the eighteenth-century General Hospital and a familiar name in the Midlands when coupled with Lacy, as the firm of Ash and Lacy have been for many years great industrialists in the heart of industry in the Birmingham area; there are still a number of engineering works in the locality operating under that name. The restoration and regeneration of Packwood became so well known that Queen Mary visited during the late 1920s, some years after the death of Mr Ash senior, to see for herself the works being performed; the room in which she rested during this honour of a visit has been named after her. At this time Graham Ash was High Sheriff for the County of Warwickshire.

Restoration as a word falls short when considering the amount of replacement from floorboards to panelling, from ceiling beams to ceiling boards, which took place when the father and son of the Ash family had possession. The sympathetically installed materials were not bought off the shelf but were sought out and obtained one way or another from other old houses; they were of the period of the original and subsequently the replacements look, feel and smell like the original. The materials, tapestries, antiques and so many objects of art were collected from all over Britain and the Continent. There was one new innovation and that was during the 1930s when a nearby cow-byre was converted into a classical great hall complete with minstrels gallery which, in truth, was the old hayloft.

In 1941 Mr Graham Baron Ash donated Packwood, together with a generous endowment, to the National Trust for permanent preservation with the request that the house and contents remain as presented without disturbance. Do the father and son justify being included in a book entitled *People of Property?* Considering the amount of tender loving care exercised during their short tenure it is confirmed that they do just that.

Chapter XVIII

Lacock

Relatively few of the great ecclesiastical houses which existed at the time when the King's Commissioners were on the rampage raising money to discharge Henry's debts could have proved so difficult to fault; could provide nothing by way of excuse for confiscation and destruction. But these difficulties did apply to an abbey founded 300 years previously by the wife of an illegitimate son of a king. The abbey was Lacock in Wiltshire, and because of the good lifestyle and great charitable works performed the Commissioners postponed their usual destruction until receiving instructions to restrict their claim for compensation by way of fines only.

The Abbey was not sacked as occurred with so many, but its function was suppressed by 1539, one of the last abbeys to suffer this fate. The building physically having been spared from destruction was, however, commandeered and became the property of a political rogue who, nevertheless, converted the building to a private residence sympathetically. A hundred years later, although the owner of the day was a Royalist, by favourable terms being agreed with the Parliamentary forces, the building remained in tact. Was the ghost of the founder of the Abbey acting as guardian angel? Further owners from time to time made structural alterations but still with a certain amount of due reverence and this continued well into the nineteenth century when the owner used his considerable knowledge as both an antiquarian and architect to preserve the remains of the monastic building. More than seven and a half centuries after the founding of Lacock Abbey there remains much to see and appreciate.

Ela Devereux inherited both the title Countess of Salisbury and her father's estate at Lacock when she was eight years of age, which would have been in the year 1194 or thereabouts. It is known that about 1149 a feudal lord of Wiltshire named Patrick de Salisbury was created Earl of Salisbury but the relationship with Ela is not proven. However, it is thought that Patrick, or his kinsman, was the same Norman on whom

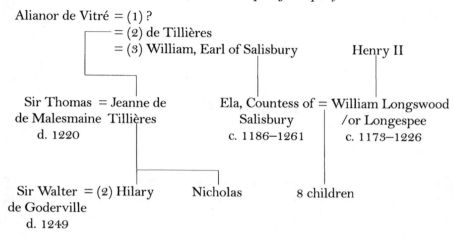

Alianor de Vitré = (1) ?
　　　　　　　 = (2) de Tillières
　　　　　　　 = (3) William, Earl of Salisbury　　　　　Henry II

Sir Thomas = Jeanne de　　　Ela, Countess of = William Longswood
de Malesmaine Tillières　　　　　Salisbury　　　／or Longespee
　　d. 1220　　　　　　　　　c. 1186–1261　　　c. 1173–1226

Sir Walter = (2) Hilary　　　Nicholas　　　8 children
de Goderville
　　d. 1249

William the Conqueror bestowed lands in Wiltshire, and Ela could have been his great-granddaughter. A marriage was arranged during the time Ela was a ward of court because she had been orphaned at an early age – she was still a child when the marriage took place to William Longswood (or Longespee), the illegitimate son of Henry II, who was thirteen years her senior.

By all accounts it was a happy marriage, she spending time at her inherited property while he served king and country fighting in France – obviously the couple met at intervals as they had eight children. It was on one of his return journeys that a miracle was performed – or so it would appear. A storm arose with such ferocity that it was feared the ship would be lost with all hands. An apparition of a fair maid was seen by those on board and this gave them faith to struggle against the elements with such success that the boat landed safely, but on the wrong side of the Channel. There was then further delay awaiting improvements in the weather and during this enforced lengthy absence from the Countess the Earl's rival in love made advances to her Ladyship, these being firmly rejected.

This rejected suitor was a nephew of the all-powerful Hubert de Burgh who became Chief Justiciar after a period as Chamberlain to King John, but because of his revolutionary tendencies with other nobles the royal favours he received fluctuated during the reign of Henry III. It is known that a future relation to Ela by marriage, namely Sir Walter de Goderville, had dealings with de Burgh as it is recorded that at one time de Goderville acted as constable for de Burgh at Montgomery Castle, but during the following year Sir Walter was one of the knights enforcing imprisonment of de Burgh at Devizes Castle. This would be during the period of the Barons' Wars. When the Earl eventually returned home he had an altercation with his rivals and when he mysteriously died a couple of years later, it was suggested that the de Burghs had had a hand in the act by using poison. Ela would have been about forty years of age when she was widowed but never remarried. Accepting some of the responsibilities previously satisfied by her husband she acted as High Sheriff for Wiltshire – the first woman to hold this office. Ela, despite being orphaned at an early age, obviously developed into a very special lady with immense faith. For a time she and her husband accepted the wardship of Sir Thomas de Malesmaine's children after his death in 1220; they were of course related to Ela as step-niece and nephew. As de Goderville had been granted the Manor of Chippenham and Sheldon, Hilary a few years later lived at the nearby estate of Sheldon.

Was it the miraculous saving of her husband at sea, or was it as a memorial to him that Ela founded and endowed an Augustinian house for canonesses at Lacock? Whatever the reason it may have been on the same day that she founded Lacock she travelled sixteen miles to lay the foundation for a second religious house, this time for men, at Hinton Charterhouse. Some years after the founding of the Abbey Ela joined the canonesses and for about seventeen years held the post as Abbess. From this she retired early providing the opportunity for a younger member to take the reins, but she continued to be a member of the community until she died aged about seventy-five years.

Ela's connections with the city of Salisbury were many. In addition to the name of Salisbury which she inherited, and subsequently her husband accepting the same name, both laid foundation stones for the new cathedral which was to be a replacement for that built, or attempted to be built some two miles away at what is today the site of Old Sarum – the former name for the two towns. For many years they became known as Old Sarum and the other New Sarum. There are a number of stories as to the difficulty of building the cathedral on the old fortified hill, but in truth the main reason for the move was possibly the lack of a water supply. Of the number of peculiarities appertaining to the 'new' Salisbury Cathedral the most important is perhaps that it was unusual in that it was built all at one period rather than piecemeal over the centuries. Between 1220 and 1280 witnessed the construction, except for the spire which was not included in the original plan, but added in 1334; the tallest spire in England. The famous treasured clock was installed within a few years and is reputedly the oldest working mechanism in the country. The actual consecration took place in 1258 and today can be seen one of the very few cathedrals where the interior is visible without interruption for the whole length; it was at this church that the Earl was buried and one of Ela's sons became Bishop of Salisbury.

After the Abbey was made obsolete and the communicants had been pensioned-off the estate was sold for a very reasonable sum to a wealthy, although ethically questionable, merchant called Sir William Sharington who became entangled with Thomas Seymour, the Lord Protector and others during the period of the noblemen's revolt. Thomas in his position as Lord Admiral connived with the practice of piracy; one of the acts it would have been his responsibility to suppress. He also accepted illegally obtained money, much of it from debasing coinage by Sharington during his term of office as Vice-Treasurer of the Bristol Mint. Both men were found guilty of offences; Thomas lost his head on Tower Hill whilst Sharington was sent to the Tower and his properties confiscated. Sometime later he was pardoned and for a price allowed to repurchase the Lacock properties. £8,000 has been quoted as the price he had to pay, which was an immense amount in that day particularly remembering that initially Sharington only paid £783 for the property after the Abbey closure. Embezzlement may have been his forte in business but his conversion of the Abbey building was carried out in a fairly sensitive manner. John Chapman was employed to work on the site during the period 1540 to 1549 and the result was the Sharington Tower and other parts using the latest fashionable details with much continental influence. The Tower balustrade work was built in a similar manner to Somerset House in London and Longleat in Wiltshire. The latter, Longleat, was at the time dominating the building work in the district as the client was John Thyme, Steward to the Protector Somerset. Chapman's work was of a high standard, he was after all one of the King's masons and completed work at royal properties. Various parts of Lacock continued to be converted from abbey to residence until Sharington died during the 1550s at which time, as he left no issue by either of his wives, his brother Sir Henry inherited. Some of the artistic fabric work arranged by Sharington has left a legacy of great interest; one particular item in the Tower is the Chapman stone table with satyrs and other embellishments which may have Normandy bias.

It was Sir Henry's daughter Olive who married into the Talbot family by her union with Sir John Talbot of Salwarp in Worcestershire. Olive succeeded her father and during her grandson's proprietorship, that was Sharington Talbot, the former abbey was besieged by Parliamentary forces.

This Royalist stronghold surrendered on reasonable terms and this saved the property from being damaged; a fine amounting to £1,100 was however charged by the anti-Royalists. Staunch Royalists the family continued to be and John, the son of Sharington Talbot, was knighted by Charles II at the Restoration. Years later Queen Anne is said to have visited the house.

As Sir John's son, another Sharington, predeceased his father without issue as a result of a duel after Sedgemoor, it was a daughter by his second marriage, Anne, who married an Irishman, Sir John Ivory from County Wexford and after the wedding adopted the name Talbot thus continuing the Talbot succession. Sir John and Lady Anne's son, who also adopted the name Talbot, lived to a ripe old age of eighty-five, and lived at Lacock for about sixty of those years. It was during his time that one of the famous amateur architects of the Gothic design worked at Lacock, namely Sanderson Miller. Gothic of one type or another was fashionable and many estate owners were dabbling in the concept. Horace Walpole perhaps brought the image to the fore with the first part of his Strawberry Hill project, whereas Miller, who was a Warwickshire squire, practised the theme at properties belonging to his friends, and at his own house of Radway Grange before he ventured into sham castles, summerhouses and follies mostly with Gothic appearances. His largest work was for Lord Lyttleton at Hagley but as that was a pure Palladian edifice it had little interest for him, it was Gothic which had the fascination and the new hall at Lacock is perhaps his best surviving example.

After the ownership of Lacock had again passed through the female line by way of Martha Talbot – daughter of John Ivory – who married the Reverend William Davenport, and their son married a Lady Elizabeth Fox-Strangeways, the name of the next heir was William Henry Fox Talbot. This gentleman is perhaps the most famous of the Lacock inheritors in modern times for his pioneer work with photography, and the tithe barn near the entrance to the house gardens is devoted to his, and other people's, very early equipment used in this field. William Henry's son, Charles Henry, had a great interest in history and archaeology and devoted part of his quiet life to continued restoration of the monastic remains of the house. Charles Henry bequeathed the property to his niece who, like those before her, adopted the name Talbot, and it was she who passed ownership of house, gardens and the village of Lacock to the National Trust for preservation.

The village which has not been mentioned above as it has little to connect it with a single person of property, but it is, and always has been, an integral part of the estate. Here there is a near complete village – it was fully complete at the start of this century – which contains architecture dating back to the twelfth century although much is of the seventeenth and eighteenth centuries. The heyday could be cited as the fourteenth and fifteenth centuries when the town developed from the wool trade and this and agriculture were how most of the inhabitants made a living.

For a period of almost 400 years the former abbey, the park and the village have been in the hands of the Sharingtons and their descendants, and before their time it is known that Lacock was owned by the Salisburys, possibly as far back as the eleventh century. There is today a property which clearly shows evidence of all these periods, together with the living village which originally was developed and survived on the local trade of wool.

Chapter XIX

Ice-houses

Chapter VI of this book provides an insight into dovecotes and their place in a civilized society, illustrating the use, advantages and disadvantages of such constructions. Another vernacular building which was for centuries considered an essential part of any reasonably sized property was the ice-house, a domestic requirement, which was equally as important to many as the dovecote, but an item so mundane a building it has received little if any recognition in its own right. There is of course an understandable reason for this lack of interest. A dovecote stands proudly above ground, the variety of designs, colours, shapes and forms appeal to the eye. It is an attractive building and it provides shelter for a defenceless bird, whereas an ice-house is a cold utilitarian object more often than not buried in the ground or covered in such a way as to be unattractive to the eye. Most constructions result in a greater proportion of the building being buried in the ground out of sight than the proportion visible, a physical requirement to serve the purpose for which it is intended.

Having been the poor relation of the vernacular buildings for so many years there is now a resurgence of interest in this part of building history. They do represent part of the history of estates, part of the history appertaining to the people of property, an integral part of the history of people considering the value of ice for medical reasons, for pure pleasure or for the essential need of food preservation.

It may be stating the obvious to mention that ice-houses were devised to store ice in such a way that it could be available months after nature had naturally frozen the available water and thus improve lifestyles both medically and for food consumed. The importance of a cooling medium can be appreciated when considering the dairy installed to feed the many people on the estate, and where large volumes of milk, butter and cheese required coolness. This many years before mechanical aids and ice became produced artificially.

At a very early stage of civilization a few basic facts were appreciated, one being that both heat and cold could be conserved better if the components were stored en masse; secondly that appropriate available materials could be utilized from that produced by nature; thirdly by the use of the same insulation which conserves heat so in the same way it will preserve cold. The first two points were the basis for the construction of the ice-house, or more simply in the early days, ice-pits – that literally meant a pit dug into the ground large enough to allow for the consolidation of a quantity of solid ice collected during the winter months, and covering this with a simple shelter or roof whether it was of heather, bracken or thatch according to the growth to hand. It was the third point which lead to the converse of the ice preservation – that is the method of keeping items hot such as that which gave rise, initially particularly in Norway, Sweden and America but later to be used throughout the modern world – the hay-box used for cookery and subsequently for transporting hot cooked food great distances a system used when feeding forces in the field et cetera, and a system maintained well into the twentieth century. The principle of insulation was well and truly accepted many centuries ago. There is ample evidence of ice storage facilities in the Middle East a few thousand years ago and even the Romans, that most civilized of societies, considered it an essential ingredient for life in Britain. People from warmer climes entering a cool country still considered it essential for their well-being. The ardour for ice, as indicated by records, waned after the Roman period and wars and strifes affected the interest in this type of building, and others. As an example there were virtually no special buildings for the storage of ice constructed during the seventeenth-century Civil Wars. At the height of the unending series of wars between England and the Continent over the years ice-house construction must have been considered an unnecessary luxury if the records indicating years of building are accepted. With the exception of royalty the gentry probably had more important matters to consider. During times of peace, construction and usage came to the fore and it was not purely a whim of nobility as communal and commercial ice-storage depots were in use, a number for the supply of ice for preservation of foodstuffs being moved from one end of the country to the other. Scotland's production of salmon, for instance, was packed in ice for transportation during the eighteenth century; in fact Scotland was probably the largest user of ice in Great Britain and possibly for the longest period – starting in the mid-eighteenth and by the mid-twentieth century the outer regions were still making use of naturally produced ice. In addition there were many demands for ice during this period for industry as well as for the food preparation trades. The candle makers found it necessary for keeping wax cool during production, and later the chemical industries required ice and latterly for import and export by containerized transport for frozen commodities such as meats. With the introduction of the railways there was an even greater demand when transporting foods.

As indicated by the reference to the Romans in Britain the ice trade was initiated long before the eighteenth century. It had been discovered by the sixteenth century that by the use of compacted ice delicate foods could be produced, many not dissimilar to ice cream as known today – in fact the change in the actual method of manufacture of ice cream is remarkably slight, accepting that in modern times chemicals have replaced the compacted ice component. The introduction of the small modern domestic ice-cream-making machines are based on the principle used as far back as the seventeenth century, and by the following century a dinner host would be sadly lacking if some courses, particularly the desserts, did not incorporate a dish of frozen iced cream, or similar, mainly served in one of the numerous moulds which were widely available. Both ancient and modern methods for the production of such delicacies relied on the basis of agitating the ingredients in an inner container within a very cold outer receptacle. Originally the space between the inner and outer containers would be filled with crushed ice, in modern equipment the ice is replaced by a chemical which is cooled before use. In a similar manner throughout the ages a custard ice-cream, as an example, was made by the use of eggs cooked and heated, and cooled before being inserted into the twin vessels. By the end of the seventeenth century recipes were being written and published by notable cooks including those serving royalty and these followed the pattern above. With the lack of mechanical aids it was the preparation of the ice which was important, sometimes the addition of salt was used and the whole equipment was soundly insulated usually with straw, and this produced a frozen dessert within four hours or so.

The continentals were aware of these intricate food preparations before the British – it could therefore be suggested that the luxury was probably experienced by gentry who travelled on their grand tours and even royalty spent time across the Channel, and thereby expected similar luxurious fare on their return home. In the earliest times such expensive desirable tastes may well have been confined to the 'top-table' diners only.

The small estate ice-house may have been supplied from natural sources or from ponds specially built for the purpose but the commercial demand had to be satisfied from further afield. In the days before ice could be produced mechanically very large quantities were imported from other countries. During the nineteenth century America was exporting ice to

Europe, Asia and as far as Australia but their home demands increased to such a level, once the population had become accustomed to domestic use, there developed a shortage for the home market and other countries had to look elsewhere for supplies. At this point in time the Norwegians filled the gap between the age of natural ice being the only available product and artificial manufacture. By 1860 machinery was being invented to supersede this expensive import and this artificial manufacture has continued ever since.

The above illustrates the importance over the years of these most insignificant buildings, but important they were. Why they have been neglected, apart from the previously mentioned hidden location, is because they did not rank amongst the architectural achievements for any period; they were not designed by architects, even if one or two did fall under the instructions of a few landscape gardeners; in the majority of cases they were purely the responsibility of the 'out-door' staff for construction, maintenance and servicing. Despite their fascinating diversity of designs, all were constructed for a single purpose but illustrating the wide variety of thoughts given to the aim of maximizing the insulation and protection from natural heat and light, serious writings on the subject are rare. There are records listing well over 2,000 traceable ice-houses although this is far from complete as there are many more which are not included in these lists. A large number of detailed surveys have been written by a variety of learned individuals and august bodies including universities, councils, archaeological societies, schools, historical societies and many private individuals, and in some cases the owners, but in each case the results of these findings require a search by people who are interested in the subject. Specific guide books to properties rarely if ever mention the ice-house, and even the great architectural historian Nikolaus Pevsner did not consider them important vernacular buildings worthy of mention when completing his writings on the big estates – at least not within the volumes inspected. Pevsner was by no means alone in this omission as other lengthy descriptions appear to avoid the subject, almost treating ice-houses as an entirely separate being disconnected from the body of the whole.

A review of the information which is available on the subject – a subject of such novelty and importance as to have been the topic of a paper presented to the Royal Society in the mid-seventeenth century – will show interesting figures. For example there were more ice-houses built during the periods of increased wealth, whether it be for titled gentry or merchants; it also indicates geographically where the wealthy estates were concentrated. However, all the figures which can be found do not complete the picture as different areas have been subjected to surveys of varying degrees and importance. In addition, of course, many of the buildings themselves have been lost through the mists of time. Exactly where any single site can be located may be readily available by searching, but there remains the question as to physically making a visit. Some, even though listed, are no longer worth viewing as materially there is no longer anything of note in sight, particularly in the many cases where most of the superstructure has been demolished and the hole filled in; others — and this applies to the majority — are contained within private grounds, but some still remain in the grounds of historic houses many of which are open to the public.

One of the National Trust properties, Hanbury Hall in Worcestershire — and there are others — has a fine example of an eighteenth-century structure which has been preserved and which can be seen by prior arrangement. Here an ice-house, which had the capacity for storing twenty-four tons of ice, is in situ together with the pools for providing the water and a freezing pool. How else would the wine coolers be cooled?

Of the thousands of ice-houses built over the centuries it would be interesting to view a few of these small constructions which were an integral part of the lifestyle of years gone by.

Chapter XX

Treshams of Rushton

Throughout history man has constructed buildings to satisfy his needs whether simply for protection against the elements, for security and defence, to be fashionable, to compete with contemporaries, or for his own gratification, or indeed to transmit a message to others. Many of the buildings, both great and small, in Britain have been built over the centuries by or for individuals who have taken a pride in pronouncing to the world their thoughts on style or appearance and this has provided a legacy probably second to none throughout Europe. Crofts and the like can still be seen as the rudimentary shelter, as indeed can many of the great castles built during the periods of unending internal – or in some cases international – strife. The large country houses represent the various stages of fashion and illustrate how the differing gentry vied one against the other to show wealth and power, whereas the structures representing a message can be seen at a number of different properties and are usually small by comparison.

The 'message' builders have provided the basis of their story in a number of places within the British Isles. One such building in Leicestershire takes the form of a church on the estate of Staunton Harold. Here, during the period when Cromwell was on the rampage in the seventeenth century and was fully expecting the gentry to financially support his cause, Sir Robert Shirley chose to spend his money on the rebuilding of the family church rather than delegate it to raising an army for what he considered to be an unnecessary act. It cost Sir Robert dear as he lost his life at an early age whilst in the Tower of London.

This part of the book is not however about Robert Shirley – although his story is well worth the telling – but it is about another landowner and his exploits about fifty years before the building of Staunton Harold church. This story is about a few buildings erected within the county next to and south of Leicestershire, that is in Northamptonshire.

The Tresham family, although well documented from John during the latter part of the fifteenth century to William of the mid-seventeenth century when the baronetcy became extinct, may not be very well known but they were much involved in events in history during 200 years and some members of the nine generations were interesting characters. They left for posterity a number of widely differing buildings from the principal family seat of Rushton Hall to the small buildings, declaring a message, of the Triangular Lodge and Lyveden New Bield.

Perhaps Thomas of Rushton and Sywell was the founder of this particular dynasty and his son William, who married Isabel, daughter of Sir William Vaux of Harrowden, may have created a record by holding a parliamentary career which extended over twenty-six years and sixteen parliaments. He was involved in the legal affairs for Henry VI but years later was murdered by the retainers of the Lancastrian Edmund Gray near Moulton whilst on his way to meet Richard, Duke of York in 1450. His son, who became Sir Thomas, was with his father when the cruel act took place, but it did not deter Thomas from being involved in life at Court. Like his father before him, he became Speaker of the House of Commons. Being devoted to Henry VI, in whose household young Thomas had been brought up, he was later appointed Comptroller for the King and also acted as Member of Parliament representing Buckinghamshire. Sir Thomas's wife was Margaret daughter of Lord Zouch of Harringworth. After the Battle of Tewkesbury the troubled times continued and, although a pardon was promised by Edward IV, Sir Thomas was beheaded along with other Lancastrians in 1471. The next heir was John who married Elizabeth daughter of Sir James Harrington of Hornby in Lancashire, and John fortunately had his father's estates restored to the family.

As the names of the head of family alternated for five generations, the next in line was another Thomas and he was a staunch Roman Catholic who married twice; his first wife was Anne, daughter of Sir William – later Lord – Parr of Horton, and secondly Lettice, relic of Sir Robert Lee. For many years he accepted his position very seriously and acted as Sheriff for the county more than once; during his terms of office he received licence to empark about 420 acres of land, part of which was at Lyveden. Because of his religious faith Thomas joined the Queen Mary faction on the death of King Edward before dying in 1558 or 9, after a very full life; he was buried in St Peter's Church in Rushton. John followed in his father's footsteps socially and married Eleanor Catesby. It was John who subsequently started the construction of the 'New Building' at Lyveden of which more will be mentioned later.

On the death of John there followed the last of the Thomases who was born about 1543, and married Muriel, daughter of Sir Robert Throckmorton of Coughton Court in Warwickshire; it should be mentioned here that a sister of Thomas married a gentleman by the name of Vaux – not the first intermarriage between the two families. It may be of interest to point out that the names of the marriage partners have deliberately been mentioned being such as Vaux, Catesby, Throckmorton, as they were some of the names of the infamous people involved in the Gunpowder Plot of 1605; as indeed was the name Tresham.

Thomas was a minor, being only fifteen years old, when he succeeded his grandfather in the Rushton and Lyveden estates. Advantage of his minority appears to have been taken to bring him up a Protestant and in 1573–4 he served as Sheriff of Northamptonshire and in 1577 was knighted. In 1580 Thomas announced his return to Catholicism, said to have taken place by the influence of the Jesuit Robert Parsons. During the following year, for harbouring Edmund Campion, he was tried in the Star Chamber and committed to seven years' confinement, first in the Fleet, then in his own home at Hoxton and then at Ely. He was duly released on bail but again imprisoned for recusancy (refusing to conform with the Established Church) in 1597 and 1599, and annually had to pay enormous fines. His intervals of freedom must have been employed in extensive building work including a market-house at Rothwell and the Triangular Lodge under the direction of John Thorpe. Thomas proclaimed James I at Northampton in 1603 which indicates that he remained actively involved with the Crown. When he died on 11 September 1605 like his grandfather he was buried at St Peter's Church, Rushton. The date of death was significant in that it was a couple of months before what is now known as 'bonfire night'.

Thomas's eldest son was given the name Francis and he married Anne, daughter of Sir John Tufton of Hothfield in Kent by whom he had two daughters called Lucy and Elizabeth; the latter married Sir George Heneage. Francis had two sisters one being Frances who married the 9th Baron Stourton, and the other Elizabeth who married William Parker, Baron Monteagle and Morley. There was also a brother called Lewis who was knighted in 1612, and it was Lewis who eventually inherited the estates after the death of Francis, but unfortunately Lewis only had one son after whose death the baronetcy became extinct. It is significant that Francis had two titled brothers-in-law as that fact alone may well be the reason why the Gunpowder Plot failed. There was no doubt that Francis was well involved with the 'plotters' and that some of his father's money – for which he made many appeals – was used to finance the treacherous actions, but on his father's death his attitude appears to have changed and with the lives of two close relatives being at risk there is, on the face of it, a case for the belief that Francis really did betray other members of the Plot. As in so many events of history the truth may never be clear and categorical, but, nevertheless, although Francis was not treated as a traitor at the time, after his death his corpse was decapitated and his head set over the gate of Northampton. Justice was seen to be done in those days – or was it? Francis' lands were forfeited although later eventually restored to brother Lewis.

Appreciating the fact that this book is on the subject of *People of Property*, in order to fully realize the potential of the people it may be an advantage to briefly incorporate the types of buildings for which they were responsible. In this story it is particularly the buildings which can be remembered and seen, and which will continue as part of the heritage of the country, rather than just a memory of those mortals long since departed this world. On the contrary there is with the Tresham family the annual reminder on the fifth of November that such characters did exist even if nearly 400 years ago. It is gratifying to know that so many of the Tresham-instigated buildings remain and most are preserved for future generations to enjoy. Some have already been mentioned above and there are others. The main family seat of Rushton Hall was referred to within the paragraph appertaining to Thomas and William of the fifteenth century, with the building begun about 1500 but modified during successive generations. It is now in the hands of the Royal National Institute for the Blind being used as a school for blind children. Hiding places for secretive accommodation for supporters of the Catholic faith during the periods of persecution are still to be found within the building.

It is quite remarkable that a landowner should be so fanatical about erecting new buildings during a period in history recorded as being one of those when unrest amongst the populace was almost at its worst. The sixteenth and early seventeenth centuries became renowned for problems; problems which developed from more than one cause. There was the lack of stability within the ruling monarchs, the enforcing of the new religion, the extreme usage and poor conditions of the workers, and the continuation of the enclosing of land thus depriving the lower order of natural foods, pasture for their limited livestock and fuels. The village of Brigstock which was in the region of one of the Tresham manors at Lyveden was a site where protests were held; this was not entirely the fault of the Treshams although Sir Thomas in particular was very unpopular because of his treatment of tenants, but also about the same time such as Sir Robert Cecil emparked part of the Rockingham Forest preventing the wild deer from being used as food by the locals. Neither Treshams nor Cecils were of course hesitant about moving homes of peasants – even if it involved a whole village – should those buildings of the lower orders spoil the view from the mansion.

In addition there was during this period the problems of enforcing the new faith. Most of the executions of Catholics took place before 1580 but nevertheless between 1581 and 1603 something like 130 priests and sixty lay people were executed; fines, taxation and loss of opportunities for high office also had drastic effects. Searches of houses where supporters of Catholics were suspected would be brutal, and horrific tortures were performed in an attempt to obtain confessions. Frequently these tortures were followed by hideous deaths. And despite all these difficulties a man of substance pursued what was almost a career in building the profane.

In fact Sir Thomas Tresham, who is the main person of this narrative, chose a most difficult time to change his faith and thus alienate so many people of authority. A decision which cost him considerable sums financially and many years of freedom; and even after release from prison he was confined to virtual house-arrest, or at best restricted to travel limited to within five miles of his residence. In fact Sir Thomas was never the builder of a large house but devoted his efforts to modifying manors and had constructed a number of relatively small buildings. He instigated the building of a county library, a town house in Rothwell before his change of faith, between his terms of imprisonment the construction of the Triangular Lodge and some years later the new building of a lodge or supplementary house at Lyveden. It is not surprising that he accumulated debts in the region of £11,000 by the time of his death as, apart from the fines he evoked estimated to be about £8,000 pounds, there were the costs of his building obsessions and he had six daughters who required marriage settlements; he also entertained in a lavish fashion.

The buildings being modified were the two manors, one at Rushton and the other the old hall at Lyveden, and also under construction the Hawkesfield Lodge, improvements to Rushton Church, a dam at Pipewell and new bridges at Rothwell and Rushton. There are two particular buildings of fanciful design which may today seem completely out of character with anything of the period but which were perhaps not so outlandish in the age of extreme enthusiasm for buildings at the time. One is the Triangular Lodge and the other Lyveden New Bield as it is now called, the former in honour of the Trinity, the latter the Passion.

It would be interesting to know exactly where the inspiration for these two particular buildings emanated. The religious implications of the triadic form may well have come from the devout Sir Thomas but converting that to the structural application may have required outside influence. Symbolic buildings were the fashion of the moment and some source of technical ability may well have come from a man called Thorpe. There was a Thomas Thorpe who died about 1596 and he was the principal mason at Kirby Hall in Northamptonshire; this was one of the most expensive of the Elizabethan houses of the period built for Sir Humphrey Stafford. John his son is perhaps the most famous name amongst the officers of works in Queen Elizabeth's reign – probably because his famous book of architectural drawings was saved and is in the Soane museum. His name has correctly, or incorrectly, been associated with many of the great building projects of this era. The book gives a number of designs for the quaint, the symbolic and religious buildings including the triangular Longford Castle in Wiltshire with three corner towers being the medieval symbol for the Trinity, begun in about 1580 for Sir Thomas Gorges.

Near the town of Oundle, a few hundred yards from the old Tresham home at Lyveden, stands the unfinished 'New Bield' begun in the 1590s in the shape of a Greek Cross. It could have been intended as a lodge or subsidiary house with many delicately carved emblems of the Passion. Unroofed and standing open to the elements it is within grassed lands in which there are faint traces of the ambitious garden layout including mounds, terraces, a series of canals and an extensive diamond-shaped patterned knot garden; it is one of the oldest surviving garden layouts in England. It is now in the care of the National Trust.

The Triangular Lodge, which is preserved by English Heritage, stands within the grounds of the former main house of Sir Thomas at Rushton – there are separate entrances to the Lodge and to the Hall. The extraordinary small building, although referred to as a lodge may possibly have been intended as a banqueting hall rather than as a lodge. Construction work progressed slowly as it took place over four years with the ironstone being obtained from a quarry newly opened in addition to those which existed at Pipewell, Pilton and Weldon. Building work commenced about 1594 and it has been suggested that it may well have been one of the meeting places for the Gunpowder plotters but how that deed can be reconciled with the 'message' the building is attempting to give is difficult to understand. The 'message' is in no doubt as being the celebration of the Trinity. The representative number of three is illustrated in every conceivable fashion from the basic three-sided building, each side being thirty-three feet long, of three floors, to three gables on each side, to the inscription around the building having thirty-three letters contained within the three equal sections. The use of three continues in every conceivable way and the whole is eccentric but a unique work of art which should be seen to be believed.

The last two mentioned buildings are as memorials to the Tresham family, or particularly to Sir Thomas. They are outstanding and will remain a testament to a man of faith who could hardly have chosen a more dangerous time in history to flaunt his devotion.

Chapter XXI

Clifford Family

Chapter VII of this book relates the story of a remarkable woman who started life of lowly birth and around eighty years later, having married four times, at the time of her death justified the title Elizabeth, Countess of Shrewsbury. That was the story of 'Bess' of Hardwick. This chapter tells the story of another woman who was born, far from lowly, nearly twenty years before the death of Bess, but both women can best be described as indomitable.

Bess was born in the county of Derbyshire, whereas the new story heroine is Anne Clifford of the north-western counties, born of titled nobility who acquired three titles in her own right from two marriages. The county name of Cumberland is associated with the Cliffords, albeit the earls of that name survived less than 120 years, through four generations. The name of Cumberland has regrettably been lost because of twentieth-century administrative changes, but gained the name Cumbria to absorb Cumberland, Westmoreland and Furness; the former name did have prominence for both dukes and earls. The dukedoms lasted somewhat longer than the earldoms, in fact for about 270 years; it was awarded to nobles such as Prince Rupert in the seventeenth century, the husband of Queen Anne, a son of George II, brother, son and great-grandson of George III, before being lost to the Hanovarians and subsequently being finally struck off the peerage roll in 1917.

But it is the earldom which is the subject of this narrative and in order to provide an insight into the character of the great Lady Anne Clifford it may be of interest to give brief details of a few of her predecessors but restricting the comments to the earls and their immediate family. The accompanying family 'tree' shows the line from 1st to 5th Earls indicating that the 5th Earl was nephew of the 3rd Earl, Lady Anne's father. There were many marriages to families of title and this increased the holdings within the family; much in the way of wealth and possessions was gained by this means and possessions, particularly of land, provided more wealth and a gaining of power.

Henry de Clifford, 10th Baron of Westmoreland m. (1) Anne St John m. (2) ?

Henry de Clifford, m. (1) Margaret Talbot   other
1st Earl   d.s.p.   children
(1493–1542)   m. (2) Margaret Percy

Henry de Clifford, m. (1) Eleanor Brandon m. (2) Anne Dacre
2nd Earl   (d.1547)   (d. 1581)
(d.1570)

Margaret (b.1540) Henry Charles   Sir Ingram Clifford Knt 4 daughters
m. Henry Stanley   d.s.p.

George Clifford, m. Margaret Russell   **Francis Clifford,**   3 daughters
3rd Earl   (d. 1616)   **4th Earl**
1558–1605)   m. Grisold Hughes

Anne Clifford m. (1) Richard   m.(2) Philip   **Henry** m. Lady Frances
(1590–1676)   Sackville,   Herbert,   **Clifford,**   Cecil
                3rd Earl of   4th Earl of   **5th Earl**
                Dorset   Pembroke &   (1591–1643)
                (1589–1624)   Montgomery
                                (d. 1650)
                                d.s.p

3 sons   2 daughters   Elizabeth m. Richard Boyle   other
                                                                children

Henry de Clifford, the 1st Earl's father, was not only 10th Baron of
Westmoreland but also held the titles as 14th Lord Clifford and 1st Baron
Vesci; the 1st Earl's mother is recorded as de Clifford's first wife – Anne,
daughter of Sir John St John of Bletsho – but records of his other wife
have not been traced.

Henry, born about 1493, was the eldest son and as was the norm in
the North of England at the time of the Cliffords, wars of many kinds,
both local in the manner of fracas and more serious encounters with
invading Scots, occupied most people's time and resources. The Cliffords
performed their duties financially and provided men-at-arms for any incursion of the day – certainly this applied to the four years from 1522
when Henry was Sheriff for the county of Yorkshire. The title Earl of

Cumberland was awarded to Henry during the year King Henry VIII made his illegitimate son, Henry Blount, Duke of Richmond and Somerset. Henry Clifford was like his contemporary nobles in that he frequently disputed and enforced his rights whether by contention over authoritative rights of Carlisle Castle, or merely disputing condition of office for the Sheriff of the county. With the many problems created by the King and his series of dissolved marriages, Clifford was involved in the divorce of 1530. Some years later there was an interesting event when the English Pilgrimage of Grace, lead by the infamous Robert Aske, was besieging strongholds in the northern districts, and Clifford rescued from Bolton Abbey confines to the safety of Skipton Castle a son's wife and child for which devotion the earl received into his possession several manors and lands, including Bolton Abbey, being some lands previously owned by the Church before the monasteries were dissolved. The following year Henry was made a KG. After his death in either 1542 or 1543, the 1st Earl was buried at either Appleby or Skipton, but records are not very clear on this point. They are however clear on the subject of his two marriages and the benefits from them. His first wife was Margaret Talbot the daughter of the 4th Earl of Shrewsbury (another Bess of Hardwick connection) – there was no issue from that union – but his second wife, by whom Henry the next holder of the title Cumberland was born, was another Margaret, a daughter of Henry Percy, 5th Earl of Northumberland hence the Cliffords became lords of all Craven. In addition to Henry and four daughters there was Ingram who received a knighthood but produced no children.

Henry the 2nd Earl, before his father's death, was conferred with the honour of Knight of the Bath at the time of Anne Boleyn's coronation; he was then styled Lorde (*sic*) Clifford. On his father's death he continued to hold the titles of Lord Clifford (16th), Baron of Westmoreland (12th), and Baron Vesci (3rd). His first wife, Eleanor, was a daughter of one of the most powerful of the gentry, Charles Brandon, Duke of Suffolk, and she produced Margaret who ultimately married Henry Stanley who later became 4th Earl of Derby. Sons Henry and Charles both died young. Henry's second wife was Anne, daughter of William, 3rd Lord Dacre of Gilsland and by this marriage there were two sons who became the 3rd and 4th Earls of Cumberland; there were also three daughters. Of these three, one of them, Frances, married Philip, Lord Wharton, but the other two, being named Eleanor and Mary, both died young. It was perhaps unfortunate that about this period in history Queen Elizabeth I was 'rearranging' her advisers and consultants – favouring much younger men for many offices – and subsequently custody of properties was being gained and lost; in this respect Lord Dacre lost much of his inheritance which was conferred on the Duke of Norfolk. The 2nd Earl of Cumberland died at Brougham Castle and was buried at Skipton.

Records appertaining to the 3rd Earl, George, appear to be remarkably inadequate apart from the known marriage to Lady Margaret Russell, third daughter of Francis, 2nd Earl of Bedford, from which union there was one child named Anne. The 3rd Earl is perhaps best remembered for his plundering of the Spanish Main, and his involvement with the Armada. More detail will be written later about Anne as the main topic of this story; let it suffice, at this stage, to mention the next two Cliffords, which includes the last of the line.

As stated above, the 4th Earl, Francis, was brother of George, 3rd Earl, and this second son of Anne Dacre married Grisold, daughter of Thomas Hughes of Uxbridge and widow of Edward Nevill, Lord Bergavenny. They had one child who became 5th Earl of Cumberland and his marriage was to yet another member of the hierarchy being to Lady Frances Cecil, daughter of the most important Robert, Earl of Salisbury, a descendant of Lord Burghley. That same year, when Henry Clifford was about twenty years of age, he was created Knight of the Bath, and less than ten years later he was appointed a member of the Council of the North, a group consisting of nobles in the district. Their only daughter Elizabeth married Richard Boyle, Earl of Dungarvan, a member of the famous Irish titled family, and she became Countess of Cork; all the other children died young. Although the 5th Earl died in middle age he lead an energetic life holding positions of office such as joint Lord Lieutenant for Northumberland, Cumberland and Westmoreland, at that time separate counties, during which time he occupied Carlisle Castle for the King's cause; in addition he acted for the King at York and became Commander-in-Chief for the county. He actually died in York but was buried in Skipton Church. As a notable amateur writer his memory lives on as some of his manuscripts are held in the Bodleian. On his death the earldom became extinct and with the absence of any male children the large family estates in the north reverted to Lady Anne Clifford under the terms of the will of her father, the 3rd Earl of Cumberland.

At this time Anne was married to Philip, 4th Earl of Pembroke, and Philip was made Earl of Montgomery prior to his marriage to Anne and thereafter the earls have born the double title, thus Lady Anne, Countess of Dorset eventually – that is seven years after the death of the 5th Earl – became Lady Anne Clifford, Countess of Dorset, Pembroke and Montgomery.

Neither of the marriages of Lady Anne appear to have been romantically happy even given the increase in title and possessions, although it is reputed that she greatly admired her first husband. Her most devoted personal affiliation probably remained with her mother, the former Margaret Russell, and it was at her Mother's home at Augustine Fryers in London that she was married to Richard Sackville 3rd Earl of Dorset. Anne was about nineteen years of age, and he no more than a year older. The young couple lived at his home of Knole in Kent and today there are preserved a few of her diaries written whilst living there for fourteen years. Unfortunately the Sackville family trait must have been one of spending money realized from the sale of inherited effects and Richard's predecessor held the family title and wealth for merely one year. During the fourteen years of Richard's incumbency, the first few years were devoted to dispensing with the fortune inherited then raising a mortgage on the property and selling the London lands, after which an almost continual battle raged between husband and wife in the hope that Lady Anne's assets in the northern counties could be converted to cash. This thought created two problems; the first being that Lady Anne herself who had no intention of relinquishing title of her family lands, and the second was the doubt of ownership of the estates. Her father had died four years before the wedding and Anne's mother, on behalf of her daughter had, during the intervening years, devoted nearly all her considerable resources in arranging litigation to obtain ownership of the estates. Nevertheless it is reputed that the Earl connived many times to persuade his wife to provide funds to satisfy his gambling debts, even to the extent of exiling her from the marital home or excluding her from the company of her daughter; all attempts of which failed. The Earl of Dorset's death occurred when he was in his mid-thirties and this brought to a close an unhappy period in the life of Lady Anne, and her happiness was not improved by neither the death at an early age of her three sons – although her two daughters both later married into titled families – nor by the death of her mother which took place about eight years prior to the death of husband number one. As Lady Anne had lost her legal stalwart with the death of her mother she continued to handle lawsuits against her Uncle Francis and a cousin, all regarding the family estates. Another similarity with Bess who devoted much of her time and money to litigation.

The second marriage did not take place until six years later when Lady Anne married Philip Herbert, 4th Earl of Pembroke and Montgomery, and the family home was, like the new husband, of a very different nature. Wilton House being the ancestral seat of the Pembroke family was first built by Sir William Herbert, 1st Earl of Pembroke and it was on the lands given to the Herberts by Henry VIII after the Dissolution of the Monasteries, formerly abbey land. King Henry was a patron of Herbert. The marriage took place at Chenies in Buckinghamshire in 1630, by which time her ladyship was nearly forty years of age and there were no children by the union. The marriage did however last about twenty years and when it came to a natural end by the death of Herbert, Lady Anne took advantage of her marital freedom and all the benefits of her vast wealth and lands and absorbed herself, during the last twenty-six years of her life, in the subject she must have treated almost as a passion – the building or rebuilding of many of her properties and indeed creating new buildings for the social good of so many of her devotees.

One of the first castles to fall under her spell was her birthplace of Skipton which henceforth remained an important Clifford seat. Skipton in modern times is the site where many modern roads converge and running through the town is the main Leeds-Liverpool canal. The castle of Norman origin was built initially by Robert de Romille and one of the gateways remains as of original Norman construction. Much of the rest of the building is of fourteenth to seventeenth centuries thanks to the Cliffords. There were many other castles which, in brief, included Brougham, and Brough a castle built by William II on the site of a Roman fort; and Pendragon which was once owned by Sir Hugh de Morville one of the murderers of Thomas à Becket in the twelfth century; later in the fourteenth century it was partly destroyed by the Scots. It is recorded that Lady Anne stayed in this castle in 1663, but the fortification is again in a ruinous state. Barden Tower and a number of churches and chapels also received her attention including the chapels of Brougham, Ninekirk, Mallerstang and Barden. Appleby, the old county town of Westmoreland on the River Eden, received special devotion with the founding of St Anne's Hospital as almshouses still in use by retired ladies, and more restoration work was completed to both the castle and the church of St Michael in Bondgate and of course the partly Norman church of St Lawrence in which there are the tombs to mother and daughter. The town castle existed during the early part of the twelfth century, fell to the invading Scots army of William the Lion, and came into Clifford ownership late thirteenth century. The keep which Anne restored is said to be larger than William's White Tower at the Tower of London. Part of the rebuilding was completed by Anne's son-in-law, the Earl of Thanet, using some of the stone from other castles such as Brough and Brougham. Commercially the castle is open to the public and houses Clifford family portraits including one of Lady Anne. It is maintained under the auspices of the Rare Breeds Survival Trust and on display are collections of birds of many types, together with Roman armour and even rare bicycles. At each end of Boroughgate a cross shows Lady Anne's motto of 'Retain your loyalty, preserve your rights'. There is little doubt that this lady performed both duties without question. Further work was initiated to the almshouses originally built and endowed by Anne's mother at Bethmesley. This philanthropic work extended beyond the Yorkshire county and in the little church of Beckington in Somerset a monument was raised to her former tutor, the Taunton-born poet Samuel Daniel who for the last sixteen years of his life lived on a farm near Rudge, which is near the Somerset and Wiltshire borders. Perhaps the most poignant of Lady Anne's construction works was a simple pillar erected on the road between Penrith and Appleby at a place where she and her mother last saw each other.

In widowhood her Ladyship dressed in a most frugal manner and made it known to all and sundry that she opposed unnecessary expenditure on personal attire for both dress and sustenance and was clearly against the luxury of items such as wine. Apparently she had a sympathetic nature to those around her, even generous, unless she did not receive that which she considered her just rewards. This was very evident when dealing with legalities and in a number of instances she would spare no expense to prove her right on, what to many, would have been a minor issue. Lady Anne's mother, Margaret, Countess of Cumberland, illustrated over a period of years the value of taking advantage of the accepted right of women to pursue their inheritance in the courts; this applied to the actions filed attempting to obtain such rights against close relations resulting in a lengthy Chancery action. Lady Anne followed in her mother's footsteps and had no compunction when dealing with legal matters. There is the classic instance, much quoted in many writings, of the expensive legal wrangles against a man called Murgatroyd of East Riddlesden Hall who was the tenant of premises near Skipton. In addition to the rent annually there was due to her Ladyship a payment of one hen, this being arranged by customary right during the previous 400 years – perhaps a relic of the tithe payment system! Murgatroyd decided, for one reason or another, to overlook this due payment and the claim was pursued at the York Assizes. Lady Anne did receive her just reward of one hen but the cost to each of the parties was estimated to be £240 with the legal fees – in the early seventeenth century this represented a considerable sum. Perhaps an insight into the mentality of the girl with inbred ethics passed through so many generations of nobles.

Having in many ways a frugal attitude there was little in the restricted expenditure during the latter years of her life when she lived in the style of a medieval magnate. As chatelaine to so many properties the rebuilt castles were used and lived in by alternation for almost fixed lengths of time each year. During her young days Anne attended the Court of Queen Elizabeth and that would be good grounding for learning the ultimate in living styles. It is recorded that the movement between one property and another was somewhat on the style of a military operation and the entourage would consist of herself in a litter, followers being the local gentry accompanied by tenants and neighbours. Treating her staff as a family there would be, in addition to the basic indoor and outdoor workers, two gentlemen, eleven other male servants, a male housekeeper, and a male clerk. Lady Anne was one of the few women to hold office in the north of England generally regarded as the prerogative of men, by holding positions of Justice of the Peace, County Sheriff, and she was certainly High Sheriff of Westmoreland in both 1660 and 1670.

It is evident that Lady Anne learned much from the past and the history of the family, and she perhaps made a deliberate decision to spend her time and wealth on her beloved northern estates. She, and to some degree the earls following her father, the 3rd Earl, were aware of the excessive costs of attending the Royal Courts and although the Earls of Cumberland were one of the few remaining families loyal to the monarch, the high living at Court brought them to near financial ruin. The Earl made various attempts to cover funds including privateering but most measures failed as the bulk of any bounty was commandeered by the Crown.

Lady Anne Clifford, Countess of Dorset, Pembroke and Montgomery, after a widowhood which lasted nearly twenty-six years, died aged eighty-seven at one of her great restored castles at Brougham. She was finally buried in the vault which she had built especially for the purpose at the church of St Lawrence in Appleby; the church in which Margaret her mother was entombed and for whom there is an alabaster effigy. This was yet another building which had benefited from Anne's tender loving care.

Bibliography

AA, *Hand-Picked Tours in Britain*, Drive Publications Ltd, 1977.

AA, *Illustrated Guide to Britain*, Drive Publications Ltd, 1971.

AA, *Illustrated Guide to Britain's Coast*, Drive Publications Ltd, 1984.

AA, *Treasures of Britain*, Drive Publications Ltd, 1968.

Adair, John, *By the Sword Divided*, Century Publishing Co Ltd, London, 1983.

Airs, Malcolm, *The Tudor & Jacobean Country House*, Sutton Publishing Ltd, Stroud, Glos, 1995.

Anthony, John, *Discovering Period Gardens*, Shire Publications Ltd, Aylesbury, 1972.

Baines, Edward, *History of the Cotton Manufacture in Great Britain*, Frank Cass & Co Ltd, 1835.

Barnard, Derek, *Merrily to Frendsbury – A History of the Parish of Frindsbury*, Rochester City, 1996.

Barnett, Correlli, *Marlborough*, Eyre Methuen Limited, London, 1974.

Beamon, S. P., & Roaf, S., *The Ice-Houses of Britain*, Routledge, London, 1990.

Bird, Vivian, *Exploring the West Midlands*, B T Batsford Ltd, London, 1977.

Birmingham, *Weekly Post*, 1926.

Bisgrove, Richard, *The National Trust Book of the English Garden*, National Trust, 1990.

Black, J. B., *History of England – The Reign of Elizabeth*, Oxford University Press, 1992.

Blakeway, Rev J. B., *Notes on Kinlet*, Shropshire Historical and Archaeological Society, 1908.

Bradley, E. T., *The Life of Arabella Stuart*, Richard Bentley & Son, London, 1889.

Briggs, A. S. A., *A Social History of England*, BCA, London, 1994.

Bryant, Julius, *Robert Adam – Architect of Genius*, English Heritage, 1992.

Burford, *The Church of St Mary, Burford, Shropshire*, Church Publication, 1990.

Burke's, *Peerage and Baronetage*, 105th Edition, 1970.

Butler, Ewan, *The Cecils*, Frederick Muller, London, 1964.

Chandler, John, *John Leland's Itinerary*, Alan Sutton Publishing Ltd, Stroud, 1993.

Coats, Peter, *Great Gardens of Britain*, Artus Publishing Co, London, 1977.

Davies, Godfrey, *History of England – The Early Stuarts*, Oxford University Press, 1991.

Dixon-Scott, J., *England Under Trust*, Alexander Maclehose & Co, London, 1937.

Eagle, D. & Stephens, M., *Illustrated Literary Guide to GB & Ireland*, Oxford U P 1981.

Edwards, E., *Hen & Chicken*, Birmingham, 1878.

Fedden, Robin, *The National Trust – Past & Present*, Jonathan Cape, London, 1968.

Fedden, Robin, and Joekes, Rosemary, *The National Trust Guide*, Jonathan Cape, London, 1973.

Fothergill, Brian, *The Mitred Earl*, Century Hutchinson, London, 1974.

Fraser, Antonia, *The Gunpowder Plot*, Weidenfeld & Nicolson, 1996.

Fraser, Antonia, *Mary Queen of Scots*, Weidenfeld & Nicolson, London, 1969.

Girouard, Mark, *Life in the English Country House*, Yale University Press, London, 1978.

Greeves, Lydia and Trinick, Michael, *The National Trust Guide*, The National Trust, London, 1973.

Hammerton, J. A., *Harmsworth's Universal Encyclopedia*, Educational Books, London, 1920s.

Hammond, R. J. W., & Lowther, K. E., *Complete Dorset and Wiltshire*, Ward Lock Ltd, London, 1976.

Havins, Peter J. Neville, *Portrait of Worcestershire*, Robert Hale & Company, London, 1974.

Head, Victor, *Hereward*, Alan Sutton Publishing Limited, Stroud, 1995.

Hessayon, Dr D. G., *The Armchair Book of the Garden*, pbi Publications, Waltham Cross, 1986.

Hibbert, Christopher, *George III: A Personal History*, Viking, London, 1998.

Hibbert, Christopher, *The English – A Social History 1066–1945*, Grafton Books, 1987.

Hibbert, Christopher, *Cavaliers and Roundheads*, English Civil War, HarperCollins, 1993.

Hopkins, Mary Alden, *Dr Johnson's Lichfield*, Peter Owen Ltd, London, 1956.

Inglis-Jones, Elisabeth, *The Lord of Burghley*, Faber & Faber, London, 1964.

Jones, A. E., *The Story of Carshalton House – now St Philomena's*, Sutton Borough, London, 1980.

Kain, R. J. P. & Prince, H. C., *The Tithe Surveys of England & Wales*, Cambridge, 1985.

Kerrigan, Michael, *Who Lies Where*, BCA, London, 1995.

Lambert, Anthony, *Settle to Carlisle*, Parragon, Bristol, 1997.

Lane, Margaret, *The Tale of Beatrix Potter – a Biography*, Frederick Warne & Co Ltd, London 1946.

Laurence, Anne, *Women in England 1500–1760*, Weidenfeld & Nicolson, London, 1994.

Leach, Francis, *The County Seats of Shropshire*, Shrewsbury, 1891.

Leatherbarrow, J. S., *Worcestershire*, B T Batsford Ltd, London, 1974.

Lees-Milne, James, *National Trust Guide – Buildings*, B T Batsford Ltd, London, 1948.

Leighton, Stanley, *Shropshire Houses; Past and Present*, London 1901.

McCormick, Rev. M., Article, St George's, Dunster, Somerset, 1960s.

McLaughlin, Rev. E. C. L., *Burford Parish Church (Salop) and the Cornewall Monument*, 1912.

Mackie, J. D., *History of England – The Earlier Tudors*, Oxford University Press, 1992.

Marshall Cavendish, *Encyclopedia of Gardening*, Marshall Cavendish, Crawley, England, 1969.

Mee, Arthur, *The King's England – Staffordshire*, Hodder & Stoughton, 1938.

Mee, Arthur, *The King's England – Worcestershire*, Hodder & Stoughton, 1938.

Morgan, Kenneth O., *Illustrated History of Britain*, Oxford University Press, 1992.

Morrill, J., *Illustrated History of Tudor & Stuart Britain*, Oxford University Press, Oxford 1996.

Mowl, Timothy, *Horace Walpole The Great Outsider*, John Murray, London, 1996.

Muir, Richard, *The Lost Villages of Britain*, Michael Joseph, London, 1982.

Murray, Peter, *A Village in Wiltshire*, PMA Lacock, 1975.

Murray, Peter and Linda, *Dictionary of Art and Artists*, Penguin Books, London, 1959.

National Trust, *Properties of the*, The National Trust, London, 1973.

Neillands, Robin, *The Wars of the Roses*, Cassell plc, London, 1992.

Norris, Ian & Bohm, Dorothy, *A Celebration of London*, Andre Deutsh, London, 1984.

Palmer, Alan, *The Life and Times of George IV*, Weidenfeld & Nicolson, London, 1972.

Parker, John, *A Guide to the Lake District & its County – Cumbria*, Bartholomew, London, 1977.

Pearson, John, *Stags and Serpents*, Macmillan, London, 1983.

Bibliography

Pevsner, Nikolaus, *The Buildings of England – Shropshire*, Penguin Books Ltd, Middlesex, 1958.

Pevsner, Nikolaus, *The Buildings of England – Herefordshire*, Penguin-Books, Middlesex, 1958.

Prebble, John, *The Highland Clearances*, Penguin Books, 1963.

Property Guides for individual properties.

Richards, J. M., *NT Book of English Architecture*, NT & Weidenfeld & Nicolson, London, 1981.

Roberts, Sir Samuel, Bt, *Cockley Cley Iceni Village & Museum*, The museum, 1988.

Ross, Estelle, *Oliver Cromwell*, George G Harrap & Co, London, 1915.

Rowse, A. L., *The Early Churchills*, Harper & Brothers, New York, 1956.

Salter, Mike, *The Castles of Hereford and Worcester*, Folly Publications, Malvern, 1989.

Sampson, George, *The Concise Cambridge History of English Literature*, University Press, 1945.

Senior, Michael, *The Age of Myth and Legend*, Weidenfeld & Nicolson, London, 1980.

Soames, Mary, *Clementine Churchill*, Cassell of London, 1979.

Stephen, Sir L., & Lee, Sir S., *The Dictionary of National Biography*, Oxford University Press, 1921–2.

Street, Pamela, *The Illustrated Portrait of Wiltshire*, Robert Hale Ltd, London, 1971.

Stroud, Dorothy, *Henry Holland – His Life and Architecture*, Country Life Ltd, London, 1966.

Summerson, John, *Architecture in Britain 1530–1830*, Yale University Press, London, 1993.

Tennison, Alfred Lord, *The Lord of Burleigh*, 1833.

Thacker, Christopher, *The Genius of Gardening*, Weidenfeld and Nicolson, London 1994.

Thomas, G. S., *Gardens of the National Trust*, The NT and Weidenfeld and Nicolson, 1979.

Thompson, Nicholas, *Moccas Court*, Country Life, November, 1976.

Timpson, John, *Timpson's England*, Jarrold Publishing, 1987.

Treasure, John, *Burford House Gardens – History and Garden Guide*, Treasures of Tenbury, 1995.

Trevelyan, G. M., *English Social History*, Longman Group Ltd, London, 1978.

Trevelyan, G. M., *England Under Queen Anne – Blenheim*, Longmans, Green and Co, 1930.

Turner, Barry, *A Place in the Country*, Sphere Books Limited, London, 1972.

Verney, Peter, *The Standard Bearer*, Hutchinson, London, 1963.

Waterson, Merlin, *The National Trust, The First Hundred Years*, BBC Ent. Ltd and NT (Ent), 1994.

Watkins, David, *A History of Western Architecture*, Laurence King, 1986.

Watson, J. Steven, *History of England – The Reign of George III*, Oxford University Press, 1992.

Watson, S. J., *The Cottage Countess*, Allen Figgis & Co Ltd, Ireland, 1974.

Welfare, Humphrey, *NT Histories Wessex*, Willow Books, London, 1984.

West, *Warwickshire*, 1830.

Williams, Penry, *History of England – The Later Tudors*, Oxford University Press, 1995.

Williams-Ellis, Clough, *On Trust for the Nation*, Paul Elek, 1947.

Wilson, John, *The Chorleys of Chorley Hall*, Sherratt and Hughes, Manchester, 1907.

Index

(Numbers indicate chapters.)

People

Places

General